100 GREAT
IRISH RUGBY
MOMENTS

First published 2019
by Black & White Publishing Ltd
Nautical House, 104 Commercial Street
Edinburgh, EH6 6NF

1 3 5 7 9 10 8 6 4 2   19 20 21 22

ISBN: 978 1 78530 253 4

A CIP catalogue record for this book is available from the British Library.

Typeset by Iolaire Typesetting, Newtonmore
Printed and bound by CPI Group (UK) Ltd, Croydon, CR0 4YY

100 GREAT
IRISH RUGBY
MOMENTS

JOHN SCALLY

BLACK & WHITE PUBLISHING

CONTENTS

To Irish rugby's number-one fan:
Fionn Golden
May the rugby gods smile on you
and keep you safe and healthy.

FOREWORD

by Jack McGrath

This book opens with Ireland's 2018 Grand Slam win. As someone who was lucky enough to be part of that great adventure I am very conscious of how privileged I was, especially because so many great players to wear the green jersey down through the decades missed out on this fantastic achievement.

One of the reasons why fans have such great affection for rugby is that it has the power to create incredible and special memories. One of the greatest games I was involved in was that historic day when we beat the All Blacks in Chicago in 2016. It was such a magical moment to be part of the first Irish team to beat the mighty All Blacks. I know the fans who were there will never forget it. And of course, the first time to beat them at home two years later was maybe even more special!

There are so many wonderful moments, like that game, in the rich history of Irish rugby that brought great joy to so many people. It's very important for us to celebrate them. However, it's also important to recall some of the players that we lost much too soon in tragic circumstances. That is why it is right and fitting that these pages also pay homage to the likes of Nevin Spence and Axel Foley.

Irish rugby has produced many extraordinary moments. It has featured so many exceptional and world-class players. And, of course, it has showcased some of the greatest characters in the history of the game worldwide.

This book is a well-deserved and fitting tribute to the great moments, great players and great characters of Irish rugby.

INTRODUCTION

I failed as a cook. Even when I boil water it gets burnt.

That is one of the reasons I became a vegetarian. *Slán go feoil*.

As a consequence, I have tried to channel all my energies into one area – and I did this so effectively that since Joe Schmidt came to Ireland I have developed a new syndrome.

I have been clinically diagnosed as an A.R.S.E.

A. Rabid. Schmidt. Enthusiast.

Writing this book is part of my treatment for this addictive condition.

When Eamon Dunphy said that 'rugby is the new sex' he was reflecting the prominent place rugby has developed not only in Irish sport but in Irish life as a whole.

Inevitably a collection such as this can only be a personal one. No two rugby fans would pick the identical 100 great moments of Irish rugby. Many of them are obvious and pick themselves. I am very happy to include these. However, I was determined to also include a few less obvious ones – which perhaps give an insight into the totality of the humanity, humour and history of the Irish rugby story.

For that reason, I did not want to turn this book into a collection of match reports but rather give the reader an insight into the stories behind the games through the eyes of the men and women who made them happen.

Health and safety influenced the writing of this book. If I was to reveal the name of the prominent rugby personality who told me the joke where the punchline was: 'You are from Limerick and you have a smartphone?', his health and safety would be at risk the next time he visits Shannonside.

PART I
Magic Moments

The rugby gods roll the dice, their eyes as cold as ice. Before the 2019 Six Nations, England's coach Eddie Jones was, in his own words, 'throwing grenades' again. This time he was complaining about Johnny Sexton being 'on his bat phone to referees'. For his part, Joe Schmidt warmed up for the tournament by becoming an honorary Cork man at the Cork Person of the Year awards and by receiving a Republic of Cork passport. But then the England assistant coach John Mitchell stirred the pot again a few days before Ireland's game with England by saying that Ireland's plan to beat his side was to 'bore the sh*t out of them'. Their comments reflected their pain at Ireland's comprehensive victory over them on their own patch the previous St Patrick's Day – a magic moment not just in Irish sport but in Irish life.

Of course, the boys in green have produced many individual moments of brilliance, like Joey Carbery's thrilling break against Scotland in Murrayfield in 2019 which set up Keith Earls' try. It created headlines like 'Joey the Slip' and 'Joey's Scot the Lot'.

Sadly after the 2019 Six Nations, Alison Miller (the daughter of Laois GAA royalty, Bobby) retired after a glittering career. She produced many a thrilling moment in the green jersey.

While Ireland's 2019 Six Nations campaign, which began with such great expectations, was a massive disappointment, nonetheless, with our Under-20s winning the Grand Slam, the hope is that we can look forward to many more glory days for Irish rugby in the immediate future.

This section celebrates some of the most magic moments in Irish rugby.

1

IT'S ALL GREEK TO ME

Ireland Win the 2018 Grand Slam

My first exposure to Joe Schmidt came when he generously agreed to speak to a class I was teaching in 2013. At the time, speculation was rife that he was going to succeed Declan Kidney as Irish coach. He confided to us that he couldn't stay as long as he would have wished because he was rushing to a meeting with Brian O'Driscoll to persuade him to continue playing for another year. A short time later it was announced that 'Drico' had committed to one more year.

It was the former English teacher who spoke to that class, with Schmidt expressing his passion for reading. I wondered if many of the Leinster rugby team shared his enthusiasm for books.

'Some of them were good readers. I would say Lee Child was probably the most popular author with the players.'

He went on to tell us that one of his own favourite books was Harper Lee's 1960 classic *To Kill a Mockingbird*. He recalled that in the novel, the hero Atticus Finch, a lawyer of immense integrity, defended an Afro-American man who was wrongly accused of raping a white girl at a time when racism was endemic in American society. An angry mob gathered at his house to tear him apart limb by limb. As the first man strode forward ready to attack him, Atticus's young daughter, Jean Louise, or 'Scout', called out the man's name. He froze on the spot. Then little Scout told him that she was in the same class as his child. The man looked embarrassed and meekly turned around and walked away shamefaced. The anger in the mob was immediately dissipated like a bicycle tyre with a puncture and each of them turned around and walked silently to their homes with their heads held down in mortification at the thought of the awful crime they had almost committed.

When he was deputy principal of Tauranga Boys' College in New Zealand, Joe Schmidt faced a different challenge. Students across the country had called a strike. All the students in the local girls' school had already gone out on strike. When he heard that the boys in his school were about to do the same, Schmidt rushed out with all the other teachers and lined them up to block off the entrance so that the boys wouldn't be able to walk out. It was a classic face off. Then to his horror, Schmidt saw that there was a gap in the school fence which had not been protected. His heart sank because he knew immediately the name of the one boy who was going to walk out through the gap.

Sure enough, the boy in question saw the gap and made his move. Hundreds of eyes were on the boy and a sudden hush descended. If he went through it, all the other students were going to follow him. Schmidt's brain was whirling. Then the scene from *To Kill a Mockingbird* came back to him. He shouted out the boy's first name. The boy froze. Then Schmidt looked him in the eye. And the boy meekly turned around and walked with his head down back into school. Every boy in the yard then quietly followed him.

Crisis averted.

I knew after listening to that story that, with his unique amalgam of intellect, emotional intelligence, problem-solving skills in high-pressure situations and capacity for lateral thinking, Schmidt was going to be a success as the Irish coach.

Who is the man most responsible for Ireland's Grand Slam in 2018? Johnny Sexton for the drop goal against France? Jacob Stockdale for all his tries? Conor Murray for giving a masterclass in each of the games? Joe Schmidt for masterminding it all?

Perhaps Schmidt himself is the best person to ask. Typical of the man, he does not give a predictable answer. He gives the credit to a man who died over 2,000 years before – the celebrated Greek philosopher Aristotle, elegantly summarised by philosopher Will Durant in the mantra: 'We are what we repeatedly do. Excellence, then, is not an act but a habit.' The Grand Slam victory would be testimony to Aristotle's wisdom.

So how did Schmidt create a winning culture?

'When we brought the group together before the Six Nations we asked them three questions:

1. How are you travelling? Had they injuries, niggles, domestic issues, etc?
2. What can you contribute? We wanted them to tell us that they had a specific contribution to make. If they didn't feel that they had something distinctive, they would have been no use to us.
3. What do we need to do to go forward?

'We had a group discussion around that. We didn't want to dictate to the players. If it was going to work, it wasn't going to be the management telling them what to do. It had to come from them and be driven by them, not us. They had to have ownership, and to be fair to them, they did take ownership of it, and that is one of the main reasons why we were so successful.

'The one specific area where we did give them direction was on the importance of discipline – both on and off the field. The need for discipline on the field was obvious in terms of not giving away penalties or, worse, stupid yellow cards which could cost us dearly. The discipline off the field was in relation to diet and "sleep hygiene". I have to confess that these were two new words to me. We wanted, even needed, all of them to get plenty of sleep. Sleep hygiene refers to creating the right conditions for sleep, which means shutting off all computers and electronic devices before trying to sleep. We encouraged them to read a book instead.'

Schmidt showcases a nice sense of humour when asked about the French match. 'We were completely in control for most of the match, to such an extent that we thought, *This is getting boring* – so we decided to allow Teddy Thomas to waltz through for a try just to make it interesting!'

Johnny's Sexton's drop goal was clearly the pivotal moment. 'We did it the opposite way to 2009 when the Grand Slam was won by Rog's drop goal at the very end. In 2018, Johnny's score was the critical one that everyone remembers, and it came in the very first match.

'Johnny rightly gets the credit for his nerves of steel in such a big moment – but it wasn't just Johnny. As most rugby fans know, there were forty-one phases before his drop goal. After the match was over we showed a version of the move to the squad and we broke it down to show a clip of each player on the pitch doing something well. Johnny was involved three times, and everyone also remembers Keith Earls' catch from Johnny's cross kick – if Keith missed that very difficult catch we could forget the Grand Slam. Likewise, if Iain Henderson had not caught the ball at the start of the move, we were beaten. It was so tense that most people have forgotten that Fergus McFadden made the most fabulous clearout from a ruck. It was nothing as eye-catching as Johnny's kick but it was absolutely critical.'

Schmidt still winces at the memory of one moment from the Italian match. 'Before he touched down for that try I was shouting at Robbie [Henshaw] not to score that try which saw him have to leave the pitch with that serious arm injury. I have seen that type of injury happen often and I was pleading with him not to touch it down because I could see what was going to happen. I knew that meant that he was out for the rest of the campaign, and I was devastated because he is such a quality player, and I felt he was going to be a huge loss for us.

'So what happens next? We bring in Chris Farrell to replace him for the Wales game and in his first competitive match for us he wins man of the match. It seems that he is in fairy-tale land but then he gets injured and is out for the next two matches. So we have to bring back Garry Ringrose, who had played little or no serious rugby for months, earlier than we would have wished. Garry then plays superbly against Scotland and England and looks as if he has never been away.'

Schmidt not only led Ireland to the Grand Slam, he did so while integrating Jacob Stockdale, James Ryan, Bundee Aki, Chris Farrell, Andrew Porter, Joey Carbery, Jordan Larmour and Dan Leavy into the first team.

The Welsh coach Warren Gatland had tried to play mind games before their showdown but the Irish coach didn't bite. 'I tried to make a joke about it to Gats afterwards but he didn't laugh.'

How does Schmidt react to the suggestion that Ireland were lucky against Wales? 'Sometimes you can be lucky but other times, as in this case, you have acquired habits that make you look lucky. I would refer people to the consistency of our performances just before and after half-time against Wales, Scotland and England. People might think they were coincidences but they weren't.'

Schmidt's attention to detail is legendary, but there was one thing he had not bargained for.

'Everybody remembers that we beat England in Twickenham on St Patrick's Day but what some people forget is that it was played during an unseasonal snowstorm both here and in England. It was Artic cold and there was a vicious wind. Our forwards coach Simon Easterby had prepared our line-out calls and had them on a table in our dugout before the game on three sheets of paper, and this huge gust of wind came and blew two of them into the English dugout, which meant that the English had most of our line-out calls – except the short ones. So we used our short ones for most of the game, and in the weather conditions it was the right strategy, so that was a case of something that might seem to be a big disadvantage for us working in our favour.'

Celebrations were such that even Johnny Sexton was living up to his role in his Mace ad and 'going the extra smile'. However, there was a setback. The weather ensured that not only was the Grand Slam homecoming scheduled for Lansdowne Road cancelled, but the players were late in leaving London, as Schmidt recalls: 'We got delayed four times because of the "Son of the Beast", and I'm not talking about Billy Vunipola!

'At 10 a.m., everyone had finished breakfast and it was very sedate – slightly hungover but very sedate. Then we got news that we had been delayed forty-five minutes. We said, "Lads, chill out and have another coffee." We got to about 10.30 a.m. when we saw the first pints starting to be shared! We thought, *That's okay, we'll get out of here in fifteen minutes*. Delayed another forty-five minutes … cocktails! Cocktails – times have really changed.'

2

HISTORY MAKERS

Ireland Beat New Zealand for the First Time

It was a shock of seismic proportions that reverberated around the rugby world.

In 2017 when the Black Ferns (the New Zealand women's team) were selected by an elite group of eight giants of the game like Brian O'Driscoll and Richie McCaw ahead of the All Blacks to lift the gong for the team of the year (and Limerick's Joy Neville won referee of the year), it represented two powerful affirmations of the growing international prominence of the women's game. That year the Black Ferns had won their fifth World Cup in Ireland compared to the All Blacks' three. The fact that the Black Ferns enjoy such dominance in world rugby makes Ireland's victory over them in the 2014 Rugby World Cup all the more remarkable.

Indeed, Ireland set the Women's Rugby World Cup alight by defeating reigning champions New Zealand 17–14 in the sides' first ever meeting in Marcoussis. The Black Ferns, coming into the fixture with a 20-match unbeaten World Cup run since the 1991 semi-finals, led 8–7 at half-time thanks to a Selica Winiata try – which even they would probably have conceded went against the run of play. Ireland's scores in the first half came from a Heather O'Brien try and a Niamh Briggs conversion. Kelly Brazier's second penalty of the evening extended the Kiwis' advantage to 11–7 under the watchful eye of Joe Schmidt and Jonathan Sexton in the crowd.

Irish coach Philip Doyle had clearly imbued the fighting Irish with great resilience and in a tight third quarter Niamh Briggs countered brilliantly to set up Alison Miller for a wonderful try. To rub salt into the New Zealand wounds, Briggs aced a stunning conversion from the touchline. Brazier managed to bring New Zealand level at 14–all with another penalty, but a final penalty from Niamh Briggs with ten minutes left sealed the Irish victory. Their second successive triumph in Pool B meant Ireland effectively qualified for the semi-finals for the first time. England brought an end to the fairy-tale story for Ireland in the semi-final before convincingly beating Canada to claim the World Cup.

Irish rugby legend Ollie Campbell was thrilled by the success.

'When I started playing, the only acknowledgement of women in the game generally came in after-dinner speeches when some dignitary would invariably say something patronising like: "And of course we must thank the ladies in the kitchen for all their hard work." Thankfully those old attitudes are gone out with the ark. Now women's rugby has become an important feature of Irish sporting life. I certainly see the evidence of that in my own club, Old Belvedere, where the women's game is thriving.

'Everybody loves a winner and when Ireland beat the Black Ferns in 2014 following up on their Grand Slam win that year, the Irish sporting nation sat up and took notice. When Sophie Spence was nominated for World Player of the Year, it was a sign of how far the game has come in this country. Thankfully, on the heels of those great triumphs, Ireland's matches are now shown on television. Young people get their heroes from television, and it's great that the stars of the team like Niamh Briggs, Joy Neville, Fiona Coghlan, and Lynne Cantwell have become household names. It is wonderful, too, that Fiona and Lynne have also gone on to become excellent television analysts, on the men's game as well as the women's, where they follow the tradition of the great Fiona Steed. It was great to witness all the hype here before the World Cup in Ireland in 2017, but it was a bit disappointing we didn't fully capitalise on it by going further in the tournament.'

Jack McGrath is also a big admirer. 'We have had the odd bit of contact with them so we have got to know them. They are so dedicated and so talented. They don't get the profile they deserve, but it is slowly changing for the better. Having the World Cup here was a real boost, and they just need to get their place in the shop window. It would be nice to think that they get the recognition their tremendous talent deserves.'

Tony Ward is another fan. 'It was a real feather in the cap for the women's game that they beat New Zealand before our men did, and of course they also won the Grand Slam. They have been a golden generation, and the hope is that they inspire the next generation to take up the game. Unfortunately, there is a drop off in participation among young women from the mid-teens onward in sport generally, but hopefully the great players we have seen and are seeing, like Nora Stapleton and Claire Molloy, will inspire others. As a former teacher, and as someone who continues to be heavily involved in schools' rugby, I would love to see the interest and participation that there is in rugby boys' schools replicated in girls' schools.'

The last word goes to Joy Neville: 'To tell a woman what she cannot do is to tell her what she can.'

3

THE WINDY CITY IS MIGHTY PRETTY

Ireland v New Zealand

Joe Schmidt had not intended to be a rugby coach. When he took up his first teaching position, he was told he would be expected to be involved in the extra-curricular life of the school. His response was: 'Fine. I'll coach the basketball team.'

At the time Schmidt had built a reputation for his prowess as a rugby player. So the headmaster didn't blink an eye and told him: 'That's fine. Your work with the basketball team won't affect you coaching the rugby team on Saturday mornings.'

There was much to learn for the young coach. 'One of the bits of advice I remember most was that the most important player in any squad was the tighthead prop and the second most important person was the reserve tighthead prop.'

Schmidt would use the skills he acquired to telling effect against his native country. Ireland produced a thrilling display to record a first ever win over New Zealand at the 29th attempt and end the All Blacks' run of eighteen straight wins in November 2016. Tries from Jordi Murphy, C. J. Stander and Conor Murray helped the Irish to a 25–8 half-time lead, then

Simon Zebo scored his side's fourth try in the corner. The Kiwis fought back to move to within four points but Robbie Henshaw's late try ensured the victory. This was Ireland's first success over the All Blacks in 111 years and it came about in sensational fashion as Ireland repelled a stirring second-half comeback by Steve Hansen's side. T. J. Perenara, Ben Smith and Scott Barrett added to George Mola's first-half try for the New Zealanders, but despite some sustained late pressure, Ireland held strong.

From the outset, the Irish effort appeared to be fuelled by the memory of Anthony Foley, who had died suddenly the previous month. Prior to kick-off, Ireland lined up in the shape of a number eight, the jersey worn with pride by Foley for many years, while their opponents performed their traditional pre-match haka.

Joe Schmidt was unfazed that in the run-up to the game, the media had created an aura of invincibility surrounding the All Blacks. He ignores them as much as possible.

The one time he couldn't ignore the media was when there was a lot of speculation some years ago that Seán O'Brien was signing for Toulon. Schmidt believed that nearly all the stuff in the papers was made up and that the Tullow Tank's agent must have been applauding every paper. But as far as Schmidt was concerned, O'Brien was never going to Toulon.

After the 2017 Autumn Internationals, I spoke with Joe shortly after Simon Zebo had announced that he was leaving Munster. Press speculation was rife that C. J. Stander in particular, but also Tadhg Furlong and Peter O'Mahony, might be about to follow him out of the Ireland set-up. When I asked him about the rumours, he said: 'Don't worry. None of them are going anywhere.' Weeks later it was announced that all three had signed new contracts to stay in Ireland.

Schmidt is a great believer in partnerships. His marriage to Kellie is living proof of that, and the Conor Murray and Jonathan Sexton partnership has been key to much of Ireland's success under Schmidt.

Beating the All Blacks was a massive team effort but Tony Ward was taken by one performance above all others.

'The out-half is the general of the backline and more often than not of the whole team. He is like the midfield general in soccer or the quarterback in American football. He performs a pivotal role with the responsibility of deciding whether the backs should run with the ball or whether he should kick for position to secure the best advantage for the team. In the modern game, he also has to be a solid tackler, as his area of the field is the one most sides choose to attack first. In the majority of cases he is also the guy who kicks the goals. For these reasons, the out-half is the glamour position on the rugby pitch.

'I thought about this in Chicago where I had the great good fortune to be present for Ireland's historic win over New Zealand. Of course, much of the credit for the win has to go to Joe Schmidt, but Joe is lucky in his general and there is no doubt that Jonathan Sexton is Joe's general.

'We saw the evidence in Sexton's first-minute penalty, his touchline conversion after Jordi Murphy's try, his peerless line punt to the corner that set up the five-metre line-out that led C. J. Stander to power home for Ireland's second try, the bouncing ball from Sexton's delightful kick which allowed Conor Murray to score a try, his delayed flat pass which gifted Simon Zebo a walk-in. I could go on but I think the point is made. Great as Sexton is, with Conor Murray beside him when both are on song he is even better.'

For Jack McGrath, winning the game 40–29 was one of the high points of his career.

'There have been some great moments playing for Ireland. Winning my first cap was incredible. A really special moment was the day we won the Grand Slam. The stars were all aligned. It was Ireland going to win the Grand Slam in Twickenham on St Patrick's Day with all the historical connotations associated with that. When I play for Ireland, my father does not come to the games because he prefers to watch them away from all the bustle, at home. Before that game, though, I told him it was a once-in-a-lifetime occasion and that he should come to watch. He did, and it's fair to say that he really enjoyed it.

'The other match that stands out was beating the All Blacks. To end an 111-year wait and be part of the first Irish team to defeat the aristocrats of rugby was stupendous. The match was played in front of a capacity crowd of 60,000 at Soldier Field in Chicago, a venue chosen in an attempt to increase the exposure of the sport. It was right and fitting that the win came only three days after the Chicago Cubs ended a 108-year drought to land baseball's World Series. Five million people flocked to the Cubs' victory parade on Friday, and after beating the All Blacks, the scores of Irish fans in town were fully able to join the party – and they brought a real Irish tinge to it. A great sporting occasion and a wonderful party. Someone said it was like a great night in Coppers – only on a massive scale.'

4

THE WEST'S AWAKE

Connacht Are Champions

'The Crazy Gang have beaten the Culture Club.'

This was legendary BBC commentator John Motson's famous comment when Wimbledon shocked Liverpool to win the 1988 FA Cup final. Had Motty commentated on the 2016 Pro12 Final he would probably have said something similar. For the first time in their 121-year history, Connacht claimed a major trophy as they brilliantly won the Guinness Pro12 title in May 2016 in front of a record final crowd of almost 35,000. Moreover, Pat Lam's side utterly deserved their 20–10 win as they outclassed Leinster with a scintillating display of attacking rugby at Murrayfield. The Westerners had booked their place in the play-offs by topping the league table, but before the game, few gave Ireland's least successful province much hope against the European aristocrats.

That Connacht collective story was brimming with great individual tales.

Though born in Paris, and raised there until he was seven,

Ultan Dillane is a real Kerry man. It was his time with Ireland Youths that saw him head to Connacht, rather than Munster's academy in Limerick. His progress was faltering with Munster as he lost out on the big selections for the important games, but coach Pat Lam loved Dillane's driving, ferocious-tackling, athletic style of play. Dillane secured a senior contract with the province and by the time the Pro12 title had come around, played for Ireland.

Bundee Aki arrived in Galway, aged twenty-four, having spurned a chance of representing the All Blacks. He was an instant fan favourite, tearing into defences and bringing Connacht to the cusp of the Champions Cup. By the end of his second season, he had not only been the inspiration for Connacht to win the Guinness Pro12 title but was also named the league's best player. He really bought into Connacht's team ethos.

This was most tellingly revealed when Robbie Henshaw had his laptop stolen. There was a tracking device on the computer so Aki rounded up half the team and went in search of the thief. A short time later they showed up at Henshaw's door and handed him back the laptop. Details of their exchange with the thief are as strictly guarded as the third secret of Fatima.

The icing on the cake for the romantics was that man of the match went to Connacht's most iconic player, the 33-year-old John Muldoon – a man who always gave his all for the province. The game marked Muldoon's 275th cap for the Westerners. An emotional Muldoon said afterwards: 'We had a bet earlier in the year that if we won I wouldn't cry – but that is the best €20 I have ever spent. Phenomenal, and I would like to thank all the support who have come over.'

Alan Quinlan played against Muldoon frequently. 'I have to confess there were times when I thought, *Ahhh, not that Muldoon ba*tard again, does he ever f**king stop?* It didn't matter what you did to John Muldoon – you could kick him, punch him or drive him into the turf – he would always come back for more. Nothing could halt him from pulling down mauls, hitting rucks, making tackles, trying to poach the ball and giving plenty of verbals too. I was regularly labelled a nuisance, a bit of a pest on the field, and for years I didn't know whether to take it as a compliment or not. As I got older, however, and could see some of my most difficult opponents had such similar traits, I began to understand how effective and enjoyable it can be to play the role of Chief Unsettler. Muldoon didn't start playing rugby until he was fourteen, taking an unconventional route to the professional game, and that probably contributed to his on-field attitude from the outset – he was desperate to prove he belonged at the top level; that he could mix it with the best in the country.

'Reputations meant little to John Muldoon. And he made sure you were aware of that from the off, particularly on his home patch. Heineken Cup winner? Ireland regular? Lion? It didn't matter, he was always confident he could compete with the best, for he had spent most of his rugby career proving himself in spite of difficult circumstances. Muldoon has said that being a one-club man is what makes him most proud when he reflects on a provincial career that concluded with his 327th game – which appropriately finished in a demolition of Leinster in Galway.

'And that decision to spend his entire career at the province further varnishes his legacy as one of the greatest Connacht players in history and enhances the esteem he is held in by his fellow professionals. It's not easy to stay with the same club for that length of time in such a fickle industry, particularly when the bad days often outweigh the good so substantially as they did at Connacht. Muldoon wasn't short on offers; other provinces came knocking, as did clubs in England and France, yet the Portumna man stayed put with his beloved side through thick and thin, even though a switch would have brought more money, or potentially more international caps than the three he won in 2009/2010.'

5

LEINSTER LIONS

Leinster Win Their First Heineken Cup

Michael Cheika has to take much of the plaudits for Leinster's first Heineken Cup win, a 19–16 win over kingpins of England, Leicester in 2009.

Rugby fans often forget the good games, but the minute you have a bad one everyone remembers it. To a handful of rugby fans, the abiding memory of Felipe Contepomi will be his apparent implosion in the 2006 Heineken Cup semi-final against Munster. He deservedly went into the match with a glowing reputation on the heels of a series of vintage performances for Leinster that season. However, Ronan O'Gara gave the perfect answer to those who felt that Leinster had the advantage at out-half, crowning the performance with a try in the last few minutes in Munster's 30–6 triumph. In boxing parlance, Contepomi and his teammates, who had given so much to the tournament in the build-up, were quite literally punch drunk long before the end.

Critics who believed Leinster to be a team of style and no substance had all their prejudices confirmed in that game. They were sometimes unfairly seen as the Anna Kournikova of rugby – talented, very pretty to look at, but never quite fulfilling their potential. The cultural contrast between Leinster and Munster was never more apparent than in that game. Hence the joke that the Leinster squad couldn't make it because there was a sale in Brown Thomas, while the Munster squad prepared by having a raw bullock for their lunch.

Yet to be fair to Contepomi that game was an aberration. His sharp brain worked on both the instinctive level and the broader tactical level where opponents shape the game for you. He read the game with absolute assurance. His ambitions had few limitations. His hands were sure and he had a full range of kicks.

It is to Michael Cheika's great credit that he generally got the best out of the Argentinian. Mind you, Felipe would probably want to forget his signing for Leinster, given the high-profile administrative error which caused him not to be registered to play in the Heineken Cup in his opening season with the province.

He was one of the greatest natural talents that Cheika had come across. The big problem with him was that he wasn't a natural out-half. He was a natural footballer but not a natural playmaking number ten. Munster capitalised on that in that Heineken Cup semi-final when they put him under pressure and exposed weaknesses in his game.

He was much more a natural number twelve than a ten. Cheika would have probably liked to have played him at number twelve for Leinster, but they had such a class centre partnership of Brian O'Driscoll and Gordon D'Arcy that he was reluctant to break it up.

You want all your best players on the field, and Leinster got the best out of their playing resources when Cheika used

Contepomi at ten and Darce and Drico in the centre. With the way the modern game has evolved, the out-half is no longer like the quarterback in American football. He is still a playmaker, but he needs other playmakers at twelve and thirteen, as the responsibility is now shared. New Zealand's Dan Carter was acknowledged as the best in the world at the time and rightly so, but he got great support from Aaron Mauger, who was the think tank in the side.

The fly-half is the one player who reflects the attitude and the potential of the team he stars in, and nobody personified Leinster's exuberant new running style under Michael Cheika better than Contepomi. Cheika wanted his side to play with freedom and so liberated his Argentinian import and empowered him. It was all very different under Declan Kidney's tenure as Leinster coach, when Contepomi's face didn't seem to fit.

His game was based around his ability to create space for others and his awareness, typified in his role in the try O'Driscoll scored against Toulouse in the Heineken Cup quarter-final. O'Driscoll took all the praise, and he deserved a fair share of it for the line he took, but it was Contepomi's awareness and his sensitivity in the pass, where he weighed it just perfectly for O'Driscoll to come on to it, that was key. You cannot buy that kind of ability. You can practise on the training ground and you can hone your gifts, but essentially, they are skills you are born with.

He had a temperament where he was prepared to attack from anywhere. Some people saw it as a failing in his game, but Cheika saw it as a strength. He did outrageous things and sometimes they backfired, but when they worked it opened up defences. Contepomi often came up with something outlandish: be it a chip under his own posts, a sidestep on his own twenty-two or an outrageous dummy, and no opposing coach can legislate for that.

The unique spirit in the Leinster camp was fuelled by much good-natured banter. Naturally O'Driscoll was a primary target. Such were his commercial opportunities that his colleagues joked that he could afford to live in an area that was so posh that the fire brigade was ex-directory. The ribbing particularly intensified when O'Driscoll famously dyed his hair blond. His teammates spun the yarn that Drico had entered a Robert Redford lookalike contest. He was knocked out in the first round, beaten by a Nigerian.

There were many stories in the Leinster camp about Malcolm O'Kelly's lack of organisation and his capacity for being late. The standard line in Leinster was: if you're behind Mal in the airport, you've missed your plane. A particular favourite in the squad was about the time when Mal was spotted wearing a black shoe and a brown shoe. When this was discreetly pointed out to O'Kelly, he shrugged nonchalantly and said: 'Don't worry. That's the new fashion. I've another pair at home exactly like that!'

Shane Byrne had a reputation in the squad for being 'careful with money'. Hence the joke among his former Leinster colleagues that he installed double-glazed windows in his home so that his children wouldn't hear the ice-cream van.

There has never been a nicer or more modest player for Leinster than Victor Costello. Yet Victor was widely quoted within the squad as boasting that Bono had asked him for his autograph.

There is a fine line between self-confidence and arrogance. Keith Gleeson stayed on the right side of that line. That didn't stop Contepomi and the other Leinster players from recounting a tale he tells of going for a walk one night and bumping into a Stena Sealink! They also claimed that he was writing a book called: *Famous People Who Know Me.*

25

Cheika brought Leinster to the top prize in European rugby through a unique amalgam of flair, his newly created work ethic in a province which had previously relied on skill, and a vibrant team spirit. The other unique contribution of Cheika that was critical to the success in 2009, and to all of Leinster's big wins through to the unique double in 2018, was to persuade Isa Nacewa to sign for the province.

6

HER MOST IMPORTANT TACKLE

Hannah Tyrrell Becomes a Campaigner

Thursday afternoon in the Avila Retreat Centre in Donnybrook and a group of teachers are gathered for a conference about how they should respond to the growing problems they are facing with students struggling with anxiety. On her way to doing a training session with the national team, Irish rugby star Hannah Tyrrell arrives to speak. Some of the teachers know nothing about rugby but within minutes they are converted as Hannah shares her story.

It is a compelling tale of a life in need of transformation, as she has so powerfully articulated in her role as a spokeswoman for the Irish Rugby Union Players' Association's Tackle Your Feelings mental well-being campaign. From the age of twelve, she grappled with eating disorders which, in turn, led to self-harming. She was consumed with such self-loathing that harming herself, she says, was a form of punishment. It was a desperately difficult time for the young woman who bottled it all up and, for a lengthy period, sought no help. Sport was her only release, her safety net, at a time when the greatest danger was that she would isolate herself and withdraw from life.

She begins her talk by getting straight to the point. 'I actually suffered with my own mental-health problems. I struggled with an eating disorder and self-harm, all throughout my teenage years.'

Suddenly the atmosphere is electric, like a revivalist meeting with a touch of fanaticism. The crowd hang on her every word like a presidential candidate at a party convention. As she speaks all eyes are on her, seemingly transfixed.

She then details how the particular eating disorder she struggled with affected her.

'I first began restricting my eating when I was around twelve or thirteen. I remember feeling like I wasn't good enough at anything I put my hand to: school, sport, friendships. Changing how I looked was a way to change how I felt, and in turn how others felt about me. I started counting calories and skipping meals, but also bingeing and vomiting after eating. These disordered eating tendencies eventually developed into bulimia, as I continued to do anything to try to lose weight. It was a dangerous cycle. I would binge, purge and self-harm, but I never actually spoke to anyone about how I felt. Nobody would have guessed that anything was wrong because I was so good at keeping up a front. My eating disorder was bulimia, so my weight only ever fluctuated by about half a stone, and I still looked healthy.

'Any time that I didn't get the weight-loss results I wanted, I'd be very hard on myself, and I soon turned to self-harm. If I felt things hadn't gone right that day, if I didn't see the weight I wanted on the scale, if I ate something that I shouldn't have or if I binged and purged, I'd punish myself by self-harming.

The temporary feeling of relief it gave me was addictive, but the feeling never lasted long and would soon be replaced by more shame and guilt. It was an endless cycle. Over time, I began to withdraw from everybody and everything except sport, which I played all through school. I didn't tell a soul what I was doing to myself. Nobody realised what was going on for years.

'It wasn't until I was in my final year of school that I finally began to open up, first to my school guidance counsellor and then to someone from Pieta House. Initially, I was very reluctant to share what I was going through with anyone. I felt I was broken and couldn't be fixed. In my head, other people needed help more than me, and I didn't deserve to be helped.

'I began getting help when I was seventeen or eighteen, but it was mostly for other people – I still didn't think there was anything really wrong. It was only when I was twenty or twenty-one that I started to take it seriously. It was very hard for me to start expressing the feelings I had bottled up for so long. Eventually, by talking to doctors and counsellors, I was able to develop more positive coping strategies to use when I was having negative thoughts about my body.'

Throughout this period, Hannah was playing underage inter-county football for Dublin, and although the bulimia affected her football 'in terms of moods and energy levels', sport was her only escape.

'It was the only thing that gave me a bit of relief from the constant battle that was going on in my head. It was nice to be able to get away from my thoughts for a couple of hours and be with friends and to enjoy something I loved. Because of my eating disorder and the self-harm, I didn't want to communicate with anybody. It has a tendency to make you withdraw from people, but the sport didn't allow me to. That social bond with the girls was something that kept me coming back to training and kept me sane at the time. At those times when I would have struggled with my performance . . . I often thought, *Imagine how good I could be if I didn't have an eating disorder; imagine if I really put 100 per cent into it*! Sometimes people say "that must have been tough growing up for you", but I don't think I would change it because it has made me the person I am today.'

It was a long road, but once she took her first steps, Hannah knew it was a battle she could win. Just talking about it all, she says, was the beginning of that rehabilitation.

'And that's why I was so happy to get involved with the campaign. It was something I felt was the right thing to do. It was an opportunity to speak about my mental health, to share my story, open up, and to hopefully help others, maybe get through about something people might be struggling with. It's probably one of the best things I've ever done. The amount of people who have contacted me saying how much it's helped them has just been phenomenal – there's been an amazing response.

'I know it would have massively helped me to have been able to hear someone I looked up to talk about how they were struggling with things, that things aren't always perfect but they'd come through it. That you can have bad times but you can come through it, and good things can still come about. I just hope people can take something from what I've talked about. And the most important thing is that you talk to someone, reach out. I have a different outlook on life now; I know what I have been through and what I have come through. It has made me the person I am, and for that reason I wouldn't change anything.'

Hannah noted that figures show up to forty-five per cent of teens self-harm, and it is also the strongest risk factor for later suicide. This is not just a girls' issue. The rate of self-harm among boys as young as ten soared by forty-four per cent in just one year.

Her parting words were for her twelve-year-old self: 'Communicate – don't isolate yourself. Bulimia and self-harm feed off isolation and want to cut you off, but it's so important to talk to family and friends about how you feel. It's hugely positive to see that they care and want to be there.'

7

LEINSTER'S HOUDINI ACT

Leinster v Northampton

Testicular fortitude was called for as never before.

Johnny Sexton was not found wanting.

Some games leave you scratching your head. The 2011 Heineken Cup Final was one of them. There have, statistically, been bigger second-half comebacks in rugby union, but there have been none in which a team have undergone the extreme makeover which propelled Leinster to a second European title in three years. Lazarus was in all likelihood a Leinster man.

Leinster trailed 22–6 at half-time. Cometh the hour, cometh Jonathan Sexton.

Few half-time speeches attain instant immortality. Sexton's was one of them. He invoked the memory of Liverpool's famous 2005 European Cup comeback against Milan in Istanbul. Joe Schmidt told his players they would be remembered forever if they regrouped and dug deep. For someone like Brian O'Driscoll, this was a call to arms. 'When you said, "Go to the well, boys", he was 200ft down,' said Schmidt. 'He could dig pretty deep when the going got tough.'

Any thoughts that Leinster were down and out of this magnificent match lasted all of thirteen minutes. That was the time it took for Sexton to contribute fourteen points, converting both of his own tries, as Leinster fought their way back.

Sexton is often seen as Schmidt's general on the pitch. 'Some coaches judge on the outcome rather than the decision. If I decide to run the ball and we have an overlap, then that is the right decision for Joe.' Moreover, Sexton has claimed that he plays the game with 'two voices in his head' – his own and Schmidt's.

Northampton were turned over from the opening restart of the second half and forced to hold out for eleven exhausting phases. They never recovered. Leinster were transformed: fast, strong, purposeful and clever. Jamie Heaslip's shirt-tug on Brian Mujati was a crucial factor in the breakout which preceded Sexton's first try, the number ten leaving Soane Tonga'uiha panting on his inside. Heaslip then blocked Phil Dowson as Sexton went on the wraparound move which yielded his second score, another mortal wound to the Saints. By the time Dowson was sent to the sin bin for entering at the side of a ruck, Leinster had stormed into the lead. Not since the All Blacks led France 24–10 with thirty-five minutes left in the 1999 World Cup has there been a more dramatic reversal of fortune.

The epic finish was also a notable personal triumph for Leo Cullen, Leinster's captain. It was noted that only four clubs had won more than one Heineken Cup and they all had been led by second-row forwards.

Leinster had pulled off the Houdini act of the decade to ensure that it was an Irish province for the fourth time in six seasons who won the Heineken Cup. Sexton was named man of the match, but it was the game itself which merited the ultimate celebration.

Joe Schmidt was conscious of the weight of expectation before the game.

'Everyone expected Leinster to beat Northampton in the Heineken Cup that year, but at half-time it was looking very bleak for us.'

With the benefit of distance Schmidt is happy to shed new light on the half-time events. He laughs when it is suggested that there must have been a lot of bad language used. 'Unlike Munster we don't actually swear in Leinster. But since I've become Irish coach and am dealing with the Munster lads I'm coaching, I've had to learn the swear words so they can understand me!'

Schmidt usually leaves the pre-match team talks to his players. All his work will have been done by then, though he may issue a few reminders to players on an individual basis.

He shares the accolades that were given to Sexton but not in the conventional narrative that has emerged about the game. 'Johnny's speech was good, but in my memory it was Jenno (Shane Jennings) who gave the most forceful speech. The thing about Johnny though was that he delivered on the pitch immediately after half-time, and that is what really mattered.'

However, Schmidt has a third name to add to the equation about the half-time speeches: 'Everyone knows about Johnny's half-time speech, but Jamie Heaslip also made a very impassioned short speech. It was twenty or twenty-two or twenty-four words long. I can't remember exactly what was said, but I know it was an even number of words, because every second word was the same!'

8

LEINSTER LIONS ROAR

Leinster Win Their Third Heineken Cup in 2012

In 2012, Leinster crushed a spirited Ulster by a record Heineken Cup Final-winning margin of 28 points to become the first side to win three titles in four years. Leinster set a new final record of five tries and became only the second team, after Leicester ten years previously, to successfully defend the Heineken Cup, and the second after Toulouse to win more than two European titles. Leinster's 100 per cent record in their three finals and the style in which they won them have seen them acclaimed in some quarters as the best Heineken Cup team ever.

It was a personal triumph for Brian O'Driscoll. The legendary centre, who'd had keyhole surgery on his knee only eight days previously, showcased his genius after thirteen minutes through a delicious offload out the back of his hand to the charging man of the match, Seán O'Brien, leading to the second try.

Denis Hickie remarked, 'Ulster attacked from everywhere and were competitive and fierce, but they've come up against one of the great European teams playing an incredible style of rugby. I'm not sure anyone could have lived with Leinster today.'

For Joe Schmidt, it was a vindication of the culture he had created in Leinster. He liked to keep the lads entertained, and one of the odder games he had was not to celebrate scoring tries, his rationale being that they were paid to score tries, and a postman does not celebrate when he delivers a letter! Initially he brought it into training and then quickly extended it into matches. But the lads had great fun when a player celebrated scoring a try, as he would be doing laps for the rest of the training match while everyone else got on with playing the game. Any chat at all to Schmidt when he was reffing a game, e.g. 'That was a knock-on' or 'He celebrated' resulted in immediate removal from the game for the offender and the starting of laps!

Discipline was and is absolutely key to Schmidt's modus operandi – if you cannot be disciplined in training, how can you expect to be disciplined on the field of play?

The one time he overlooked the try celebrations was when Mike Ross scored his one and only try. 'He never even scored a try as a kid, so I was happy to let that one pass!'

Schmidt is very proud of the fact that Leinster won the fair play award two out of the three years he was in charge – and it was an after-match citing and ban for one player late in the season that cost them three from three.

They had a system of internal fines and penalties for misde-meanours, where the players imposed penalties on each other for indiscretions, however small. Once a week they all gathered to dish out the punishments. Eoin Reddan was the adminis-trator and called out the offenders. They rolled a massive dice, and whatever number they rolled decided the punishment. The players thought the worst one was a €250 fine, and they went crazy with excitement whenever someone got this. Schmidt believed that showed they were really a bunch of big kids!

The other one they hated getting was 'Suits for two weeks',

i.e. every day for training they had to arrive in a suit, shirt and tie, and after training they had to put them all back on.

One of the small things Schmidt copied from his Clermont days and introduced was shaking hands when you meet someone for the first time that day. This was something the players really took to. Jamie Heaslip in particular was a big fan and went out of his way to shake hands with all the young academy lads he met, which gave them a huge lift. When Joe talked to the young lads, a good few of them said how a Jamie handshake really gave them a huge boost and a strong feeling of belonging to a group. It was affirmation of one of Schmidt's most cherished dictums: little things can have a big impact.

9

ON THE DOUBLE

Leinster Win the Cup and League

Irish rugby had its best year ever in 2018 with a Grand Slam and a series win down under. For Jack McGrath though, his biggest match came off the field when he married Sinead Corcoran, daughter of much loved RTÉ commentator, Michael. As he is such a big fan of Munster Today FM's *Gift Grub*, they did a hilarious sketch of Michael's father-of-the-bride speech – which, in essence, questioned why she was marrying a Leinster player when she could have married a Munster one – even a 'blow-in' like Joey Carbery.

The season had not begun particularly well for McGrath.

'I had won three Lions caps in New Zealand in the summer of 2017. That was all my childhood dreams come true, but my form dipped at the start of the autumn. Up to then my career had been upwards all the way, and that was tough, so the finish of the season with two pieces of silver was particularly sweet.'

McGrath believes that personalities were key to Leinster's Champions Cup and League double in 2018.

'I am very serious about my game. When things aren't going

well, I am very hard on myself and get very serious. A lot of the lads are the same, and then the likes of Johnny (Sexton) aren't exactly a bundle of laughs when we lose or when we make mistakes. That is why you need a few personalities in the camp who are more extrovert. Fergus McFadden was always like that. When you're beating yourself up about a match you lost or a mistake you made, Fergus will always be there with a laugh or a joke, and that gives everyone a lift.

'Once James Lowe came into the squad, things kicked up a whole new level in that respect. He's not one to get down, and he's able to lighten the mood when things get too serious. He is very chilled and is a welcome counterbalance to the other personalities in the group, and that light touch amid all the seriousness helps create that winning culture.'

An indication of Lowe's personality came before Leinster's match with Wasps in October 2018. Somebody tried to break into his car. To the amusement of the Gardaí when he reported the incident, Lowe asked if, when they found the culprit, he could be left alone with him for ten minutes!

If you go to the library every day you will eventually read a book, and McGrath believes there is an analogy there for Leinster rugby.

'Culture is also crucial in Leinster. When I was starting off I saw Joe Schmidt creating a new culture. Joe spoke about the habits that would lead us on to excellence and said we would learn the habits of winners. He absolutely drilled those habits into us. I think some of Joe's legacy lives on in Leinster and that is part of the reason we won the double.

'We were brothers. I got injured at the start of the 2018–19 season and immediately I was gutted because I could see myself missing out on the start of the European campaign with Leinster and the Autumn Internationals with Ireland. In the event, the injury wasn't as bad as I feared and I was back playing much quicker, but I hated the idea of not being able to play with my friends at Leinster. They are my second family.

'Of course, a big part of our double win was that we had an excellent coaching ticket. Leo (Cullen) and Stuart (Lancaster) work so well together. Stuart talks about hitting the sweet spot between structured and unstructured rugby. We hit that sweet spot often that season.

'Another reason we had success is that we worked really hard in training. We couldn't do it in big games if we didn't put it in training. Above all we had a huge number of great players.'

Rob Kearney furnishes a telling insight in that respect. 'On the morning the team is announced, it's very quiet now. Most players are a bit nervous because there is so much quality throughout the squad now that nobody is sure what our best team is anymore.'

10

SIMPLY THE BEST

Ireland Win the 2009 Grand Slam

Ireland claimed their first Grand Slam in sixty-one years in a sensational 17–15 win over Wales in Cardiff. The Irish over-turned a 6–0 interval deficit with early second-half tries from Brian O'Driscoll and Tommy Bowe.

Rugby has opened a lot of doors for Brian O'Driscoll. A bit like Harry Potter, he was capable of producing every trick in the book.

'I loved the chances to play for the Barbarians because they play a seven-man game with fifteen players on the pitch. That's the way I'd describe it. My first experience was very exciting; even the build-up was exciting, and playing with players you'd never have the opportunity to play with was amazing. Just to experience it was incredible. Training with Carlos Spencer, who was a childhood hero of mine, was great. Seeing the tricks he was doing in training left me flabbergasted, but I had to pretend to be taking everything he was doing in my stride!'

Which rugby player would he most like to be compared with?

'If I had to be compared with anyone I suppose I would like

to be compared with Australia's Tim Horan. He could mix his game a huge amount and was in the World Cup-winning side of 1991 at a very young age. The fact that he could mix running skills and hard-tackling makes him the complete rugby player, and a lot of his skills I tried to emulate.'

O'Driscoll's career was filled with highs. A major landmark came in March 2004 when he captained Ireland to their first Triple Crown in nineteen years.

'In the Scotland game, we had to wear them down a bit. These Six Nations matches aren't easy and a lot of the time you mightn't pull away 'til the end, which was the case in this one. There was another agenda in this game. Matt Williams was coming back to Lansdowne Road. He had a point to prove because Scotland's campaign up to then had been so disastrous. Add to the mix that he literally knew the way the wind blows in Lansdowne from his time as Leinster and Ireland A coach and his intimate knowledge of so many of the players he once coached on the Irish team. There had to be an element of proving the critics wrong.

'We weren't second-guessing what was going on in his mind. We were concentrating on playing to the best of our ability and we felt that if we were to do that, we could and would win the game.'

There was perhaps one notable low in O'Driscoll's career. Girvan Dempsey was understandably wary when I asked him about Gary Ella's reign as Leinster coach.

'It's a tricky area. Gary has given his side of the story to the media and his criticisms of senior players like Brian (O'Driscoll), Mal (O'Kelly) and Victor (Costello) have been widely reported. He had a tough year insofar as the internationals were away a lot and he had a lot of injuries. To be fair to him, he brought on young players like Shane Jennings and Gary Brown, and they probably have a lot to thank him for. I think the internationals found his laidback attitude a bit strange. We were so used to Matt's authoritarian style and him telling us what to do all the time. Gary was inclined to leave it to us and maybe we needed a bit more direction.'

The high point of O'Driscoll's career, even surpassing perhaps the honour of captaining the Lions on the ill-fated 2005 Lions tour, came when he led Ireland to victory over Wales in 2009 to claim the Grand Slam. Was he nervous before the game?

'Personally, I was probably more nervous going into that game than others because the stakes were so high, but I was determined not to let my teammates see that.'

What was the secret of O'Driscoll's brilliant form in 2009?

'The best piece of advice I've ever been given was from my old coach in UCD, Lee Smith. Lee always wrote out a couple of sentences on a piece of paper for each player before a match saying what he wanted you to do and what your role on the team was, but when he came around to me he said: "Just go out and play your own game." Such a small thing made a big difference and inspired me and gave me a lot of confidence to go out and play well because I thought very highly of Lee and I still do.'

Tony Ward feels that much of the credit for Ireland's triumph in 2009 must go to their coach Declan Kidney.

'To this very day one of my most powerful memories is of playing an under-13 game for St Mary's against Willow Park. My opposite number was way bigger than me and I let him run riot. At half-time our coach's face was beetroot red because he was so furious. He shouted at me in front of the whole team: "Where's your party dress, Ward?" That degree of humiliation could have put me off rugby for life.

'One philosophy I have is that I never, ever transmit negative comments to kids on the field. The day I do that is the day that I hang up my coaching boots, so to speak. Certainly a few days later I will point out the mistakes that were made on the training field. No player goes on the field deliberately trying to make a mistake, and I do get very annoyed when I hear teammates chastising a player on the field or, worse still, a coach shouting abuse at a kid from the sideline. Declan Kidney came from a teaching background, too, and he shares that ethos. His talent is man management and the 2009 Grand Slam is the product of a patient teacher who extracted the very best out of his pupils. He had a group of big personalities and he created the environment to bring home that coveted trophy that had eluded us for sixty-one years.'

11

THE BULL'S TEARS

Ireland v England, 2007

It is a defining image not just of Irish rugby but of Irish life.

'Today is so much more than a game of rugby,' said BBC's rugby anchor John Inverdale with no hint of hyperbole. Saturday, 24 February 2007 transcended the realm of Irish rugby perhaps in a way that no other Irish sporting event has ever done. The French had already banished Ireland's Grand Slam dreams a few weeks previously, but the French connection didn't have any of the historical baggage that an English team did. Fears of playing *'God Save the Queen'* on such sacred sod in the Irish psyche had supporters, administrators and players on edge. Eighty-three thousand were lucky enough to be there, but demand for tickets was such that they could have sold ten times that amount.

Ireland's 43–13 win against England, featuring tries from Girvan Dempsey, David Wallace, Shane Horgan and Isaac Boss is still fondly remembered. It was a record defeat of our historic enemies. However, what is forever firmly embedded in the national consciousness is the singing of the anthems. Despite all the trepidation about the playing of *God Save the Queen* at Croke Park, eighty-seven years after Bloody Sunday, the singing of the national anthems and, in particular, the respectful reception of them was magical, breathtaking and unforgettable.

I wanted to get an independent appraisal of the event so I spoke with the head of the Irish Sports Council John Treacy, himself a former Olympic silver medallist.

'For an amateur organisation, it's a staggering achievement to have created an incredible stadium like Croke Park, especially in the middle of Dublin. The GAA have shown incredible leadership. They have adapted to the changing times. They are keenly aware of the need to bring modern marketing methods into Gaelic games. The Economic and Social Research Institute produced a report on the social-capital aspect of sport and it's basically ninety pages of a glowing tribute to the GAA and the way they have harnessed the voluntary capacity.

'However, their finest hour for me was when they revoked Rule 42 and opened up Croke Park to Ireland's soccer and rugby games while the old Lansdowne Road stadium was being demolished and the Aviva was being built. Nobody will ever forget the extraordinarily unique atmosphere that day Ireland played England in that never-to-be-forgotten rugby match. The emotion that day was unreal, as evidenced by the sight of big John Hayes bawling his eyes out while the anthems were being played. You could hear a pin drop when they played *God Save the Queen*. The respect was phenomenal. It was a day when everybody was so proud to be Irish. A special day in the history of a very special sporting body and one I take my hat off to. The fact that we hammered the old enemy in the match itself was just a bonus – but a very nice bonus!'

12

MIGHTY MUNSTER

Munster Win the 2006 Heineken Cup

Tony Ward was left feeling old after Munster won their first Heineken Cup.

'I suppose it was most forcefully emphasised to me that year, on 20 May to be precise, how much time has moved on after Munster won the Heineken Cup in Cardiff. Just before the match I went up in the lift with Ned Van Esbeck. When I got out, there were hundreds of Munster fans around and needless to say we got involved in friendly banter. No praise is high enough for what these supporters do for this country's image around the world. They are something else, with Cardiff that day the zenith of everything good to date.

'Shortly after, Gareth Edwards came along and stopped for a chat with us. He looked great, but what stunned me was that not a single Munster fan recognised the legend in their presence. This is the man who is the acknowledged greatest player of all time, the Pelé of rugby and scorer of *the* try. Despite the great depth of knowledge of Munster fans and the fact that they were in his home city, which is adorned by a Parnell-style monument of Gareth the Great in the city centre, the 500 or so Munster fans who were milling around him were blissfully unaware of who he was. Yesterday's heroes are quickly forgotten. Yet if Gavin Henson, a player with only a fraction of Gareth's talent, had walked into that gathering, everyone would have recognised him straight away.

'I must be getting old but that saddens me. It does illustrate though the importance of television to the game today. The profile of rugby is massive in Ireland at the moment and while mighty Munster's astounding achievements are hugely responsible for this, television coverage has played a vital role too.'

Ward felt more positive emotions too.

'We were ready to pass the baton! For 27 years I, and fourteen others, had the great good fortune to bask in the glory of one of the great moments in Irish sport when Munster beat the All Blacks.

'It was time for us to take our rightful place in the shade and pass the torch to the new high kings of Munster: Ronan O'Gara and company. As Tom Kiernan, coach in '78, so rightly said when throwing his arm around me in Heathrow on the way back, "Ward, we're buried".

'Saturday, 20 May 2006 became the high point of Munster rugby when the red army finally claimed the Holy Grail of European rugby by defeating Biarritz 23–19 in the Heineken Cup Final at the Millennium Stadium in Cardiff. Bearing in mind that from conceding seven points in the opening few minutes, Munster went on to outscore Biarritz 17–3 in the remainder of the half to the break, it represented their most convincing half of rugby in the three finals to date. As Mick Galwey said to me at the break, they were converting pressure into points, unlike their previous finals. They pushed the bounds of fitness, conditioning and most of all commitment beyond anything they had in the past. This was new territory and, given its context, the biggest single achievement yet in the long and proud history of Munster rugby.

'Ronan O'Gara masterminded Munster's mighty performance with confidence and assurance. He and Peter Stringer were majestic and marked the biggest difference in tactical appreciation between the two sides. Of course, they had thirteen heroes beside them, not least one of Ireland's two universally recognised world-class players. None of the Munster players take the field with fear but such was the force of Paul O'Connell that when he walked on the pitch, it was fear itself that was afraid!'

A great weight had been lifted from some of the sturdiest shoulders in world rugby. For so long it had seemed to be the destiny of that Munster team to be always the bridesmaid but never the bride. Each year since 1998–9 they had reached the knockout stages of the competition: losing three semi-finals to Stade Français, Toulouse and Wasps and, heartbreakingly, two finals to Northampton and Leicester. As Declan Kidney with typical shrewdness observed: 'Experience is what you get when you don't get what you want.'

Not surprisingly some of Ronan O'Gara's happiest memories are of Munster fans' greatest day.

'That game wasn't just about the final. It was about seven years of hard work. You get so close to something and you're denied that and it makes your resolve even greater. We just wanted to win so badly.

'We kept our composure. It was 7–3 and I know hindsight is a great thing but myself and Axel (Foley) made a great call to go for the corner. We needed to make a statement. We'd learned that you need tries to win finals. If we kept tapping penalties away it would have been 7–6, then 9–7. That wasn't what we needed. The boys tore into them and Trevor (Halstead)'s try was a great result for all that hard work.

'I don't think we took our foot off the pedal but for twenty minutes in the second half they dictated it. They'd a purple patch as you'd expect from a team of their quality. But we finished well. We had to get out of three-point range. There's a big difference between one and four points. With four points, you can retreat and make sure they don't cross your line. I think we took the game into our own terms and that's exactly what you've got to do.'

In any other game Ronan's superb performance would have won him the man of the match award, but after the final it was his half-back partner Peter Stringer who got the accolade. O'Gara was happy to see his friend's contribution recognised.

'Of all the games for him to pull out one of the best tries ever scored in the red jersey – it was incredible. When he made that break, he probably fooled all of us as well! It was a huge lift for us at the time to get those seven points. He's been criticised in the past because pundits said he wasn't able to make a break, but in fairness to Strings he stood up on the biggest occasion of all. My view of pundits is that it's easy to talk, but the real judgment on a player is not what is written in the papers but what he does on the pitch, and I think Strings has proven himself where it matters most.'

Although down the years Stringer has had a hard time from a number of rugby pundits, the fans have a very different view of him. This was perhaps most strikingly illustrated at the homecoming celebration for the Heineken Cup-winning Munster team in Cork. In the large crowd that night were some young ladies with a poster saying: 'Peter Stringer, we want to have your babies.'

It was a great help to O'Gara to have had such a long associa-

tion with Stringer. There is a famous photo in the Cork Consti-
tution dressing room with O'Gara and Stringer sitting beside
each other, having won a European under-12 competition.

Overall, 2006 was a year to remember for O'Gara. As if a second
Triple Crown triumph and a Heineken Cup win were enough, he
met his perfect match in July when he married his long-time love,
Jessica. Unusually for a Cork man, on that day Limerick rugby
fans were happy to sing 'There is an Isle' for Ronan.

The sweetness of the win was magnified for Paul O'Connell
by the fact that there had been so many disappointments on the
journey.

'I picked up a shoulder injury playing for Munster in the
run-up to the Heineken semi-final against Castres. The morning
of the match I had to do a fitness test. That is a test I will never
forget because my shoulder was standing up well and I was
hitting a tackle bag which Declan Kidney was holding. The
problem was that I hit it so hard at one stage I knocked out
one of Declan's teeth! He was due to do a TV interview three
quarters of an hour later so he had to go to the dentist to get it
stuck back in. The shoulder was fine, but I probably wasn't one
hundred per cent fit. We won the game, but in a warm-up match
before the Heineken Cup Final I damaged my ankle ligaments.
I did manage to play against Leicester in the final, but with my
shoulder and ankle problems I didn't play well.'

There was a lot of criticism of the side after that match. Was
that hard to take at the time?

'We knew that we had a lot of potential in the side and that's
why talk of "brave old Munster" had no interest for us. We
wanted to win and weren't satisfied anymore to play heroically
but to lose. I think criticism is brilliant. It only makes you a
better player, if you are mentally strong enough to take it. If
someone has a go at me personally in the press, and I respect

him, I think I can learn from that. If you don't respect him but he's speaking the truth, you have to take it on board, but if you know it's not the truth you just ignore it.'

O'Connell believes that much of the credit for the triumph must go to the coach.

'I am forever indebted to Declan Kidney. He gave me my first big break with Munster. I had a bit of a discipline problem when I was younger and I suppose I was lucky that he took a chance on me. I was getting too many yellow cards and if you're doing that, you don't get picked, and if you don't get picked, you don't get selected, and if you don't play, you don't get selected for Ireland and your career goes nowhere.

'Declan was a good motivator. He was always looking for the psychological edge. I remember at one stage in Munster we were conceding too many penalties and the odd soft try because of a lapse in concentration. Declan got white T-shirts for us to wear in training with "concentration" written on the front and "discipline" written on the back. You couldn't escape the message wherever you looked on the training pitch.

'My favourite story about him though goes back to 2000 before I joined the Munster squad. On the way to the Heineken Cup Final against Northampton, Munster had to play Saracens away. Saracens were a club without a tradition and they enlisted marketing people to tell them how to bring in the crowds.

'One of the things they did was to play the *Rocky* music whenever there was a fight or a row. When the team came on to the pitch they played the *A-Team* music; when the opposition came on they played 'The Teddy Bears' Picnic'; when the Saracens placekicker faced up to a penalty the crowd put on fez hats and had a little routine to guide the ball over the bar, and the tee came on in a remote-controlled car. To play against Saracens, you have to face a lot of distractions.

'Before Munster played them, the Munster squad were watching a Saracens match as part of their video analysis. With about two minutes to go on the video, Declan turned on a ghetto blaster and had the *A-Team* music blaring, put on his fez hat and started playing with the remote control and the lights. After a minute or so Declan turned off the television, took off his hat and turned off the ghetto blaster and he asked: "What happened in the last sixty seconds of the Saracens game?"'

13

TOULOUSE TOPPLED

Munster Win Their Second Heineken Cup

Ronan O'Gara pauses for thought when asked about the high point of his career.

'So much has happened in the last few years that there has been very little time for reflection. You don't get the luxury of looking back because you have to be looking forward all the time. You can never sit back and rest on your laurels but must always be looking for new goals and challenges. Every game you win with Ireland is a high point. We've had some great wins over France which were memorable. Beating Australia was a fantastic thrill. It was sweet to beat Argentina in the 2003 World Cup. Probably a match that stands out was beating England in Twickenham in 2004. Without wanting to sound arrogant, once we won that game, I knew that the Triple Crown was on. The Grand Slam was great but few days surpassed winning the two Heineken Cups with Munster.'

Tony Ward believes that Munster would not have won a second Heineken Cup (16–13 on 24 May 2008 against Toulouse in the Millennium Stadium) without O'Gara.

'What is it about Cork Con that they have produced three of the

54

greatest tactical kickers in the game, certainly in Ireland: Barry McGann, Ralph Keyes and Ronan O'Gara? Tactical kicking was probably Ronan's greatest strength. In terms of the diagonal kick to the corner, especially to the right-hand side of the pitch, generally, he had no peer. He was better at it than either Jonny Wilkinson or Dan Carter. He also excelled at appreciating the needs of his pack or of his team, or of playing for position or of pinning the corners. In those respects, as Carly Simon might have sung: nobody does it better. Ronan was the best.

'He was, for obvious reasons, the key piece in Declan Kidney's Munster jigsaw. He played the game that suited the Munster pack to perfection. He made life so easy for them but such a nightmare for the opposition. It's really soul-destroying for a pack when they are turned around and put on the back foot all the time. Ronan performed this task immaculately for Munster and Ireland, and that is why Eddie O'Sullivan rated him so highly for Ireland.

'There is another less obvious factor. I know for a fact that both Brian O'Driscoll and Gordon D'Arcy loved playing alongside him because of his ability to put players through the gaps. He had a long pass off either hand and had lovely, soft hands which enabled him to distribute the ball brilliantly. He could disguise his pass perfectly and release either O'Driscoll or D'Arcy on the outside defender with a long pass or on the inside defender with a short, popped pass. He really was a fantastic and much under-rated distributor.'

Ward accepts O'Gara had the odd flaw in his game too.

'Like myself, Ronan had weaknesses in his game. His Achilles heel was his inability to protect the ball when he was tackled after a break because he lacked the physical strength and requisite acceleration at the highest level. It was something he worked on.

'One criticism that was sometimes levelled against him concerned his so-called defensive frailties. People cite examples like the first Test against New Zealand in 2006 when Luke McAlister, a powerful out-half with a low centre of gravity, ran through him. A similar incident happened in one of the early games for the Lions in 2005. In modern parlance, he was targeted with an attack down his channel. That's the way the modern game is going, where any perceived weakness in any position on the field is targeted. It is not a defensive weakness. Technically Ronan was a very good tackler and wasn't afraid of tackling, but physically he was at times blown out of it.

'Firing on all cylinders he was an outstanding player. Kicking wise, off the ground, from the hands, drop goals – his record speaks for itself. He was just a brilliant out-half with a fantastic temperament and that is why both Munster and Ireland were so fortunate to have him.'

For his part Ronan O'Gara is happy to pay homage to the man of the match in that game. 'The player I most liked to have on my team going into battle was Alan Quinlan. He was a very under-rated player and had a great inner steel to him. He was dirty in a good way!'

Quinlan in turn gives part of the credit to a retired colleague.

'Early in my Munster career we were playing a training match and I was caught in the ruck. I felt this pain in my leg. I looked up and saw that The Claw (Peter Clohessy) was shoeing me – in other words standing on my hamstring. I said to him, "Claw, I'm on your side." He looked down dismissively at me and said: "Take your shoeing like a man."

'He was sending me a message that I needed to toughen up. It was also about helping me to understand that I was part of a culture where I literally had to be on the front foot. Playing for Munster was like going to war. Having only come on as a sub and played four minutes of our first Heineken Cup win, I was ready to go to war that day.'

14

MR D'ARCY

Ireland Win the 2004 Triple Crown

Few players have ever announced their arrival on the Six Nations stage with a louder blare of trumpets than Gordon D'Arcy in 2004. If there was one moment that will forever define his impact that season, it was the last minute of the match against Scotland which sealed Ireland's Triple Crown. Eddie O'Sullivan was making a bench clearance and D'Arcy was one of the players to be called ashore. Having scored two tries and having consistently tormented the Scottish defence with his powerful and intelligent running, the cheer for D'Arcy was almost deafening.

From the start of that campaign, Irish rugby followers took to him with extraordinary warmth, and not just because of the subtlety and invention and spirit of adventure that enabled him to terrorise opposing defenders. Above all they loved his all-action style, like a mighty atom, and relentless pursuit of every chance of taking off on an incisive run. Allied to that his creativity on the ball, his genius for penetration and his killing finish all commanded their respect. The fusion of great commitment and dazzling skills would be the stuff of cult status and instant sporting legend. It wasn't always clear though that he was going to light up the rugby landscape so dramatically.

Before 2004 there had been a number of hints in newspaper articles that D'Arcy had a problem with his attitude. How accurate was that perception?

'When I first started playing rugby, I had a very blasé approach,' D'Arcy recalls. 'I enjoyed playing rugby, but I was carrying that casual attitude into my preparation and training and it just gave off the wrong vibe, and it took me a while to realise that more commitment was needed. When you have established yourself consistently as a top-class player, you don't have to be too worried about the vibe you give off, but when you're trying to break into a new team, it's important because other people make judgements about you on the basis of that rather than what you can do on the pitch. It took me a while to adjust to that.

'I don't think saying I had a bad attitude was the most accurate way of portraying it. I just had my own way. When I look back at it now, I came straight out of school and into a professional set-up. I probably wasn't given the direction initially. I probably should have been put into an under-21 squad or on a regimented programme where someone said: "You're a stone and a half overweight – you need to lose that, then we'll work on your fitness, etc." Instead it was very haphazard. I was here and there working with different people but nobody was actually telling me what to do. When I look back at it now, I think: I wasted a lot of time then. It wasn't that I was resisting anybody or had a bad attitude because people like that don't last in sport.

'What amazed me was that certain people in the media were looking for a story to latch on to and a story about Matt Williams finding me drunk got legs and started turning up everywhere. My attitude though was that one incident doesn't sum me up as a person. I was doing things my way. I was playing exciting rugby in my eyes like running the ball from my own five-metre line – sometimes it came off, sometimes it didn't. As a nineteen-year-old the consequences of your actions aren't all that relevant. People said, "He was a crazy, crazy kid." I wasn't. I was just a regular nineteen-year-old.'

What then is his assessment of Matt Williams?

'Mattie has his pros and cons. He gave me a little correction and said I wasn't professional enough. I thought I was but I wasn't. I didn't see the need to kick because I thought I could run my way out of trouble but he said no – you have to be able to kick with both feet.

'Mattie probably did more for the set-up in Leinster in general than for any player in particular. There was a lot of talk that he resurrected Reggie Corrigan's and Victor Costello's careers, but I don't think that's true. There's a great saying that when you're down and out and on the ground, nobody can pick you up. People can hold out their hand but, in the end, you have to pick yourself up off the floor. Matt gave us a lot of the tools to help ourselves. When he first came he brought in revolutionary changes like us having a sports massage every Monday morning. At the time, we were all saying: that's crazy. He revolutionised Leinster rugby and fought hard for the players. He told us that he would shout and curse at us behind closed doors but in public he would defend us to the hilt. In fairness to him, that's exactly what he did.'

D'Arcy was controversially omitted from the Irish World Cup squad in 2003.

'That will go down as one of the low points of my life. I always said when I made the first World Cup in '99 I would like to play in four World Cups. It was between Paddy Wallace and myself for the one spot. It was a call that had to be made, and you live and die by those calls. There were calls that went my way afterwards, like when Brian (O'Driscoll) was injured before the France game in 2004.

'I remember I was inconsolable when I heard I'd missed out on the squad. I was talking to a schoolteacher friend of mine and I asked in a wailing tone, "What's going to happen to me now?" He calmly said: "Well, you're going to be able to play eight games at full-back for Leinster and you're always saying that you want to play at full-back." It helped me to start thinking positively again.'

The popular perception was that missing out on the World Cup was the catalyst D'Arcy needed to finally get his act together and fulfil his true potential. Not for the first time in his career, the real story was more complex.

'It was easy for people to write that missing out on the World Cup was the spur that made me perform in 2004, but that is not the case. When I wasn't getting picked for Ireland, I lost my enjoyment of playing rugby, and I lost the things I enjoyed about the game – like beating a man one-on-one and putting in a good tackle. During the World Cup, I started to enjoy my rugby again, because at Leinster I was playing with my friends and a coach I got on brilliantly with, Gary Ella. He gave me literally a free role. I asked him before one game: "Is there anything you want me to do?" And he said: "If you see it, do it."

'"Is there anything you don't want me to do?"

'"No, not really, mate."

'"Okay."

'I was just smiling after a game and I was training well because I was so looking forward to playing again and that was re-energising me. I didn't consciously say "I'm going to get my place on the Irish team" or "I'm going to train harder" – I was just enjoying it more.'

His international redemption came almost by accident.

'There wasn't much cover in either Leinster or Ireland for the centre positions. In the run-up to a Leinster game Gary Ella casually asked me one day: "Do you want to go thirteen?" It really was as casual as that. We were walking on to the pitch and we were having a little banter. I replied: "Well, do you want me to play thirteen?"

'"Well, what do you think?"

'"Yeah, okay. We'll see how it goes."

'It seemed to work for Leinster and Eddie O'Sullivan gave it a try against France.'

Brian O'Driscoll's injury allowed D'Arcy to take his place on the Irish team in the opening Six Nations fixture in Paris. Yet some shook their heads and said it would be too high a jump to move into the cauldron of such a match. It was an extraordinary burden for such an inexperienced player to carry but, driven by a fierce determination, and that most magical of qualities, a big-match temperament, D'Arcy would not buckle under.

'I had five caps before I started the Six Nations game against France in 2004. The experience of those caps and of being in and out of the Irish squad probably helped me for a start.'

D'Arcy came into a side with a clear mission.

'People said we were a "nearly team" before we won the Triple Crown. I remember Brian O'Driscoll saying when we beat Australia in 2002: "Let's not be the nearly team, let's not get the good win now and again but let's strive to beat the big guns consistently." I think we did that winning the Triple Crown. We had beaten France in 2000, England in 2001 and Australia in 2002, but we hadn't strung enough good results together against top opposition. Winning the Triple Crown took that monkey off our back and gave us a base to build on. When we went on tour to South Africa after winning the Triple Crown, a good performance was no longer to lose by only ten points. A good performance was nothing less than a win.'

Five years after winning his first cap against Romania in the '99 World Cup, D'Arcy was to finally stamp his distinctive mark on international rugby.

'There were a few moments before the France game that stand out for me. You trained at the start of the week with a squad of thirty. Then on the Wednesday a squad of twenty-two players was announced. I was in the twenty-two and I went: "Wow. I'm going to be on the bench." I presumed they were going to go for a different combination in the centre, but I was pretty sure that I would win another cap at some stage in the match by coming on as a replacement.

'Then the team was called out. I heard: "D'Arcy, thirteen." I was in a state of shock. After that we went to training and Eddie (O'Sullivan) said to me: "Relax. Play your game and when you get the ball run hard." It was the best advice I ever got.

'The other thing I remember is going to the stadium before the match. I had heard a lot about it but never been in it. I remember when we turned a corner on the team bus, there it stood in front of us, and I actually couldn't see as far as the top of it because it was so huge. I walked out with Malcolm O'Kelly to throw the ball around. You nearly had to look straight up to see the sunlight.

'As the game started, I just wanted the ball. From the kick-off, we went straight at them, but two defensive mistakes, two simple things, cost us fourteen points and the game. I went to Kitty O'Shea's afterwards and met my brothers and sisters, who had travelled over for the match, and that was great.

'The Wales game for me personally was massive. It was my first start at home for Ireland and I felt really in the zone. Your first home game is amazing, and it was also Brian's first game back from his injury. Playing with Brian made my job a lot easier. Everyone knows he was a great player, but I honestly think people don't fully appreciate how good he was and all the things he did on the pitch. People remember the flashy stuff he did, like the tries, but they don't see the amount of bread-and-butter stuff he got through in a match. If people only knew the amount of work he got through on the pitch they would be in awe. From a selfish point of view, his great value was that he created more space for me. He actually created more time on the ball for you.

'The English game was special. All week everybody was "locked and loaded", as Eddie liked to put it. The great thing was that the squad – players and staff – was so well gelled together, and our play on the field reflected that. Brian made a throwaway comment that he hoped Ireland might make the Twickenham crowd "choke on their prawn sandwiches". Of course, the English media whipped up a storm about it but we didn't let it faze us in the slightest.

'Before the game we did a warm-up and you could feel the energy running through the side. Rog (Ronan O'Gara) was playing so well and was able to give Brian and myself the type of ball we needed, and that made a huge difference. A big part of the game plan for that match was for Rog to throw a wide, flat pass to Brian and myself. When we came in at half-time the question was asked: "Is anybody tired?" The answer was an emphatic no from everyone. This is the Six Nations and we are going to win. They can't beat us. The try we scored from our own twenty-two was one of my favourite Ireland team tries ever. I remember speaking to Eddie that evening and saying: "I'd say that put a smile on your face."

'"What?"

'"That try was exactly what you were getting us to do during the week."

'"Yeah."

'He wasn't saying it in a smug way, but he was just satisfied that everybody had done exactly what they were supposed to do.

'I know I got two tries in the Scotland game but, going on the stats, my best game was against England in terms of ball-carrying and so on. I was more satisfied with my performance in the England game than the Scottish game. I was fourteen the last time Ireland had won in Twickenham in 1994, when Simon Geoghegan got that try in the corner. I was jumping up and down and I didn't even like rugby then! So that was a big one to win.

'The England game was the critical one that season. From one to twenty-two we had a belief that we were going to win that game. The preparation had gone well all week, the self-belief was there – which was a huge thing. The popular view was that we were underdogs but, in the squad, man for man, we didn't believe that. We felt we were as good as them.

'The problem with the Scottish game was that they were like a cornered dog. It was going to be a five-game whitewash for them, so we knew it was going to be a tough game. Down through the years one of the things that has always bugged me about Irish sport is that we're not comfortable about being favourites. We're much happier as underdogs, grinding out a result. You have to get used to being favourites. People say it's a weight around your neck. I think it's time we saw it the other way – as something you wear on your shoulder to make you feel taller – and we need to develop that mentality. Up to the last twenty minutes against Scotland we were grinding away at them. Finally, we pulled away from them. To win the Triple Crown is something I hadn't even dreamed about because it happened so seldom at that stage.'

What was his own highlight from that magical season?

'My second try against Scotland was the last nail in the coffin and effectively sealed the Triple Crown, but it was my first try that day that was the most satisfying for me personally because it was a much better score.'

The icing on the cake for D'Arcy was that he was chosen as the Northern Hemisphere player of the season.

15

DOYEN DEMPSEY

Ireland Shock England in 2004

Girvan Dempsey guaranteed himself a place in Irish rugby immortality when he scored the try that beat England in 2004. Against all the odds Ireland ended England's 22-match winning streak at 'Fortress Twickenham', stretching back to the 1999 World Cup when they were beaten by New Zealand. It was England's first championship home defeat under Sir Clive Woodward, whose coaching regime began in November 1997. To add the icing to the cake, the English were parading the Webb Ellis trophy at Twickers for the first time since their World Cup victory in Australia. Dempsey's try immediately entered the pantheon of greatest Irish touchdowns of all time alongside both Kevin Flynn's '72 try and Ginger McLoughlin's try in '82 in the same venue, and Ken Goodall's celebrated hoof-and-chase try in Ireland's 14–0 win over Wales at Lansdowne Road in 1970.

The try came after fifty-one minutes when Gordon D'Arcy made a classic break through the field, the ball was taken on down the left and then switched back to the right, where the pack took up the charge. After the ball was recycled, both

D'Arcy and Brian O'Driscoll threw long passes across the field and Tyrone Howe passed to Dempsey, who scythed over. Girvan feels that the only people who weren't shocked by this turn of events were the Irish team.

'Although nobody gave us a chance, we went into the game with a lot of self-confidence and felt we could take the scalp of the world champions. All week Eddie O'Sullivan had been asking: "Why can't we beat England?"

'Training had gone well all week. Going on to the pitch, the noise from the English fans was incredible. They got a try from Matt Dawson early on. Brian O'Driscoll called us together and said: "Right, lads. This is a big game. Let's buckle down." I know it's a cliché but the try was straight off the training ground. We had worked that move again and again in Naas and everyone played their part perfectly.'

Many Irish fans were very annoyed by the rash lunge Ben Cohen made at Dempsey as he scored the try.

'I know some people were very unhappy about it but I bear no ill will towards him. You have to do everything you can to stop a try. The problem was that I had to go off with a damaged right knee because of the incident. While I wasn't angry with him, I was livid that I had to leave the pitch on what was to be one of the greatest days in the history of Irish rugby.

'It was great, then, to go on and win the Triple Crown against Scotland in Lansdowne Road. Down through the years, Scotland had given us many a beating in the Six Nations, even on the days we were expected to win. They had performed poorly in the competition up to that game but, with Matt Williams in charge of them, and with his intimate knowledge of so many of our players, we knew they would raise their game.

'It was such a fantastic feeling once the final whistle went. Nobody wanted to leave afterwards. We felt it was a tangible reward for all the hard work we had put in down the years. Losing the Grand Slam decider against England the previous year had been such a massive disappointment. We'd felt that the distance between us was nowhere near as great as the scoreboard suggested. Jonny Wilkinson produced the greatest display of rugby I have ever seen that day, and the margin of their victory flattered them, so it was doubly nice to win the Triple Crown in Lansdowne Road twelve months later. Once Gordon got the try we just knew it was going to be one of those great days.'

For Dempsey, the English game was a redemption experience. After Ireland's defeat in Paris in 2004, Dempsey found his performance lacerated in the media and his abilities questioned and even derided. As Billy Keane colourfully put it, he 'got more stick than a lazy donkey during the turf-cutting season'.

'I never considered myself the same sort of flair player as Denis Hickie, Geordan Murphy, Gordon D'Arcy or Brian O'Driscoll, but my game was based on doing the bread-and-butter stuff well. In a Heineken Cup game for Leinster, and in the France match, I made a couple of mistakes I normally wouldn't make, and as a result some of the comments about me in the press were at the very least not constructive, and some were nasty. Dealing with the press is part of the job of being a professional rugby player today. It toughens the skin and makes you try harder when they write you off. The problem is that when they write nasty things about you, it's very difficult for your parents to read it – they find it very upsetting. They've been at all the games I've played in and given me great support, so they took it badly when they saw destructive comments about me. That said, the best way to answer your critics is to let your performances do the talking.'

Dempsey is keen to pay tribute to his Irish coaches for the highs of 2004.

'Warren Gatland gave me my first cap. He is an excellent coach, as he has proved since. He instilled a lot of toughness in us, though I think he was never fully forgiven for losing against Argentina in Lens in 1999.

'Eddie O'Sullivan was a superb coach. He was so meticulous and spent every waking moment thinking of ways to improve us. His analysis was so thorough that sometimes we could see our opponents' moves before they could. He was also very innovative and used imaginative ways to motivate us. A speech just before, during or straight after a game rarely means anything. It's what is done in the weeks leading up to it that wins a match for you. In the run-up to the World Cup in 2003, Eddie brought in two very different guest speakers to talk to us in the City West hotel. They were the explorer Sir Ranulph Fiennes and the former champion boxer Marvin Hagler. They both struck a chord with a number of players in the squad. Sir Ranulph talked about the preparation that was needed for a major expedition and the steps you needed to take to achieve what you wanted to achieve. Marvin spoke about the importance of self-confidence. They both really touched me and many of us found them inspirational – they were just the right choices to get us psyched up for the World Cup.'

16

MUNSTER'S MIRACLE MATCH

Munster v Gloucester

'Stand toe to toe
Trade blow for blow'

At times, it seemed Ronan O'Gara could do the impossible. On the day Ireland claimed the 2004 Triple Crown with a win over Scotland, RTÉ radio commentator Michael Corcoran observed, 'Ronan O'Gara has his boots on the right foot.'

Did he suffer from nerves before big games?

'In the build-up to big games I couldn't afford to let myself be distracted by paper talk. My main job was to stay cool.'

O'Gara's coolness was exemplified in the Millennium Stadium in Cardiff in 2003. Rog came on as a late sub in the game. Ireland led 22–21 when Stephen Jones drop-kicked Wales ahead. From the restart, O'Gara got the ball forty metres out and calmly dropped a goal to give Ireland a dramatic win. In the Autumn International with Argentina in 2004, he replicated this feat with a dramatic drop goal to snatch the game for Ireland.

His temperament was also shown on a sodden November afternoon at Lansdowne Road in 2002 when he held his nerve and his footing all afternoon and kicked the six penalties required to give Ireland an 18–9 victory over Australia, which led the Irish team to literally squelch around the pitch for a lap of honour.

His coolness would be called for like never before.

18 January 2003.

Heineken Cup pool game.

Thomond Park. Where else do you go for epic drama?

Munster face Mission Impossible.

They need to beat Gloucester by no less than twenty-seven points to qualify for the Heineken Cup quarter-final.

They also need to score four tries.

Surely it couldn't be done.

Stand up and fight.

The atmosphere was electric.

As if there wasn't enough tension, a James Bond moment takes place. A copy of the Gloucester game plan was found in the back of a taxi in Limerick. It was rushed to the Munster coach Alan Gaffney.

Is this the real thing? Or could it be a double bluff?

The game started.

John Kelly scored the first try in the right corner.

The crowd were singing.

Stand up and fight right now.

Just before half-time Mossy Lawler scored on the left.

Thomond Park was rocking.

In the second half Mick O'Driscoll scored a try.

The crowd went wild. The impossible was now possible.

Time passed.

More time passed.

The tension rose.

Time was almost up.

The tension had become unbearable.

A hero needed to save the day.

It was the 80th minute.

Stand up and fight.

Ronan O'Gara got the ball.

A characteristically perfect pinpoint kick.

A line-out close to the line.

John Kelly collected and scored the fourth try.

31–6.

Still not enough.

The conversion was needed.

A very difficult angle in any circumstances ...

But with all this tension? A cool head was required like never before.

Ronan O'Gara stepped forward.

Yet again, when it mattered most, he nailed it.

Cue delirium.

Yet O'Gara does not take the credit. One of the abiding memories of his early games for Ireland was the way the great Mick Galwey put his arms around Ronan and Peter Stringer during the preliminaries to reassure them that they were going to rise to the occasion. It's not surprising to discover that Galwey features prominently in O'Gara's list of great characters.

'I suppose the two greatest characters of Munster rugby in my time were Mick Galwey and Peter Clohessy. They were old school and are a huge loss to the game, and the freshness they brought to both the game and the Munster squad was very uplifting. Probably my most abiding memory of my days in the Irish squad was when the players and management made a presentation to Peter to mark his 50th cap. Peter responded by singing the Frank Sinatra song: "My Way". What an appropriate song! He did things his way or no way. That's why I liked and admired him so much. Without The Claw and Gallimh (Galway), Munster would never have become the force it did.

'Gallimh was on the bench during the miracle match. The night before, he really got us going with a great speech about what it meant to play for Munster. It got us all in exactly the right frame of mind. He was the spark we needed to win that magical day.'

Stand up and fight like hell.

17

BAND OF BROTHERS

Three Wallace Brothers Play for the Lions

Few scores have ever been greeted as enthusiastically as David Wallace's try against Scotland in 2004. The match was supposed to be a mere formality which would allow Ireland to win their first Triple Crown in nineteen years. However, the Scots had not read the script and had the cheek to draw level eight minutes into the second half. Irish fans started to get anxious. Wallace steadied Irish nerves when he used his extraordinary power to pivot out of a tackle and dash for the line to allow all of Ireland to relax. As he left the Scottish defence in his wake, a great roar shook the Lansdowne Road stadium. Wallace has always been quick off the mark. In August 2003, he came on as a sub against Wales in a World Cup warm-up game and scored a try after just thirty-eight seconds.

Wallace is part of a unique rugby family. Two of his brothers played both for Ireland and the Lions, as he did.

'Dad had a huge interest in rugby and we all got involved from an early age. At the school sports day, my mother won the mother's race, so I think we all got a bit of speed from Mum.'

Richard Wallace won the first of his twenty-nine caps on the Irish wing against Namibia in 1991 and his last against England in 1998. Like his brother Paul, he scored five tries in Test games for Ireland. Paul won the first of forty-five caps in the Irish front row against Japan in 1995 and the last against Georgia in 2002. Though injury forced him to retire prematurely from the game, he has found a new niche on the rugby landscape as an intelligent and perceptive media analyst.

'Richard went out on the Lions tour as a replacement in '93.' Paul remembers. 'I was only sixteen at the time and it was an incredible thrill for us as a family to see him playing with and against the legends of world rugby. I would have to say that it was also a fantastic experience to see my eldest brother, Henry, and Richard play for the Irish Colleges team together.

'To think of Richard playing for the Lions was inspirational for me, particularly as he was relatively new to international rugby. I learned a lot from him about the training and the physical preparation that is required for rugby at the highest level.'

'When Paul was selected to replace Peter Clohessy before the Lions tour to South Africa in '97 actually began,' David remembers, 'he was looking over a partition in the airport when he saw The Claw coming towards him on the way home. It was awkward for him. But the fact that he made it on to the Test team and was considered one of the stars of the tour was great for the family.'

This was also a significant year for David Wallace's emerging rugby career.

'I played in all the games on the Irish development tour to New Zealand that year, but I lost my way a bit after that in the new professional environment. I was probably in a bit of a comfort zone. The following February I won my first Ireland A cap when coming on as a replacement for Alan Quinlan against Scotland. One of my happiest memories that year was

75

being part of the under-21 team that won the Triple Crown.

'That summer I was called to the senior squad for the summer tour to South Africa. I had been recovering from injury so I wasn't at my best, and although I played in three games, I probably didn't do myself any favours. I wasn't firing on all cylinders after that so it took me two years to win my first cap against Argentina on Ireland's summer tour. It wasn't the fairy-tale debut I dreamed of and we lost, which was very disappointing. I do remember feeling a little bit nervous before the game began as we togged out, and that the crowd was very intense. I've never seen a video of the game. A week later I won my second cap against the United States. We beat them well in the hottest temperatures I have ever played in.'

The year 2001 was to prove another big one for Wallace.

'I played against Italy and France in the Six Nations, but the foot-and-mouth outbreak interrupted the championship. I had been in the preliminary squad for the Lions tour, but like other players on the Irish team I was out of the shop window at a crucial time because of the foot-and-mouth scare. I was kind of disappointed not to make the original touring party but knew that I still might make the trip because I was on standby. I won my fifth cap in a friendly against Romania but, as the Lions tour was progressing, I was starting to worry that I wouldn't get the call. I was going off on a summer training camp in Poland with the Irish team and was halfway there on a stop-off in Copenhagen airport when I got a phone call from Ronan O'Gara telling me that there was an injury and that I was going to be called up. I got a flight back to Heathrow and then another one on to Australia. I had forty-five hours of airports and planes before I eventually got there. I then had to learn about 101 squad calls very quickly because almost immediately I had to play against New South Wales.

'It was pretty unbelievable to find myself playing for the Lions and to discover that I had made history by becoming the third member of the one family to play for the Lions – which had never been done before. I discovered pretty early on though that there was a negative vibe within the camp. Players like Austin Healey and Matt Dawson were unhappy not to be playing in the Test side. You could understand why they might be unhappy, but then they vented their grievances with management in their newspaper columns, which obviously did nothing to improve morale within the squad and added to the media circus.'

What was at the heart of the problems within the squad?

'I would attribute the difficulties to two factors: the training regime and poor communication. Some of the players found that the training was excessive and didn't allow enough time for rest. Any time you have disharmony within a group like that, you can be certain that there are failures of communication.

'For my own part I seemed to gel pretty well with everybody. The squad was divided pretty much between the Test side and the midweek side, and the players on both teams tended to mix largely with the other players on "their team" rather than the entire squad. As a result, the only English player I really got to know was Ben Cohen. Before the second Test, Scott Quinnell picked up an injury and there was major doubt about him being able to take his place on the bench for the game, and I was in line to replace him. But he passed his fitness test the day of the game so I missed out on having any involvement on the Test team, which was a bit of a disappointment, as you would expect.

'I was a regular in the Irish side for the Six Nations the following season, but I got a bad shoulder injury which required surgery and I missed out on all the Six Nations in 2003. I did travel on the summer tour to Australia that year, but I was still bothered by my shoulder and wasn't playing well, which in turn affected my confidence. It had been a big goal of mine to play in the World Cup but, unfortunately, I wasn't selected for the squad. I was sitting home watching the Argentina game when Alan Quinlan got that bad injury and I had an hour or two to throw my stuff into a bag. It wasn't how I'd dreamed of getting there, and while it was good to experience the tournament, it was disappointing to be at the World Cup and not be part of the action on the pitch.

'As a child, some of my earliest memories were of Ireland's two Triple Crowns in the 1980s. It was great to play a part in Ireland's Triple Crown win in 2004. It was particularly sweet for me to score a try against Scotland in the decisive match.'

Wallace's highs and lows with Ireland have been replicated with Munster.

'I've had so many great days with Munster, especially some incredible wins against the odds on French soil. Losing two European finals was very hard to take. The one that hurt the most was losing the final to Northampton. The game was ours for the taking that day, but we left it behind us.'

18

DRICO'S DESTINY

Brian O'Driscoll's Threesome

France play their rugby with great passion, what the Welsh called *hwyl*. Never was this quality more exemplified than in the 1999 World Cup semi-final against New Zealand, one of the greatest matches of all time, when they trailed 24–10 in the second half only to win 43–31 before a bedazzled Twickenham audience. It was appropriate that Brian O'Driscoll should announce his arrival on the international stage in bold print in Paris in front of the French audience.

Brian has been in thrall to the game of rugby for as long as he can remember. It helps that his father, Frank, played for Ireland and that his cousins Barry and John also played for Ireland. A kind, passionate but polite, thoroughly delightful man, Frank recalls Brian's introduction to rugby with pure and undiluted happiness.

'I still recall going to see Brian playing his first match with the Schoolboys. I think he scored four tries that day. After the game, people were asking: who is this new kid on the block? Having been fortunate enough to play for Ireland myself, I always felt that if Brian got the breaks, he would also go on and play for Ireland. I never had any doubt about whether he had the talent, but talented players don't always make it for a variety of reasons – injury, for example.

'One of the proudest days for me was when Brian played his first game for Ireland at schoolboy level. I remember saying to my wife, Geraldine, on the way to the match, "Do you realise that only fourteen other sets of parents in Ireland are going to experience what we're going to experience today?" I was so proud of him.

'Although he has done a lot of great things on the field, I am particularly proud of him because of his discipline. He never let his social life interfere with his rugby. It was always the other way around.'

In conversation with this writer, Eddie O'Sullivan recalled his early impressions of the brightest star in Irish rugby.

'Brian O'Driscoll burst on the scene in a pretty explosive style. I remember seeing him at school in Blackrock College when I worked there for a while. He was quite small then but suddenly got this great growth spurt and turned into a fine athlete. He had something special. He was very gifted in terms of athleticism and in terms of football skills but he's also a very intelligent guy. The key thing that made him different to everyone else was that he could perform at the highest level under the greatest pressure and still come through. That's the biggest test for any athlete.'

At Blackrock College, Brian paraded all the fluent skills that would characterise his international career: great speed and an almost unique combination of attacking and defensive qualities. Those talents brought him to the attention of the international selectors.

'My debut for Ireland came in June 1999. I had been brought on the tour of Australia having sat on the bench for one of the Six Nations games. I played a few games on the tour before the first Test in Brisbane, when I was selected to play in the centre with Kevin Maggs. I was lucky to play for Ireland when I was so young. It was a huge honour for me and something that I had always hoped to rise to at some stage of my career, but for it to have come at such an early age was incredible and something I really cherished. I had mixed emotions because we got a bad beating, but at the same time I'd won my first cap. I probably got to enjoy my second Test more because we really pushed the Aussies all the way. I had heard people say that your first cap always goes by so quickly that you can't really take it all in and enjoy it. That was my experience too.

'At the start, things weren't going so well for Ireland. The low point was probably losing to Argentina in the World Cup back in Lens in 1999. That defeat was crushing. I think we panicked as a team towards the end and probably our thirteen-man line-out showed we were a bit scarce of ideas.

'I think we probably reached an equal low when we lost so heavily to England the following year. After that a lot of changes were made, the team started to improve and we began to win again. I think when you have bad losses as well as great victories you become very philosophical and realise that when you're down, the team is probably not as bad as people say you are, or when you win, you're not the world-beaters that everybody says you are.'

Happier times were around the corner and Brian dramatically announced his arrival on the world stage with a stunning performance in Paris, culminating in his three tries.

'When we went to play France, nobody expected us to even challenge them, which probably took a lot of weight off our shoulders. I look back at the pictures and see the joy on our faces for having achieved something that Irish teams had failed to do for twenty-eight years. We were overwhelmed at the end and it was really a fantastic feeling. For me to have scored three tries was a nice bonus!

'The third try sticks out most of all. What most people probably don't realise is that I shouldn't have been where I was when I got the ball. I was just trying to catch a breather before I got back into position, but the ball squirted out in front of me and I went for the gap. That try took us to within two points of them and convinced us that we could win the game. A lot of people have remarked that Émile Ntamack didn't make a great effort to tackle me – I'm only glad he didn't come crashing into me!'

Brian was fortunate in having a temperament that gets energised rather than drained by a big occasion. The bigger the occasion, the more he liked it. In fact, where he was least relaxed was when he was watching a game he wasn't playing in.

'I know some people will probably feel this is strange, but I was far more nervous watching the 1997 Lions tour of South Africa, when I was back home in Dublin staring at the television set, than I was on the field in Brisbane for the first Test in 2001. When you're playing, you have no time to dwell on things.'

O'Driscoll was lucky to have the support of such a united family behind him, particularly as he was so much in the public glare. Brian's mother, Geraldine, is all too aware of this.

'The France game in 2000, when he scored the three tries, changed everything for Brian – and indeed for us. I first realised that when I was introduced to someone after the match and they said, "This is Geraldine O'Driscoll. She used to be Frank O'Driscoll's wife. Now she's Brian O'Driscoll's mother!"

'The France game was on a Sunday and shortly after the match we had to rush for the train to be home for work the next day. One of our daughters was in Australia at the time and she rang us on the mobile, saying, "Mum, after Brian's three tries I'm now a minor celebrity here!"

19

I'M ON FIRE

Peter Clohessy Makes His Mark

Peter Clohessy's love of Limerick is immediately apparent when he is asked about the highlights of his career.

'I suppose my first highlight was winning the All-Ireland League with Young Munster in 1993. After that the other highlights were my first cap for Ireland, then beating France in Paris in 2000 and England in Twickenham in 1994.'

The Limerick bias is also evident when he's asked to name the characters of rugby: 'Mick Galwey, Philip Danaher, Keith Wood and Anthony Foley.'

Another great passion was Munster. 'The low points were losing two European Cup finals with Munster. To be so close twice and to lose on both occasions was very tough. We just seemed to always be the bridesmaids.'

The Claw has happier memories of an English World Cup hero.

'I always got on well with Jason Leonard. When we played England, there was always a bit of banter between us because we'd been playing against each other so long. With about twenty minutes to go of our trouncing at Twickenham in 2002, Jason took me by surprise when he said: "Peter, I believe you're away to a wedding straight after the game?"

'I'm not sure how he knew that but I was indeed off to a friend's wedding in Cork immediately after the match. I replied: "The quicker I get out of this place, the f**king better."'

The Claw did have some other setbacks. In 1997, he was chosen to tour with the Lions to South Africa, but although he made the trip to London to meet with the squad, he was forced to return home with injury.

Before the 2002 Heineken Cup semi-final he faced a more serious injury when he was badly burned in a domestic accident. This prompted his wife to remark: 'I always knew you'd go out in a blaze of glory, but I didn't think you'd literally do it.'

The small matter of multiple skin burns wasn't enough to deter Clohessy from playing in the game though. In solidarity with The Claw, Munster fans wore T-shirts to the game saying: 'Bitten and burnt, but not beaten.'

A happier memory had come earlier that year when his son, Luke, accompanied him as he led the Irish team out against Wales in the Six Nations to celebrate his 50th cap. To add to the occasion, he was followed closely on to the Lansdowne Road turf by his great friend, Mick Galwey, captaining his country for the first time on the famous sod. Clohessy played like a man possessed in Ireland's demolition job of the Welsh, even setting up a try for Geordan Murphy with a masterful reverse-pass. When he was substituted near the end, he received a massive standing ovation.

It was not always thus. One man's meat is another's poison. Clohessy unexpectedly found himself cast as the bête noire of Irish rugby in 1996. During a Five Nations match in Paris he 'misplaced his boot' on Olivier Roumat's head during a ruck.

The six-foot-six, 242lbs lock was himself no angel. He was once so incensed by the loud snoring of his roommate Abdel Benazzi on the eve of a Test that he ran over to his bed and punched the mighty Moroccan-born forward.

Clohessy's character was unfairly traduced after the affair, particularly considering that the amount of intimidation and provocation he was subjected to was ignored. He was quoted after one match against French opposition as saying: 'It's a bit much to have some French f**ker gouging you in the eyes without him grabbing you by the bollocks as well.'

The six-month ban that ensued and the trial by the media almost caused him to walk away from the game, but one maid in shining armour came to his rescue.

'The biggest influence on my career was my wife, Anna. After all the bashing I got in the media after the stamping incident, I was very tempted to pack in rugby, but she persuaded me to stick with it. She really got me through what was a difficult period for me. While I was suspended from rugby here, I went to play in Brisbane, Australia. That was my first introduction into playing rugby at professional level and an experience I really enjoyed.'

Some birds are not meant to be caged; their feathers are just too bright. A series of top-notch performances for Munster and Ireland quickly earned Clohessy any redemption that might have been necessary in the eyes of rugby fans, to the extent that he became a father figure of Irish rugby, especially for young players. He adhered to the motto of: 'Say little but say it well'.

How would he like to be remembered by Irish rugby fans?

'I'd just like them to think of me as someone who always played in the green jersey – or any jersey – with passion.'

History has already decreed that this is an incontestable fact, and The Claw has many happy memories from his time in rugby.

'I think the nice thing is that when I look back now at my career, what I remember most is all the good times we had on and off the pitch. Although we trained hard, we had a lot of fun. My fondest memory is before we played Scotland one time. The night before the match Mick Galwey discovered his togs were missing. There was a minor panic because nobody else had any to spare. Eventually someone got him togs. Ireland were sponsored by Nike at the time. But Mick's togs didn't have the Nike name or swish so someone gave him a black marker and he wrote the name Nike on them.

'Later that night I crept into his room and changed the word "Nike" to "Mike" and wrote "Mike loves Joan". The next day we were changing in the dressing room before the match when I saw Mick putting on his togs. He didn't notice the change but noticed I was laughing at him. He asked: "Okay, what have you done to me?"

'When I told him, he had a great laugh. It was just an hour before a big international but it was a great way of breaking the ice for us.'

20

ULSTER SAYS YES

Ulster Are European Champions in 1999

David Humphreys has seen both sides of the rugby coin. At the end of a glorious week for Irish rugby, seven days after Munster had won the Heineken Cup, Ulster claimed their first Celtic League title in 2006. Given his great service to the province, it was appropriate that the victory was sealed by a dramatic late kick by David Humphreys against defending champions Ospreys, in Wales. Humphreys slotted over a forty-metre drop goal just two minutes from time to snatch the title from Leinster.

David Humphreys MBE amassed a number of records, becoming Ireland's record point scorer and Ireland's most prolific drop-goal scorer. He received an honorary doctorate from the University of Ulster for services to the game and captained the Irish Schools side to their first Grand Slam in the Home Nations Championships, but really introduced himself to the rugby world in 1995 in the Varsity match when he scored all of Oxford's points with a try, conversion, drop goal and three penalties in a 21–19 defeat by Cambridge. He became the first Irish player to score more than 500 points in international rugby.

His running game hasn't always got the credit it deserves, like the way he skinned Aaron Persico for pace before scoring a try in Ireland's 37–13 win over Italy in Rome in 2003.

The highlight of his career came in January 1999 when he captained Ulster to victory in the European Cup, becoming the first Irish province to become European Champions.

'We didn't have a very good team, but we got on a roll. There were just a few hundred people at our first match, but our success struck a chord initially across the province and then throughout the whole of Ireland. Driving down to Dublin for the final in Lansdowne Road, all the flags of support really inspired us.

'All of Ireland got behind us as we were bidding to become the first Irish side to win the competition. I suppose it was all the sweeter for me as I was captain. Mark McCall was captain for the opening match, but he got injured and the captaincy fell on to my shoulders by default. The whole day was an incredible experience.'

It is often said that a week is a long time in politics, but Humphreys was to learn the hard way that seven days can be just as long in rugby. Exactly one week after the zenith of his career came the nadir.

'Unquestionably the low point of my days in an Irish shirt came against France at Lansdowne Road. I had a chance to win the game with a penalty very close to the end of the game, but I missed it. It was just such a horrible feeling when the final whistle went. To go from top of the world to being the villain was a very sobering experience and I suppose it highlighted just how cruel sport can be.'

A year after missing the penalty against France, Humphreys was faced with the chance to redeem himself with another penalty, which was to give Ireland its first victory in Paris in twenty-eight years.

'It wasn't like it was the last kick of the game, so the pressure wasn't weighing as heavily on me as the year before. There was still a few minutes to go, so if I missed, there was another chance. It's for situations like those that I spent hours and hours practising so that I would be able to slot the ball between the posts, and that helped me to relax as I faced up to the kick.'

From a personal point of view, another highlight came in 2002 when Humphreys scored a record thirty-seven points in a European Cup tie against Wasps in a 42–3 victory, scoring a try and four drop goals in the process.

Humphreys is one of the most amiable and articulate people in rugby. Yet at the mention of one name he is uncharacteristically reticent. After a series of uncomplimentary comments about him on RTÉ television from panellist George Hook, Humphreys allegedly refused to be interviewed by RTÉ television. What, then, is his attitude to 'The Right Hook'?

'The one subject I have never spoken on the record about is George Hook. I have no plans to change that policy.'

Humphreys retains fond memories of his teammates from 1999:

'The international players were away with the Irish squad and Jonny Bell was made captain of Ulster for a Celtic League match. Just before the game, Jonny gathered all the players around him, brought them into a huddle and said: "Right, lads, there's just two things I want from you in this game." He paused dramatically. You could have heard a pin drop as the lads were hanging on his every word. You could almost cut the tension with a knife as he said: "Honesty, commitment and work rate."

'The lads almost fell on the floor laughing at his gaffe. Ulster lost badly and Jonny's career as a captain came to an abrupt and undistinguished end!'

21

THE TIMES ARE A-CHANGING

The End of the Amateur Era

In 1995, after the World Cup, rugby turned professional, as Tony Ward recalls.

'Professionalism has dramatically changed the face of rugby on so many levels. Officially the game turned professional in 1995, but towards the end of my career the cracks in the old amateur ethos so beloved by the authorities were appearing. My only brush with the clandestine world of illegal payments came when the Welsh second row Alan "Panther" Martin invited me to play a match in Aberavon. I had got to know him very well on the Lions' tour in 1980. After the game, he slipped me a brown paper bag with my "expenses". The subterfuge about "under the table" payments was at James Bond levels for years, but finally in 1995 the genie was let out of the bottle and the professional era was formally ushered in.'

The transition was not painless. For players, the new era presented great opportunities. Many older players though still feel nostalgic about the 'good old days' of amateurism. So, was the amateur era all that different? One player's experience may serve as a microcosm.

With the retirement of Ollie Campbell in 1984, the popular opinion among rugby fans was that the stage was set for Tony Ward to return to the Irish team. Not for the first time, the selectors had a surprise in store for them.

An injury to Ward playing for Mary's against Monkstown in Sydney Parade on a dark autumn afternoon in 1984 opened the way for Paul Dean to become Ireland's out-half. Ward had been due to travel to Cork the next day to play for an Irish selection against Highfield in an exhibition. Ward's difficulty was Dean's opportunity and he played out-half to Mick Bradley. The rest of the backline comprised Brendan Mullin and Michael Kiernan in the centre, Trevor Ringland and Keith Crossan on the wings and Hugo MacNeill at full-back. They went to town against Highfield, inspired by the brilliance of Dean, a backline that was to subsequently help win the Triple Crown and win it in style.

When it came to a running, fifteen-man game, Dean was peerless. His genius was in the way he took attention off his centres, his backline alignment and speed of delivery. Few Irish players have ever been better able to straighten a backline. He was able to run incredibly straight and was also a beautifully balanced runner with an outstanding hip movement, which he used to great effect in beating the opposition and to create space for those around him. He had magnificent hands. He was rarely, if ever, seen dropping a pass. He was also an exceptionally good tackler. Although he was the lynchpin of the Triple Crown-winning side in 1985 at out-half, he initially made his mark in the green jersey as first centre, where he helped Ireland win the Triple Crown in 1982.

Ireland's summer tour to South Africa in 1981 marked Dean's

initiation into the Irish set-up. It was to prove an education in every sense of the term.

'I'm still learning what happened on that tour. There were three young lads in the squad: Michael Kiernan, John Hewitt and myself. We were going to bed very early at night, getting up early to go training and we couldn't understand why the older players were so tired in the mornings. We were on different clocks. They had a different agenda.

'The three of us were so naive and innocent. To give you an example, I roomed with one very senior player, who shall remain nameless, for four nights, but I never saw him at night-time and I was so naive I thought he didn't want to room with me because he was afraid I'd be snoring!'

Dean's rugby past is a different country. Change is inevitable, except from a vending machine, and Paul has noticed big changes in rugby since his playing days.

'When I think back, though, my diet was very different to what players have today. I was living in a flat and all I was eating was sandwiches, hot dogs and hamburgers. In 1985, we were due to pay England but the match was called off because of snow. As soon as we heard the news, we all went down to O'Donoghue's and got completely drunk. That kind of thing wouldn't happen today.

'There was an unwritten code about fair play back then as well. I saw this over two years in internationals between England and Ireland. After we played England at home, we had the post-match dinner except, for the first time, women were allowed to attend. We were then on strict instructions from our girlfriends to get to the function in a "decent state" otherwise we'd be in trouble.

'Before the dinner a lot of drink had been consumed and one of my Irish teammates was "tired and emotional" and had to go to bed. When his girlfriend came down from her room, there was an English player in the lift with her. He thought she fancied him, so he grabbed her and groped her. She was terribly embarrassed. Her boyfriend didn't get to hear about it until the following day.

'The next year when Ireland played the return fixture, a line-out took place and the call was made to the Irish forward in question. He was marking the English player responsible. The English guy jumped and the Irish player planted him and put his opponent's nose to the other side of his face. The English player huddled up his forwards and told them the next time they got a line-out to throw the ball to them so he could plant his opponent in turn. But the English players knew about the incident the previous year and told him he deserved it. That night, the English player came to the Irish lad and apologised. The basic rule was what goes around comes around. Nowadays if you struck a player like that, especially with the media coverage and video evidence, you would be sued for GBH.'

For Dean, the rugby friendships endure.

'A great character was the Scottish international John Jeffrey. He became a good friend of mine. The night before we played Scotland in 1985, we went to the cinema, as was the tradition back then. All I remember of the film was that it starred Eddie Murphy and his catchphrase was: "Get the f**k out of there." As soon as the film was over the lights came on, and when we stood up we saw that the Scottish team were sitting three rows behind us. We had a popcorn fight with them which was great fun, and they started shouting at us: "Get the f**k out of here."

'Almost as soon as the match started the next day, John Jeffrey tackled me very late. He knew exactly what he was doing. It was too early in the game for him to be penalised. As he pinned me down on the ground, he whispered in my ear: "Get the f**k out of here."

'The nice thing was that we did get the f**k out of there – but with a victory.'

Back home, Dean was particularly close with an international teammate. 'When I started with Ireland, I loved playing with Michael Kiernan because he was so fast. The problem was that, as he got older, he put on weight and started to lose his speed! My job was to make our talented backline look good, and I made Michael look much, much better than he actually was.'

Many rugby fans felt Michael Kiernan left the Irish team prematurely. For the first time, Deano can exclusively reveal the real reason for Kiernan's premature retirement. 'He left because of illness. The truth is, everyone was sick of him!'

22

STUNNING SIMON

Ireland 13, England 12

Tragically, injury brought Simon Geoghegan's career to a premature end, and Irish and world rugby were deprived of one of their most thrilling wingers.

Geoghegan's performance has not always been enhanced by his Irish teammates though. He was rooming with Neil Francis the night before the Fiji game in November 1995, Murray Kidd's first outing as team coach. Francis got thirsty during the night and disposed of a glass of water in the bathroom. The next morning when Geoghegan went to retrieve his contact lenses he discovered that Francis had unwittingly drunk them and the glass of water.

It was no coincidence that Ireland's best performances in the early '90s coincided with the best of the flying wingers, notably Ireland's 17–3 victory over England in 1993. The disappointment was that it was too late for him to claim a place on the Lions tour. When injury struck, it was his partner on the wing, Richard Wallace, and not the golden boy of Irish rugby that got the call to go south as a replacement.

Still basking in the glory of their win over the All Blacks, the English expected to extract retribution in 1994 in Twickenham, but a splendid try from Geoghegan helped Ireland to secure another shock win – this time on a score of 13–12. During these years the Underwood brothers played on the wings for England. Whenever either scored a try, the director of the BBC coverage of the English game always cut to the stands, where invariably their mother was dancing a jig with elation. After scything past Jon Callard and Tony Underwood to score that try, Simon is said to have turned to Underwood and remarked: 'I hope your mother saw that!'

Geoghegan recalls the game with undisguised affection.

'We performed excellently for eighty minutes. It was probably the first pass I received all season with a bit of space in front of me.'

23

AN EIGHTY-MINUTE ORGASM

Ireland 17, England 3

Mick Doyle was not a man to lavish praise on the Irish team with wanton abandon so when he described an Irish victory as an 'eighty-minute orgasm' one had to sit up and take notice. The performance which prompted this vintage 'Doylerism' was Ireland's 17–3 victory over England in 1993. In the green jersey, it was Mick Galwey's finest hour.

In a team performance in which all the boys in green were heroes, it's difficult to single out one player for special attention, but Galwey would have to come under that category. Six weeks before that match he lay in a Dublin hospital with his neck in a brace and his rugby future shrouded in uncertainty. At one point, he was told that his playing career was history. A shadow on his X-ray cast an ominous cloud on his prospects, and for four fear-filled days he waited for the all clear. Then it was out of hospital on to the training field.

A week later he played for Ireland against France – a game which offered promise of better things following total embarrassment at Murrayfield. The next match saw Ireland, with

Eric Ellwood making a hugely impressive debut, overcome the Welsh in Cardiff. The win was sealed with Galwey scoring a fine try – helping him to become one of only two Irish men able to secure a place on the Lions tour to New Zealand, with Nick Popplewell.

Mick Quinn tells a story about Galwey and Will Carling from that match. The famous English captain was not loved universally by his teammates, and when Ireland played England, it was a typically robust match. After a heated ruck, where boots were flying with more frequency than planes at an airport, everyone picked themselves off the muddy pitch to reveal the man at the bottom of the pile of bodies. It was Carling. He had a huge gash under his eye. The referee, slightly shocked that the English captain should be the victim of such thuggery, asked: 'Right, own up – who did this?'

Immediately Galwey piped up, 'Take your pick, ref – it could have been any one of twenty-nine of us.'

24

GIVE IT A LASH

Ireland Win the 1985 Triple Crown

In 2004 the news broke that Mick Doyle had been tragically killed in a car accident. It was difficult to comprehend that this man who gave new meaning to the phrase 'larger than life' was no longer with us.

Despite his great achievements as a player for Ireland and the Lions, he will be best remembered as coach of the Irish team that captured the Triple Crown in 1985 in such style and for the 'give it a lash' philosophy he espoused. Yet the carefree exterior masked a warm and generous nature and a great intelligence. He had a mind as sharp as an executioner's axe.

There was no disguising the pride in his voice as he talked about the Triple Crown in 1985.

'I had built up a huge dossier of information about each player. I had made up my mind if I ever was made coach of a representative side, I would give players responsibility for their own performances. The only thing I wouldn't tolerate is players not trying. I think it's fair to say I gave straight answers to players, and there was honest selection, which helped to build up the right spirit.'

In fairness, Doyler, as he was known, told more stories against himself than anybody else. He frequently joked about his weight: 'I have flabby thighs, but fortunately my stomach covers them. We have a tradition of walking in our family to fight the battle of the bulge. My uncle started walking five miles a day when he was sixty. He's ninety-seven now and we don't know where the f**k he is. I like long walks myself, especially when they're taken by people who annoy me.'

The highs of 1985 were dramatically reversed the following year when Ireland were whitewashed in the Five Nations championship, and 1987, too, was a year of missed opportunities, with rumours of discontent within the Irish camp.

'We should have won the Triple Crown in 1987. We let the game against Scotland slip through our fingers. Things were sometimes misinterpreted. After we lost that match, the then chairman of the selectors, Eddie Coleman, asked if he could sit in on our team meeting. I told him I would have preferred if he didn't but, because he was chairman of selectors, I couldn't stop him if he really wanted to.

'During the meeting, I was very critical of the players' performances and told them so in forthright terms and what I expected of them. I also said that what I had said was not for repeating outside. Some people obviously thought I was putting on a macho display for Eddie's benefit and was trying to show them up. Within a week, a journalist, David Walsh, had the story. I didn't think the "affair" did lasting damage. The mood was brilliant after we beat Wales in Cardiff and the guys, in a show of affection, threw me in the bath!

'I think it's probably fair to say that I was less tolerant towards the end, particularly during the World Cup in 1987. My period as Irish coach cost me about £750,000. Before we left for that tournament, my business was going down the tubes – I didn't have time to keep my eye on the ball. I had never experienced stress until then, but literally up to the last minute before going down under, I was frantically trying to salvage my business. I was also hitting the bottle too hard and it wasn't doing me any favours. It was the darkest hour of my life because everything I had worked for was disappearing before my eyes. Of course, what made it much worse was that I was worried about not being able to provide for my family.

'I suppose we didn't have the same off-the-cuff attitude we had in 1985. On the rugby side, things weren't going right in the build-up. We lost Nigel Carr in that horrific bomb blast, which was a huge blow. I always take too much on, and I was trying to do everything I could for the players on the organisational side. Phily Orr told me I was doing too much.

'Within twenty-four hours of getting to New Zealand, I had my coronary "incident". I should have been sent home after that. I was on tablets to sleep, tablets to wake up, tablets for hypertension and God knows what else. Most of the three or four weeks I was there I was edgy and irritable and in no way a suitable candidate for being a coach. The guys deserved a better coach than I was. I was less understanding than I should have been. Syd Millar and Mick Molloy were probably too kind to me at the time. They should have shaken me up a bit.

'When I came home, I was on the point of having a nervous breakdown, but I never quite went over the brink. That phase lasted for about six months until I started to put the pieces back together.'

Hugo MacNeill feels that Doyler was pivotal to the glory days of 1985.

'In 1985, grey clouds hung over the entire country. To those back home in Dublin in the 1980s, I was one of the rats that deserted the sinking ship. I was studying at Oxford at the time, a world away from the recession and depression at home. I was working on a thesis: 'How Do You Reduce the Irish Unemployment Problem?' It wasn't easy. There was almost twenty per cent unemployment and I always think that's why our triumph in '85 was so important, because it lifted a nation at a time when it desperately needed lifting. It wasn't just that we won the Triple Crown. It was the style we played when winning. Much of the credit for this has to go to our coach Mick Doyle. He best summed up his philosophy when he said: "I want you to run and if doesn't work out, I want you to run again."

'On a personal level, I had reason to be grateful to Doyler that season. We drew 15–15 but the match didn't go well for me. After the game, a number of journalists were calling for a change at full-back. Mick said to me in training: "Hugo, I want you in this side, okay?" We had a good chat and he made me feel confident again. He had a great gift for man management.

'Doyler had a wicked sense of humour. He was taking us for a Sunday morning training session. His prop forward Jim McCoy wasn't moving as swiftly as Doyler would have liked. Big Jim was an RUC officer and brought up in the Protestant tradition. Doyler shouted at him, "Hurry up, McCoy, or you'll be late for Mass!"'

25

CAPTAIN FANTASTIC

Ciaran Fitzgerald Leads Ireland to Double Glory

The beauty of television coverage of sport is that it can occasionally capture an image which offers a telling insight into a sporting hero. For the Irish rugby fan, an enduring image will always be Ciaran Fitzgerald's efforts to rally the Irish team as they appeared to be letting the Triple Crown slip from their fingers in 1985 against England in the wake of their dazzling and stylish victories away to Scotland and Wales. Even those who had no experience of lip-reading could clearly make out his plea from the heart, as he temporarily put aside the good habits he'd acquired as an altar boy with the Carmelites in Loughrea: 'Where's your pride? Where's your f**king pride?'

In the 1980–1 season, Fitzgerald sustained a serious shoulder injury in a club match.

'A bad situation was made worse by a doctor during the match. Immediately after the injury he tried to yank my shoulder back into place. Then I was assisted off the pitch. He put me on the flat of my back on the sideline and tried a second time. As a result of the injury and the "cure", I missed the entire international season.'

The following season, not only did Fitzgerald regain his place on the team, he also found himself taking over the captaincy from Fergus Slattery. What was the secret of his success?

'I think I'm very sensitive to people and curious about them. I was still a relatively inexperienced player in comparison with most of my pack. I knew there was no way I could use my army style to deal with these guys. You have to remember there were a lot of world-class players in the forwards like Orr, Keane, Slattery, O'Driscoll and Duggan. The previous year, Ireland had won no matches and those guys were fed up hearing from people who knew virtually nothing about rugby: "You're only a shower of…" That really annoyed them, and they were fired up to prove just how good they were.

'Whatever you say to players of that calibre has to be effective. Every player is different. The most important thing is to find out how to bring out the best of each one and find a strategy appropriate to his personality. In 1982, before the decisive Triple Crown match against Scotland, *The Irish Press* wrote a very critical article about John O'Driscoll, who was a superb player and central to our success that season. The day before the match I quietly went to him in the Shelbourne Hotel and expressed my sympathy about the article. He knew nothing about it and asked to see it. He read it but said nothing. The next day he played like a man possessed.

'The most difficult players to handle are those making their debuts. They get distracted by the press and the hype. Worst of all, though, are relatives who want to socialise with them and fill their head with all kinds of nonsense. The best way around this is the buddy system, i.e. having them room with one of the more experienced players.

'As captain, no matter what position you play in, you can't see everything that's happening on the pitch. You need guys you can quickly turn to in the heat of battle who can read the game and tell what is needed in their area. Fergus Slattery was a great player in those situations. Ollie Campbell, apart from being an outstanding player, had a great rugby brain, and I relied on him to control the game for us. His partner at scrum-half, Robbie McGrath, also played a crucial role. He was a very underrated player who never got the acclaim he deserved, and later in his career, Hugo MacNeill developed into a very tactically astute performer.

'Our coach, Tom Kiernan, was always two moves ahead of you. I often heard myself saying things which I would later get a flashback of and see that Tom had discreetly planted the thought in my mind either the previous day or a week earlier. He was a great man manager. He was always prompting you because he wanted the ideas to come from the players themselves, because they took more responsibility for their own decisions. Tom wasn't called "The Grey Fox" for nothing. I wanted the players to do more physical work, but Tom always subjected everything to a cost-benefit analysis and asked: "Was it worth it?" He always said that what exhausted players wasn't training sessions but constantly travelling up and down to Dublin.

PJ Dwyer, as chairman of selectors, was also somebody who was a great prompter of ideas.

'My clearest memory of 1982 was when Gareth Davies limped off in the Welsh game. We could see it in their eyes that they knew we were going to beat them. The England game really established that we were a side to be reckoned with. I remember travelling on the bus back to the hotel and, while everybody else was ecstatic, Willie Duggan was sitting at the back of the bus working out the practicalities of what was needed for a

Triple Crown decider in terms of extra tickets for players and so on. There were a lot of myths about Willie and Moss Keane at the time, in terms of drinking and lack of training, but it's all rubbish. I was living beside Moss at the time and was training every other night with him. I'm not exaggerating one bit when I say I was going flat out just to keep up with him.

'Moss's contribution was crucial on many levels in my view, not least of which was in telling Ginger McLoughlin: "I'm not going back." I know this is very technical but to put it as simply as I can, if the prop forward retreats, the second row normally has to as well, otherwise the prop's back is arched up. Ginger knew that this would be his fate if he didn't hold his line, which meant he went in there fighting like a tiger. It's things like that which make the difference between victory and defeat, and only someone of Moss's stature could have pulled it off.

'I believe we should also have won the Triple Crown in 1983. We should have beaten Wales, but we lacked discipline. The French match was like World War Four. World War Three was the previous year. Both sides had a lot of physical scores to settle in the first ten minutes of the game.'

26

FLOWER OF SCOTLAND

Ireland v Scotland, 1985

Having been a virtual novice in 1982 when Ireland won its first Triple Crown in thirty-three years, Hugo MacNeill was one of the more senior players when Ireland regained the Triple Crown in 1985.

'There was a great bond between the team. It was probably most evident at Cardiff Arms Park when we beat Wales 21–9. We hadn't won there for over twenty years, but I'll never forget that we linked arms before kick-off. It wasn't planned. It just happened naturally. It showed how united we were.'

However, this was not the highlight of Hugo's season. That came at Murrayfield.

'The Scots had beaten us 32–9 at Lansdowne Road the previous March and we were going into their backyard with a young team. We were whitewashed in 1984 and so many experienced players retired that year. Ollie Campbell, Moss Keane, Fergus Slattery, Willie Duggan and John O'Driscoll had all moved on. Mick Doyle asked us: "What are we afraid of?" The answer most people would have given him was the wooden spoon. But literally from the first minute, I sensed that something special was about to happen to us all. Deano moved it wide, Keith Crossan split the line, Brenny (Brendan Mullin) passed to me and the ball squirted forward as I was tackled over the line. If I'd had the ball in my other hand, we'd have scored a breathtaking try with our first attack. Our confidence was instantly lifted. We thought: *Wow, did we really do that?*

'The Scots got on top of us slowly and it looked like it was going to end badly but then we produced a little piece of magic. The back row created a position on the far side, the ball went wide and through the hands of nearly every back on the team before Trevor Ringland scored in the corner. We won 18–15.

'It was an extraordinary day, made all the more special by the scenes in the dressing room afterwards. I played thirty-seven times for Ireland, as well as for the Lions, and if you ask me to single out one moment from all those years that will live with me forever it would have to be the Murrayfield dressing room on the late afternoon of 2 February 1985. There was an ecstatic air about the place. Nobody could sit down. It was almost child-like. We had all played hundreds of championship matches as children in our back gardens, but this was the real thing. It was the most amazing feeling I ever had in my career.

'That year there was a great uncertainty and apprehension before the Scotland game. We had no recognised place-kicker and had such a young side. After our win, there was so much excitement and freshness that no one could sit down. I had come through the schools and universities with these guys and I really enjoyed the buzz.'

27

CAMPBELL'S KINGDOM

Ireland Clinch the Triple Crown

In 1982, Ireland's 20–12 victory in the opening Five Nations game against Wales raised hopes of a Triple Crown. The away fixture against England was going to be crucial to achieving this ambition. The match is best remembered for a moment from Gerry McLoughlin, the carrot-haired Shannon prop, who scored a try after he was driven over the line by the sheer weight of Irish players who were up in support. 'Ginger' claimed that he pulled the other players over with him. However, what is often forgotten is that Ireland's second try in their 16–15 victory that day was scored by Hugo MacNeill, his third for his country. On 20 February, Ireland secured a historic 21–12 victory over Scotland, thanks to six penalty goals and a dropped goal from Ollie Campbell.

In 1981, Ollie Campbell had been moved to the centre to allow for Tony Ward's return as Irish out-half. How did he react to the change?

'I never minded the idea of playing in the same team as Tony – provided I was at out-half. Playing in the centre is a very different position, and to be honest I was never really comfortable there. In 1981, we lost all four matches by a single score after leading in all four at half-time. I remember at the time Tom Kiernan repeatedly kept telling us that whatever the results, if there was to be a Lions tour that year, the country that would have the most representatives would be Ireland. I'm not sure if that was true, but it certainly kept our morale and self-belief up. That summer we toured South Africa. It was a non-event for me – concussion and a broken wrist keeping me down to about fifty minutes of rugby.'

The following season things came together for the Irish side as they won the Triple Crown. One of Campbell's enduring recollections of the game was of the fans.

'Probably my abiding memory of that whole season was the reaction of the crowd during the whole of the second half of the Scottish game, particularly in the East Stand because much of the half seemed to be played there. I think it was really the start of "Molly Malone" becoming the "anthem" of the Irish team. The atmosphere was just incredible. I heard a piece of radio commentary of the game for the first time a few years ago and it really brought goose pimples down the back of my neck.

'An interesting postscript to the match came when my aunt in Scotland asked me to send on my autograph for a local lad showing a lot of rugby promise. Later he would be a star for both Scotland and the Lions. His name – Craig Chalmers.

'There were a lot of great moments that season – I suppose most famously Ginger's celebrated try against England. On a personal level, I remember a break I made which set up Moss Finn's first try against Wales; the virtual touchline conversion of Ginger's try at Twickenham and the drop goal against Scotland. That score came from a special loop movement we had devised in January with David Irwin but kept under wraps. It should have led to a try, but I gave a bad pass to Keith Crossan and the move broke down, so we had to settle for three points.

Life for that team was never really the same afterwards. Most of them had grown up with no international success, so there was a huge sense of achievement and a bond that has lasted since.

'When we won our first match, all we were trying to do was to bring a sequence of seven consecutive defeats to an end. Two weeks later we won at Twickenham and suddenly we were in a Triple Crown situation. It was something as a team we had never thought about. But we knew we were on to something big when we saw the huge crowds watching us in training. That was something we had never experienced before. It was a very exciting week, as we had a general election at the time following the fall of Garret FitzGerald's first coalition government, but nobody seemed to care about it. Everybody was more excited about the possibility of a Triple Crown – Ireland had never won one at Lansdowne Road before.

'The tension mounted, but then Tom Kiernan, the Irish coach, decided to have a closed practise session on the Thursday before the game. Suddenly the Triple Crown match became just another game, and I have never felt so at ease and comfortable going into a game. It was a masterstroke as far as I was concerned.

'Two weeks previously, I had missed a penalty against England that would have sewn the game up. On the Sunday afterwards, I went to Anglesea Road with my five balls and kicked for two hours from the same spot I had missed from the previous day. Ninety per cent of all the kicks I took in practice over the next two weeks were from this spot. After just three minutes of the Scotland game, when the first penalty arrived, I relaxed. Amazingly, it was from exactly the same spot. I felt I could have kicked it with my eyes closed, but I didn't take the chance. We were on our way, and for me at least, never before had the value of practice been more clearly demonstrated.'

After the Irish squad were awarded professional contracts, Campbell jokingly thought of establishing a petition of ex-international players asking that former internationals be rewarded retrospectively.

28

THE KEANE EDGE

The Moss Keane Era

The entire Irish nation went into mourning in 2010 with news of the death of Moss Keane. Few sports personalities were more loved. Speaking to me about his funeral, Ollie Campbell observed, 'I've never experienced anything like it. It must have gone on for a few hours. Despite his innate modesty, Moss would have loved it. When his wife Anne spoke, she received a standing ovation. I thought of the line, "Anyone who lives in the hearts of those they leave behind will never die." Those words could have been written for Moss.'

It was only when you met someone like Moss Keane that you really understood the phrase 'legend of Irish rugby'. A huge bulk of a man, he had a penchant for straight talking and a treasure trove of stories and jokes, though surprisingly few were about rugby, more about matters agricultural.

Moss had originally made an impact as a Gaelic footballer. However, he was not known for being fleet of foot. According to folklore, after a less than resoundingly successful career as a Gaelic footballer, his conversion to rugby came when he overheard a friend saying in a pub that, 'A farmer could make a tidy living on the space of ground it takes Moss to turn.'

Stories about Moss are more common than showers in April – though few are printable in our politically correct times. Some are even true! Moss had a nice line in self-deprecating humour: 'After I left university, I found I had no talent for anything so I joined the civil service! I won fifty-two caps – a lot of them just because they couldn't find anybody else.'

Moss Keane is one of the all-time greatest characters in Irish rugby and is often associated with his teammate, the late Willie Duggan, for the way they played on the pitch and the way they celebrated off it. In victory or defeat, Moss and Willie knew how to party after a game.

One player who was Keane by name but not by nature tops Paul Dean's list of characters.

'Moss Keane always hated me getting the ball because he knew I'd pass it and that meant, in his eyes, that the backs were going to lose it and he'd have to chase it and win it back again. A common instruction from Moss was, "Jaysus, now, don't let the little fellas have it." Like Willie Duggan, he hated having to run around the pitch.

'The young players looked up to Moss as if he was God. New players from the north found his thick Kerry accent particularly difficult to decipher. The senior players devised a little ritual for those new players. When Trevor Ringland was brought on to the team for the first time they put him beside Moss for dinner and Trevor was in awe of him. They primed Moss to speak for two minutes in fast-forward mode. He was talking pure gibberish. Then he turned to Trevor and asked him what he thought of that. Trevor answered lamely, "I think you're right," not having a clue what Moss had said. Then Moss launched off again, only faster. The panic on Trevor's face was a sight to behold. He was going green. All the senior players were killing themselves trying to keep a straight face until Trevor found out he was being wound up.'

Folklore about Moss grows with every day, and distinguishing fact from fiction isn't easy. Moss was playing for the Wolfhounds and in the side was Charlie Kent, the big blond English centre. Charlie is a diabetic, and at half-time this rather puffed-up ambulance man arrived in the players' huddle and tapped Moss on the shoulder. The man asked Moss if he was the one who wanted a sugar lump. Moss said, 'Arra Jaysus, who do you think I am, Shergar?'

The definitive verdict on Moss came from Mick Doyle: 'For the first half, Moss would push in the line-outs, and in the second, he'd jump in the scrums. That would always confuse the English.'

When Moss went on his first tour to New Zealand with the Lions, he was the only player in the first seven weeks who the BBC had not interviewed because they didn't think his strong Kerry brogue would work well with a British audience. Eventually the Lions players said they would refuse to do any more interviews for the BBC until Nigel Starmer-Smith interviewed Moss. Nigel reluctantly agreed to this demand and asked on live television, 'Well, Moss, you've been here now for two months and you've played in your first Lions Test, met the Maoris … what's been the best moment of the trip for you?'

In his thickest Kerry accent Moss replied, 'When I heard that Kerry beat Cork in the Munster final.'

Internationally, Moss was a much-loved figure too, as Welsh legend Ray Gravell told me. 'Willie Duggan was an awesome player and a great man to knock back a pint with! I would probably say the same thing about Moss Keane. These guys were legends on the pitch and legends in the bar! Sometimes too much drink is not enough! It only took one drink to get them drunk. The problem was they could never remember whether it was the 24th or the 25th!'

Like Willie Duggan, Moss had a fear of flying and generally the only way they got on a plane was with the benefit of a lot of Dutch courage. As he drove to the airport for the Lions tour in 1977, he was so nervous about the flight that he crashed his car. The story goes that he rang his mother just before he took off and said, 'The car is in the airport. It's wrecked. See you in four months.'

Moss was once asked, 'Are you afraid of flying, Mossie?'

He replied, 'Afraid of flying? No. Afraid of crashing? Yes.'

Moss habitually had to sit on the back seat whenever he took the plane. Asked by Ciaran Fitzgerald why he always took the back seat, he replied, 'I've never seen a plane back into a mountain yet.'

29

OH, HAPPY DAY

Munster Beat the All Blacks in 1978

Down through the years, Munster had turned in some remarkable performances against touring sides – the All Blacks, the Springboks and the Wallabies – only to be narrowly defeated. The more senior Munster supporters could still remember the feeling of being robbed at the Mardyke in 1947 when Australia scored a last-minute try to defeat Munster 6–5, despite the suspicion that the winning try came from a forward pass. But 1978 was destined to be different.

The only biblical story which the four gospels share in common is the multiplication of the loaves and the fishes when Jesus fed the multitude and managed to have twelve baskets of fragments left over. Munster's victory over the All Blacks has spawned a similar miracle. Although the official attendance at the match was only 12,000, since then tens of thousands of people have said, often with the benefit of generous liquid refreshment, 'I was there the day Munster beat the All Blacks.'

The Clare Hills provided a scenic background for the New Zealanders as they performed their traditional haka before the game. Somewhat against the run of play, Munster took the lead in the eleventh minute – a delicate chip from Tony Ward was followed through and won by Jimmy Bowen, who made an incisive run and, as he was caught from behind, fed Christy Cantillon, who crossed the line beneath the posts. Ward kicked the conversion with ease. Then in the seventeenth minute Ward dropped a goal.

The home side hung on to their 9–0 lead until half-time but realised that a modern-day siege of Limerick awaited them in the second half when the men from down under would do all in their formidable power to protect their unbeaten record. Their fears were justified as the All Blacks exerted enormous pressure. But metaphorically and literally, the tourists didn't know what hit them as they were stopped in their tracks with a series of crunching tackles by such players as Seamus Dennison, Greg Barrett and, most notably, Colm Tucker. Jack Gleeson subsequently described them as 'Kamikaze tacklers'.

As the seconds ticked by agonisingly slowly in the second half, the crowd became more and more frenzied, sensing that here lay history in the making. 'M-U-N-S-T-E-R! M-U-N-S-T-E-R!' rang out at near deafening levels. Ward got the only score in the second-half – a drop goal – and Munster held on. It was an extraordinary team performance.

One of Limerick's best-known sons, the late film star Richard Harris, swept away by the euphoria of victory, wired the following message from a movie set in Johannesburg.

'Your historic victory over New Zealand made roaring headlines in every South African paper. I've been on the dry for ten months, but I can't think of a better occasion or excuse to reacquaint my liver with the drowning sensation of a drop. I wish I was there. I rang Richard Burton and although he extends his congratulations, I detected a tinge of jealousy.'

One of Tony Ward's most vivid memories of Moss Keane goes back to that match.

'We were leading 12–0 with only minutes left and there was a scrum close to the sideline. Our lads wheeled the scrum and drove the Blacks over the sideline, right up against the wall. The All Blacks weren't very pleased about this and a scuffle broke out. One of their players, Andy Hayden, swung out his arm to have a swipe at Brendan Foley and Moss grabbed him by the arm and said: "Don't. You'll lose that one as well." Hayden turned, smiled and accepted it. The meaning was clear.

'Moss was one of the great characters of Irish rugby. On the pitch, he was a tiger but off the field a pussy cat. I'll never forget when we played England in 1979 – he took off on a run and the crowd started chanting: "Mossie, Mossie." He was one of those characters who lifts the whole crowd and that, in turn, lifts the team.'

30

THE MAKING OF A LEGEND

Willie John Becomes the Lion King

In his final home international, Willie John McBride scored his first try for his country when Ireland defeated France 25–6. Such was the emotion generated that the crowd ran on to the pitch to celebrate the try. To mark the centenary season of Irish rugby, the IRFU arranged a match between Ireland–Scotland and England–Wales in April 1975. It was to be the last time the Ballymena man would lead out a side at the home of Irish rugby. Events took an unexpected turn after the match when he was hijacked by the late Eamonn Andrews and whisked away to become the subject of an edition of *This Is Your Life*.

It is inconceivable that a discussion on great Irish forwards should begin without reference to Willie John. The fact that it is unnecessary to use his surname says it all, and to say his rugby CV is impressive is an understatement: sixty-three caps, five Lions tours, seventeen Lions Test appearances, captain of the most successful Lions side of all time. In the 1972–3 season he surpassed the record of Scottish prop forward Hugh McLeod when he made forty-three consecutive appearances in international rugby.

Born one of six children in Toomebridge, County Antrim, he lost his father at four and was brought up by his mother on a small farm. The hardships he experienced give a lie to the perception that rugby in Ireland is only a game for those brought up with a silver spoon.

Gareth Edwards has gone on record to say that Willie John McBride was his sort of captain because of his creed of total commitment, and he would have followed him anywhere. Willie John was wont to say: 'I hate small men.' Each match was rugby's high noon for him. He believed in all or nothing – 'lay down your life or don't come with me'.

He is spoilt for choice when asked about the highlights of his career.

'Beating Australia in the Test in Sydney (11–5) was a great achievement, particularly as we had to strap up three players because of injury to get them on to the field. Our win over Wales in 1970 was also a magic moment. We had an amazing pack of forwards then, with world-class players like McLoughlin and Slattery. The team was at its peak in 1972 but politics probably cost us the Triple Crown. It was great towards the end of my career to lead Ireland to the championship in 1974.'

There was no doubt, though, that his finest hour was the Lions tour in 1974 when he was an inspirational captain.

'I was a Lion at twenty-one but losing became a habit. I'd had a baptism of fire in my first Test because I was up against two of the all-time greats in Johan Claassen and Colin Meads. I had to wait nine matches for a win with the Lions.

'The 1974 tour was like all my Christmases at once. When the tour was finished, the players presented me with a lovely engraved silver water jug which read: "To Willie John. It was great to travel with you." That is my most treasured rugby possession. There is a bond between that team that will never die.'

Willie John recalled his bonding skills for me.

'That was the biggest challenge of my life, trying to get coal miners from Wales and solicitors from London to mix together. Cracks could have appeared in the squad when we divided into a Test side and a midweek side, but those problems never arose because we kept on winning. I especially remember after Alan Old broke his leg, Phil Bennett came along to say to me: "Don't worry, I'll play as often as you need me."

'When we won the first two Tests we had the Springboks reeling. I think they made ten changes in all for the third Test. That was the big one because if we won that match, we won the series.

'When I walked into the room where the team had gathered, the air was full of electricity. Usually, I would talk about the importance of the game and the reasons for wanting to win. But this time I simply asked: "Men, are we ready?" They looked up. They were ready.

'The first twenty minutes or so were probably the toughest of the whole tour. The pressure on us was terrible. People expected us to win, which can be fatal for any team. We made it hard on ourselves by making mistakes we'd never made before. However, we finally got it together and won 26–9.'

31

CHAMPIONS

Ireland Win the 1974 Five Nations

Joe Schmidt once said to me: 'Since I started coaching Ireland there are two banes of my life. One is injuries to our players. The other is that Mick Quinn is always taking the piss out of me!'

Out-half Mick Quinn was ever present in what was then a rare Five Nations Championship success in 1974. That season provided him with his finest hour.

'My best game for Ireland was unquestionably against England at Twickenham in 1974. Although the final score, 26–21, was deceptively close, we hockeyed them that day – scoring four tries. It was such a wonderful feeling after the game to know that I had played to my very best and the team had performed to its best. I have an unbeaten record against England and Wales – not many Irish internationals can say that. Okay, so I only played against them once!'

Ireland faced England at Twickenham as underdogs. Before the game, the Irish players were running on to the pitch when they were stopped in the tunnel by an official in a blazer who had the archetypal RAF moustache. He said, 'Tally ho, boys. Tally ho. The BBC cameras aren't ready for you yet.'

The Irish lads were just itching to get on the pitch and found the waiting a pain, particularly when they were joined in the tunnel by the English team. The English were led by their captain, John Pullin, who was shouting at his team about Waterloo. The Irish players couldn't understand what Waterloo had to do with them. The English players looked bigger and stronger than their Irish counterparts. As they were always on television, they were all huge stars and had mega names like David Duckham and Andy Ripley. The Irish players were studiously trying to avoid eye contact with them, as they planned to rough them up a bit on the pitch. However, Tony Neary went over and tapped Moss Keane on the shoulder and said, 'Moss, best of luck. May the best team win.'

Keane growled back, 'I f**king hope not!'

Mick Quinn had a memorable encounter afterwards.

'After that game, a young autograph hunter said to me: "Can I have your autograph please, Johnny?" I didn't have the heart to tell him he had the wrong man so I just signed it. "To Bert. Best wishes, Johnny Moloney." As he was leaving, he looked up and said to me: "How do you keep playing with Mick Quinn. He plays like sh*t!"

'In fairness, Johnny did me a favour when we played Wales in 1974. We drew 9–9. I had a bad flu before the match and was puking all over the place. The only one who knew about it was "Shagger". I told him if he told anyone about it I would kill him.'

For his part, Barry McGann jokes: 'I got Mick Quinn his ten caps for Ireland because I was his only competition and I wasn't up to much at the time! Syd Millar was the coach then. I had the reputation of being a very laid-back player, but I was serious when I needed to be. Because of work, I was late for a training session, although genuinely I got there as quick as I could. The training session at Anglesea Road was in full swing when I got there. I went over and apologised to Syd for being late and asked him what he wanted me to do. I had a strong feeling he didn't believe I had made much of an effort to be there, but he told me to warm up. Instinctively I rubbed my hands together and blew on them and said: "Okay, coach, I'm ready." Moss Keane was in stitches but I'll never forget the bemused look on Syd's face. I think that incident probably cost me ten caps!'

After the high of the championship victory in 1974, Quinn was quickly brought down to earth.

'The one great disappointment of my career was when I was a standby for the Lions tour to South Africa. The English fly-half Alan Old got injured near the end of the tour, and I got a call at home from one of the Lions' management team, Albert Agar, who told me to get ready for the trip to South Africa. An hour later I had my bags packed and at the hall door. Then another call came from Agar, a name I will never forget, telling me that in fact I wouldn't be travelling and asking me if I minded. What a question! Of course, I lied and said no, but it was devastating. It turned out that after he had called me someone else rang Mike Gibson, who had declined the invitation to tour initially.'

32

MISSED OPPORTUNITY

Ireland 10, All Blacks 10

Barry McGann had great physical presence and was a wonderful team player, and there are a number of matches which evoke a warm glow on his face. He scored his first international try in 1969 when Ireland defeated Scotland 16–0. The Triple Crown was now on. The Cardiff Arms Park showdown is best remembered for arguably the most controversial punch in the history of international rugby when Noel 'Noisy' Murphy was sensationally floored by Brian Price. After ten minutes, the Welsh forward broke from the ruck to do his Cassius Clay impersonation. Murphy, in his final international (after winning forty-one caps and touring twice with the Lions), was left sprawling on the ground. Ireland lost 24–11. McGann remembers the game clearly.

'It was a very physical match. The press made a lot of the fact that Prince Charles was attending his first match as Prince of Wales and right in front of him Brian Price knocked out Noisy. People now will not appreciate just how sensational the incident was at the time. There wasn't a culture of sending players off then the way there is now, so Price continued on his merry way for the rest of the game. That was really the beginning of the great Welsh team with Gareth Edwards brought to the fore.

'Beating France in Paris in 1972 was a great thrill. I especially remember Ray McLoughlin's try. He was in the wrong place at the wrong time and fell over the line with the ball!

'Playing against the All Blacks was also a magic moment. We drew with them, 10–10, in 1973. Tom Grace got a try in the last moment in the right corner. I missed out on rugby fame because I officially missed the conversion that would have won the game for Ireland. The kick was so high that it was difficult to see which side of the post the ball went but, to this day, I'm convinced that the ball did not in fact go wide. Earlier that week the All Blacks had got out of jail against Munster in Musgrave Park with a penalty in injury time when we drew 3–3. Another chance of being part of history snatched away from me.'

Tom Grace collected his third cap against the All Blacks in January 1973 when he scored a dramatic equalising try in the right-hand corner to tie the match at 10–10. Some moments live in the memory and that try is one, when like a salmon-leap he sailed in a great arc through the air and scored a try in the corner with a split second to spare.

'There was a lot of speculation afterwards about whether the ball had crossed the dead-ball line or not. Thankfully the *Irish Independent* had a photographer on hand to show it hadn't. Barry McGann always says if it wasn't for him, I would have been famous. After I scored the try, he narrowly missed the conversion which robbed us of our part in rugby's hall of fame.'

33

SLAM

Ireland Win the 1948 Grand Slam

It was Irish rugby's first time to reach the Promised Land.

One of the centres on that team, Paddy Reid, recalled for me that New Year's Day in 1948 saw the opening of an unexpectedly glorious chapter in the history of Irish rugby, when Ireland had a shock 13–6 victory over France at Colombes. Reid was literally at the centre of things.

'A great character in the team was Barney Mullan. The night before the game in Paris we had a team meeting, as per usual. Barney came up with the idea that if we were under pressure during the game and got a line-out, he would call a short one and throw it out over the forwards' heads and lift the siege. True to plan, we got a line-out on our own twenty-five. The French players were huge. They looked like mountains to us, so we needed to out-think them. Mullan threw it long and Jack Kyle grabbed it, passed it to me, I fed it to Des McKee and he returned the compliment for me to score under the posts. The glory was mine, but it was Barney's tactical awareness that earned us that try.

'Travelling to Paris for us at the time was like going to the edge of the world. We were as green as grass. After our win, we were invited to a reception at the Irish embassy. Of course, champagne was the order of the day, which was a very novel experience for most of us. We were knocking it back as if it was stout! To me, the incident that best illustrated our innocence was when the Dolphin pair Jim McCarthy and Bertie O'Hanlon asked for red lemonade!'

The following Valentine's Day saw Ireland beat England 11–10 at Twickenham. The Grand Slam decider against Wales at Ravenhill was the critical one, and 13 March was not to prove an unlucky date as Ireland fought a tense battle with their nerves as much as with the opposition before emerging victorious. Reid's memories of that year were vivid. He believed that the decisive moment came when Ireland laid the Welsh bogey.

'We were fortunate to have a wonderful captain in Karl Mullen. He was great for letting everyone have their say, and the night before the Wales game we had a meeting. One of the people who had given us advice was Dave O'Loughlin, who had been a star Irish forward just before World War Two. To all of us on the '48 team he was an idol. He had played against the great Welsh scrum-half Haydn Tanner, who was still calling the shots on the Welsh team in 1948. (The previous year his late break had set up a try which robbed Ireland of the Triple Crown.)

'Dave told us that Tanner was the man to watch and assured us that he would make two breaks during the game. At the team meeting I suggested that Des O'Brien should be appointed as Tanner's shadow, to ensure that when the Welsh man broke, he would be quashed. I went so far as to suggest that if he didn't do his task properly in this respect, he should be dropped. Des wasn't too happy with this part of the plan at the time, but he was given the assignment nonetheless. Sure enough, as Dave had promised, Haydn broke twice. Both times Des tackled him superbly. In fact, so annoyed was Tanner on the second occasion that he slammed the ball on the ground in frustration. These things don't just turn a match. I'm convinced it was the difference between victory and defeat for us in the Grand Slam.'

Jack Kyle's clearest memory of the Grand Slam-winning side was of Jack Daly.

'At the time, we always faced playing the Welsh on their own patch with trepidation. In 1948 though, when we played them in Swansea, Jack sat in the dressing room punching his fist into his hand, saying: "I'm mad to get at them. I'm mad to get at them. I'm mad to get at them." His enthusiasm rubbed off on the rest of us.

'Jack was an extraordinary character. Before the war he only played with the thirds for London Irish. As he departed for combat, he said: "When I come back, I'll be picked for Ireland."

'He was stationed in Italy during the war and had to carry heavy wireless equipment on his back. As a result, his upper body strength was incredible. Before internationals he did double somersaults to confirm his fitness. Having scored the winning try to give us the Grand Slam in 1948, he was nearly killed by spectators at the final whistle. His jersey was stripped off his back and people were wearing pieces of it on their lapels for weeks afterwards. Jack was whisked off from the train station in Dublin the next day by a girl in a sports car whom he had never met but who was sporting a piece of his jersey on her blouse. He stayed with her for a week and lost his job when he went back to London!'

34

THE JACK KYLE ERA

Ireland Win the 1949 Triple Crown

Such was Jack Kyle's impact when he won forty-six caps that he literally defined the age. His glory days, when Ireland reached its rugby zenith in the late 1940s, were known throughout the rugby world as 'the Jackie Kyle era'. He was the star when Ireland won the Triple Crown in 1949 – dwarfing all who trailed in his wake as he scythed through the defence. In full flight, his hand-off gesture was like a royal dismissal to bewildered opponents reduced to looking like oxen on an ice rink. He enjoyed to the full the drama and poetic presence that was part of the most glorious chapter in Irish rugby history. His voice betrayed the nerve-tingling excitement as the great moments of the 1940s and 1950s were unreeled to me before the vivid mind's eye of memory, particularly of his fellow internationals.

'There is a big advantage in being a small country, if that isn't a contradiction in terms, in that it's difficult for good players to slip through the net because of the Interpros, the matches between the combined provinces and the rest of Ireland and the final trial. If you were any good at all, somebody saw you play somewhere!

'I wasn't a great tackler. If I had to play rugby as a forward, I would never have played the game! Our back row of Jim McCarthy, Bill McKay and Des O'Brien was so strong that I didn't have to bother too much with the normal defensive duties of a fly-half. McCarthy was like greased lightning and an incredible forager and opportunist. I could virtually leave the out-half to our two flankers. I just stood back and took him if he went on the outside.

'I was doubly blessed in that I also had Noel Henderson playing alongside me in the centre. He was a marvellous defender, performing many of my defensive duties, and I'm not just saying that because he became my brother-in-law!'

It was his brother-in-law that caused Kyle's greatest surprise in rugby.

'Noel caused a major shock one day at our team meeting. He was a very quiet man and normally was not very loquacious at those sessions. As was his custom, Karl Mullen concluded by asking if there were any questions. Noel asked: "What I would like to know, Captain, is if there's any way of knowing whether the out-half will be taking his man for a change?"

'Noel had the good fortune to be the father of four daughters. I once met the former Scottish centre Charlie Drummond, who also has a lot of daughters. When I told him about Noel he said: "We're raising good stock for future rugby players." There's a man who takes the long-term view!'

Training techniques were very different back then.

'You have to remember that it was such a different set-up then from today. We came down from Belfast on the train in the morning, and in the afternoon we went for a training session, using the term loosely, in Trinity College. Johnny O'Meara might throw me a few passes and that would be enough for me. We used an interesting word a lot at the time – "stale" – which I never hear now. Basically, we believed if we trained too hard we wouldn't perform on the Saturday. It was probably an excuse for us not to do any serious work!

'I always felt that, just as a girl who is born beautiful can only enhance her looks a little bit, you can only achieve a limited amount in rugby by coaching. It's really a question of natural ability. I only dropped a goal once for Ireland. It was from a very difficult angle. If I'd thought about it, I could never have attempted it. It was just instinctive. A lot of times we were working on a subconscious level. Another time I combined with Jim McCarthy for Jim to score a great try. I got a letter afterwards telling me it was such a textbook score we must have practised it on the training ground. Looking back now, it's amazing how the few set moves we had worked out came off.'

Former Irish and Lions forward Bill Mulcahy has one of the many stories told about Jack Kyle:

'The classic tale told about Jack concerns John O'Meara's first cap, when he was to partner Jack at half-back. He was naturally a bit apprehensive about partnering the unquestioned best player in the world and was debating how he would address Jack. Should he call him Dr Kyle or Mr Kyle? John travelled up in the *Cork Examiner* van and walked meekly into the team hotel. Immediately he walked in the door the first person to greet him was Jack, who said: "Congratulations, Johnny. Delighted to see you here. Where would you like me to stand on the pitch?" Who else would have shown such modesty?'

For Jack Kyle, Karl Mullen was an inspirational force.

'Karl was a wonderful captain. His greatest gift was to let the players play to the best of their potential. There were times though when he showed great tactical awareness. Before we played Wales, in Swansea in 1949, he gathered us around and said: "We're going to run them into the ground." We had such a fit and fast back row in particular at the time that he knew we could wear them down, and we did. There's a lot of talk today that "forward supremacy is the key", but at that time, we were always able to win the battle of the packs, which made our job in the backs all that much easier.

'I especially remember the game against Wales at Ravenhill in front of a capacity crowd of 30,000. I'd say they could have taken four times as many had there been space for them. We were all understandably a bit apprehensive but deep down felt we could win. Karl made a point of getting the team to discuss tactics and the strengths and weaknesses of our opponents before matches. He made sure that every man had his say, and it was an important part of the pre-match preparations from the point of view of contributing to the great team spirit. We also had a "council of war" at half-time and Karl kept us on the straight and narrow.'

Flanker Jim McCarthy's back-row combination with Old Belvedere's Des O'Brien and Bill McKay in those years is among the finest in Irish rugby history. He paid homage to Kyle for me.

'Karl Mullen was a great leader, but we also had the great fortune to have Jack Kyle in the side. He was a wizard. I'd be struggling to put words on him, he was such a classy player, a man apart. The strange thing about him is that for all his greatness, he was such a humble man and a real team player. I would also have to say though that we were no one-man team. There was a great camaraderie and spirit in that side, and we all pulled for each other. Bill McKay, a medical student from Queen's University, was the best wing-forward I ever saw. To me the unsung hero was full-back Dudley Higgins, who of course is a past president of the IRFU. You never had to look over your shoulder when he was on the team. He was such a great tackler he could stop a train.'

McCarthy became the record try scorer for Ireland for a forward. What was the secret of his success? 'Wherever the ball is, you be there. When I was playing for Ireland, the best place to be was two feet behind Jackie Kyle.'

35

THE PLAYERS' REVOLUTION

The Irish Squad Gain Concessions, 1949

Ireland's Grand Slam victory in 1948 prompted star flanker Jim McCarthy to engage in what the IRFU saw as extravagant behaviour.

'After we won the Triple Crown in Belfast, I sent in my expenses to the IRFU. I claimed four pounds and ten shillings but only got four pounds and seven shillings. They deducted three shillings because I rang my family to tell them we'd won the Triple Crown and because I'd gone outside the de hôte menu. I had ordered two raw eggs to eat the morning of the match. That was part of my ritual. I also took glucose. It probably did me no good physically, but psychologically it gave me an extra edge.'

Did the players receive any reward for their unique achievement?

'The only thing we got was a photo of the winning team and the team crest!'

Flushed by their success with the Grand Slam and the Triple

Crown in consecutive seasons, the Irish squad were ready to flex their muscles in 1949 and demand better conditions.

Karl Mullen's successor as Irish captain, Des O'Brien, explained to me:

'Of course, things were very different back then. We had none of the perks players have today. We wore our own club socks when we played for Ireland. The clubs liked that, as did we. Wales wore letters on their backs instead of numbers at the time. Team dinners after internationals were held in Mills' restaurant in Merrion Row – just the team and half a dozen officials. Speeches were brief as we all wanted to get to the three big dances being held from ten until three in the Gresham, the Metropole and the Shelbourne. We would be guests of all three. The night before a Dublin game we would usually take the opposition team to the Gaiety Theatre. We had to pay for our own tickets! You were only given one jersey a season, no matter how many games you played. You could be dropped if you pinched a jersey after a game!

'In my first two years, the players weren't allowed any tickets – even to buy! Before the Scotland game in Dublin in 1949, Karl Mullen was offered two tickets to buy for his parents. The team decided no tickets, no game and there was quite a scene in the Shelbourne on the Friday night – Karl got his tickets and, after that, the IRFU agreed with reluctance to let us buy two tickets each. Big deal!

'I was on the first team to take a plane to a match when we went to France. Our touring party amounted to sixty-eight, of whom forty were alickadoos!'

Another concession was a trip to exotic parts touring with Ireland to South America in 1951.

'It was a total success off the field and a disaster on it. We were the first international team to be beaten by Argentina. When we got there, we were told we couldn't play any rugby because Eva Perón had just died. They sent us down to Santiago, Chile, to teach the cadets how to play. We didn't take the playing side very seriously. After eight days, they beat us!'

PART II
What Goes on Tour

Rugby tours have a number of striking similarities with a religious pilgrimage, such as uniformity in dress codes, the chanting of familiar songs and a feeling of community and fellowship throughout. The analogy does not hold true for the Wasps' tour to Malaysia in 1992, when some of the tourists bared their posteriors for the world to see. Not surprisingly in a Muslim country, this cheeky behaviour caused outrage, and the offenders were severely fined and deported.

Rugby tours have a unique capacity to produce tales of the unexpected. This section celebrates some of them.

36

WHEN HOPE AND HISTORY RHYME

Ireland Win in Cape Town

A visit to Cape Town was high on Joe Schmidt's bucket list. Nelson Mandela's memoir *Long Walk to Freedom* was among his reading material. Not surprisingly, a visit to Robben Island was top of his agenda when he toured to Cape Town; there he saw a tiny cell which could have been a cold tomb of loneliness and despair. Inside the sterile, cinder-block cell was a toilet, a thin mattress with pillows and a brown blanket. A single window looking into the courtyard had thick white bars, matching the ones on the door to the cellblock's hallway. Yet while he was a prisoner there, even when little sunlight shone into that cell, Nelson Mandela could see a better future – one worthy of sacrifice. Standing outside that same tiny spot – now a monument to Mandela, where he was incarcerated for eighteen years during his long campaign to end the policies of racial apartheid and oppression in his country – was an intense experience for Schmidt.

The emotional impact was accentuated when, a few minutes later, he and his fellow tourists gathered in a small courtyard where Mandela and other prisoners were forced to work, and where they occasionally played sports. Along one wall stood lattices for grapevines behind which Mandela, while a prisoner, stored the pages of a manuscript that eventually became *Long Walk to Freedom*.

Schmidt's guide, who had been a prisoner on Robben Island with Mandela for five years, told them that the pages were smuggled out of the prison. Pointing to a black-and-white photograph of prisoners at work in the courtyard, the guide told them that guards once took away the prisoners' hammers and took photos to show the world that the inmates were only doing light work. Once the pictures were finished with, the hammers were soon given back.

Schmidt read with interest Barack Obama's 2013 comments in the visitors' book in the prison courtyard, that his family was 'humbled to stand where men of such courage faced down injustice and refused to yield. The world is grateful for the heroes of Robben Island, who remind us that no shackles or cells can match the strength of the human spirit.'

He wrote of trying to 'transport myself back to those days when President Mandela was still Prisoner 466/64 – a time when the success of his struggle was by no means a certainty. One thing you might not be aware of is that the idea of political non-violence first took root here in South Africa because Mahatma Gandhi was a lawyer here in South Africa. When he went back to India, the principles ultimately led to Indian independence.'

President Obama made the journey with his wife and daughters. He called Nelson Mandela the ultimate testament to the process of peaceful change and said his daughters now understood his legacy better. 'Seeing them stand within the walls that once surrounded Nelson Mandela, I knew this was an experience they would never forget. They appreciate the sacrifices that Madiba [the clan name that many people fondly use to refer to Mr Mandela] and others made for freedom.'

The symbolism of Obama's visit to Robben Island was impossible to miss: America's first African-American president, whose wife is a descendant of African slaves, stating publicly that he might not have been elected were it not for Nelson Mandela's ability to endure imprisonment and emerge to take power without bitterness or recrimination.

For Schmidt, his Robben Island visit inspired him in many ways, not least of which was to think boldly when it came to rugby. The fruit of this bold thinking came when Ireland claimed an historic first Test win in South Africa in Cape Town in 2016. The merchants of doom predicted a tough time for Ireland on their summer tour after a disappointing Six Nations and on the heels of a number of high-profile absences from the touring party, notably Jonathan Sexton.

Few saw Ireland's 26–20 win coming. The number shrank still further when South African-born and reared C. J. Stander was sent off on his first overseas tour with his adopted country for striking the head of Pat Lambie after only twenty-three minutes. Lambie's involvement in the match also came to an end, taken off on a stretcher having been knocked cold, and he was subsequently ruled out of the second Test under the concussion protocol. Stander was attempting to charge down Lambie's kick when he cleaned out the fly-half so maybe a yellow card would have been more appropriate.

Ireland dominated the Springboks early on and Jared Payne's try, after a clever Luke Marshall grubber kick, helped them into a 10–3 lead. When Lwazi Mvovo's try helped the Springboks move into a 13–10 lead within eight minutes of Stander being sent off, there looked likely to be only one winner. But Schmidt's disciples of hope responded gallantly to the challenge.

Conor Murray's try after the restart gave Ireland further belief and captain Rory Best was among those who produced a series of vital turnovers as the visitors refused to wilt in the second half. Leinster flanker Jordi Murphy was impressive in Seán O'Brien's continuing absence from the back row. Devin Toner's brilliant line-out work helped set up Jared Payne's early try and the Leinster lock seemed to be engaged in a competition with his captain Rory Best to earn the most turnovers in the second half, so it was indeed right and fitting that the Leinster giant won man of the match. Jamie Heaslip was also among other contenders, while impressive scrum-half Murray's try two minutes after half-time was undoubtedly the key score of the game.

Perhaps the most remarkable thing about Ireland's first ever win on South African soil was just how comfortable it was, barring a few tense moments at the death. All over Ireland's defensive system were Andy Farrell's fingerprints – the new defence coach clearly having a considerable impact – but the boys in green led by seven when Stander departed, and did so for most of the second half, only an intercept try from South Africa ensuring a tense finish.

'We knew to come here and get a victory would be un-believably tough and require a massive physical performance,' Irish captain Rory Best said afterwards. 'If we had sat back and kept giving them the ball, we would have eventually run out of steam, so we had to take the game to them. There are a lot of tired boys who are running on empty now after the euphoria of the win.'

Jack McGrath gives much of the credit to Joe Schmidt. 'I have been with Joe all my career – first with Leinster and then with Ireland. His attention to detail is phenomenal. Say when we are playing France we all get a two-minute video clip of thirty of the French players showing their strengths and weaknesses: what foot they like to kick with; the hand they pass off with. This kind of detail is invaluable, but the amount of work that goes into producing those video clips is unreal.

'I know people are always going on about how brutal his video analysis is. Certainly, new players coming into the squad are a little apprehensive about it. Joe won't criticise you if you make a mistake. What drives him mad, though, is when you make the same mistake a few times after he's told you about it. In international rugby, the margins are so tight that a small mistake can cost you a match, and that's why Joe is so keen on the minute detail, and Irish rugby has seen the benefit of it. He's the best coach in the world in my eyes.'

37

THE LIFE OF BRIAN

Brian O'Driscoll Becomes a Lions Legend in 2001

'They call him God. Well I reckon he's a much better player than that.'

Thus spoke Stuart Barnes during the Sky Sports commentary of one of the all-time great tries. In his first Test for the Lions in 2001, Brian O'Driscoll left the World Champions, Australia, looking as slow as growing grass as he ran half the field and scythed through their defence to score one of the greatest individual tries ever seen, the very signature of genius.

Following his vintage displays for the Lions, Brian continued his dizzying ascent to become one of the very biggest names in world rugby. The French rugby legend Philippe Sella said of him, 'Brian is like a locomotive,' while Tony Ward referred to him as 'he who walks on water'. He is to rugby aficionados what Nureyev was to the ballet enthusiast.

That game was a big one for Brian's parents Geraldine and Frank, as Geraldine told me:

'Probably the most interesting experience of all came in Australia during the Lions tour. After the first Test, when

Brian scored the famous try, Frank and I got on the bus with a gang of Lions supporters. We sat at the back of the bus and nobody knew who we were. Then the crowd burst into song. They started singing "Waltzing O'Driscoll". Frank and I said nothing. We just nodded at each other, but it was actually very emotional.'

Ollie Campbell was immediately conscious he had watched a career-changing moment.

'I remember Brian O'Driscoll was compared to God after scoring *the* try for the Lions in 2001. I remember thinking then if Brian continued in the same style that, in time, God would be very flattered by the comparison. I still get a shiver down my spine when I think about the try, even now. What struck me were the words of Ian McGeechan, who coached the Lions on three consecutive tours. He said: "You can play for your country and become a hero, but if you play for the Lions, you can become a legend." I think when Brian scored that try he became an instant Lions legend.

'Brian had the absolute instinct for the essence of rugby, which is to score tries. He knew exactly where the line was. He had an amazing strike rate at a time when defences are so well organised, and I think that says more than anything else about Brian's sniff and knowledge of where the line is.

'One of those tries was the infamous try against France in 2001, when many people were surprised that the video referee awarded it. What struck me most was that as the camera was on Brian, as we were all waiting for the video to decide whether or not it was a score, he was smiling. I think that one of the things that really appealed to me about Brian and his attitude to rugby is that he did play with a smile on his face, and he really did seem to always have fun. This is particularly noteworthy in the modern professional era when the stakes are so high, and it's a great example not only to children as to how the game should be played but also to his own contemporaries that it's still possible to enjoy yourself.

'Brian's qualities were too numerous to mention but to list some of them, he had a great work ethic and a healthy appetite for the more mundane aspects of centre play. Mike Gibson had that quality and Tim Horan, the great Australian centre, had it more recently. Brian didn't shirk the defensive responsibilities and, in fact, actually seemed to relish them. He seemed to enjoy both the offensive and defensive, which is an unusual combination – only the great players have that.

'According to Mark Ella, the great Australian out–half in the 1980s, the essence of rugby is support. Brian did seem to have that instinct to be in the right place at the right time. There's an answer for everything in rugby except pace. Brian had that explosive speed off the mark, which he seemed to sustain for more than fifteen yards. He was such a rounded player, with pretty much all the skills in abundance, not least his extraordinary evasion skills. I lost count of the number of times I saw him be incredibly effective and creative in the most unlikely situations. Somehow with his low centre of gravity he was able to dodge and weave and was able to offload to a supporting player – as often as not turning water into wine. Another of his great qualities was almost magical hands, hands that a magician would have been very proud of.

'One of the trademarks that I saw in Brian was his ability to offload in the tackle. He made it look like a very easy skill, but in fact it's extremely difficult. I am reminded of a quote from my childhood idol Mike Gibson after the Lions tour in 1971. He said that they practised and practised, playing so often that the ball became an extension of their hands. Having watched Brian so often it seemed that the ball had become a mere extension of his body. I suppose the final quality was that he seemed to have a remarkable temperament.

'When I saw him score that try in 2001, I knew immediately that Brian had the potential to have an extraordinary career. I thought if he could sustain that hunger and enjoyment of the game and his freshness, and keep himself free from injury, he could go on to join that select band of sports people who became universal household names – which of course he did.'

How does O'Driscoll himself look back on the game?

'I was aware of the crowd at the Gabba. Just looking up into that sea of red as we ran out was enough to put us on our toes, but when the Wallabies appeared and the boos drowned out the cheers, it was just unbelievable.'

O'Driscoll looks back on the tour with mixed feelings.

'If we had gone on to win the series, that first Test would probably have been a major highlight of my career, but because we lost the series it doesn't have the same glow in my memory. We were fairly surprised at what we achieved in the opening fifty minutes of the first Test in particular, but all the gaps were closed up for the next two Tests. When you're part of a tour like that, every result counts in terms of morale and encouragement. The first Test gave us a big lift, but losing the other two were crushing blows.'

38

TOUCH WOOD

Keith Wood Stars on the 1997 Lions Tour

Among the Irish players chosen on the Lions tour in 1959 was the late Gordon Wood. He was capped twenty-nine times for Ireland between 1954 and 1961 at loosehead prop, scoring one international try and forming a formidable front row in the late '50s and early '60s with Syd Millar and Ronnie Dawson. As those four great philosophers ABBA famously suggested when they won the Eurovision in 1974, 'the history book on the shelf is always repeating itself'. Thirty-five years later Ireland's tour to Australia would see the emergence of a new star – Gordon's son Keith earned rave reviews for his performances as hooker. In fact, Wood was singled out by Bob Dwyer as a potential great on his Ireland debut against Australia in 1994. As early as his first match the potential was there.

Such adulation brings its own problems. From the young player's point of view, it could delude them into fostering unrealistic delusions about their own importance – encouraged to imagine they are better than they are, only to become embittered when their careers failed to deliver what they appeared to promise. Far more damaging than anything opponents can do to them is the burden of unrealistic expectations. Yet Wood went on to realise and even surpass those expectations with a series of dazzling performances for Ireland and the Lions (in South Africa in 1997 and Australia in 2001, playing in five of the six Tests) which saw him selected as IRB Player of the Year in 2001. In the process, he won fifty-eight caps and became Ireland's most-capped hooker, having surpassed the great Ken Kennedy. Wood, though, was no ordinary hooker. He kicked like a fly-half, linked like a centre, jinked like a winger and was always inspired by his father's words – 'never be ashamed at being proud of what you're good at'.

The bald wonder first made his name with Garryowen, but in 1996, he crossed the channel and joined Harlequins. The following year he became the club's captain and then remained with the club until his retirement, except for the 1999–2000 season when he returned to play with Munster, leading them to the narrowest of defeats in the European Cup Final.

He first captained Ireland against Australia in November 1996 and immediately established himself as an inspirational leader. His motivational qualities were very evident in one of the most tangible legacies of the 1997 Lions' tour when England's John 'Bentos' Bentley made as big a name for himself off the pitch as he did on it with his critically acclaimed video account of the trip, *Living with the Lions*. Woodie's passionate outbursts before games were one of the most striking features of the video. It was as if his tactics were to try and equalise before the other side had scored.

However, Woodie's one blemish was also to emerge on the trip. Bentley had the misfortune to be rooming with him. As a result of his shoulder problems, Keith could only sleep in one position. He propped two pillows under both shoulders and as soon as he began to sleep, he started snoring loudly. After seven sleepless nights, Bentley could take no more and sought medical advice. On the eighth night, as soon as Woodie started sleeping, Bentley kissed him on the cheek. For the next three nights Woodie lay awake in case Bentley would make further advances on him.

39

HERE ORR THERE

Leinster Tour Romania in 1980

Irish rugby has seldom produced a better prop forward than Phil Orr. In fact, he became the world's most capped prop forward. Of his fifty-eight caps, forty-nine were won consecutively (one short of the Scottish international Sandy Carmichael's record for a prop forward of fifty caps) from 1976 to the match against Wales in 1986. He was recalled, though, for the last match of the 1986 championship.

In 1976, Orr made his international debut in Paris as Ireland lost by a then record 26–3, coming in as a late replacement for Paddy Agnew.

'One of the clearest memories I have is of touring Romania with Leinster in 1980. It was like entering a time warp. Most of the time we were starving because there wasn't enough food largely, because it all went up to Moscow. There was nothing in the shops except bare shelves. If you wanted an orange, for example, you had to order it the day before. One incident stands out for me. We stopped for a meal of sorts in a halfway house. As we got off the bus, what struck me most was that there wasn't the sound of a bird to be heard. I learned later that DDT had killed all the insects and the birds had migrated.'

The belief at the time was that one in every four people in Romania was an informer for the Securitate. It subsequently emerged that this was a lie deliberately put about by the Securitate to keep everyone in line, lest anyone they were talking to reported them for subversion or, perish the thought, making a joke about the dictator, Nicolae Ceaușescu.

So now his playing days are over, what is Orr's happiest rugby memory?

'On Leinster's tour to Romania in 1980 we were soon fed up with the food on offer. On a bus journey, the two big jokers in the side, Paul McNaughton and Freddie McLennan, walked up the bus with a list taking the lunch orders. We were told we could choose between T-bone steak or grilled chicken, and we had to indicate whether we wanted chips, baked or sautéed potatoes, and select from a choice of vegetables, as it all had to be ordered in advance. All the players got very excited, and great care was taken over the menu. We arrived at an impressive-looking restaurant for a big meal. There was a buzz of expectancy – which turned into a stunned silence when the food arrived. Each dish was the same: a big bowl of clear, greasy soup and in it was a huge fish head complete with eyes. Nothing was eaten. McNaughton and McLennan had to be led out – they were laughing so much they couldn't walk.'

40

CONQUERING THE AUSSIES

Ireland v Australia, 1979

Rugby tours are notorious for their unpredictability. The Irish tour to Australia in 1979 was no exception. More accurately, unpredictability was the order of the day. Consider the case of John Moloney, who went on the tour as a cover scrum-half for the incumbent Colin Patterson and won a shock call-up as wing three-quarter for the Tests.

Fergus Slattery led the Irish on the successful tour down under in 1979.

'Before the Australian tour I thought we would have our work cut out to win the Tests. I think it's fair to say Australia underperformed in the first match because we caught them on the hop, but we beat them on merit in the second game.'

On the controversial tour to Australia, Ciaran Fitzgerald made his international debut, playing in both Tests, although he went out as number two to Pat Whelan.

'At the time, there was an incredible fuss about the fact that

Tony Ward had been dropped and Ollie Campbell chosen in his place. I was totally oblivious to it all. I heard my own name mentioned when the team was announced and nothing else registered with me. A tour was a great place to win a first cap because you were sheltered from all the hype, press attention and distractions that you get at home. I was able to hold my place the following season. I never felt threatened, but I never felt comfortable. All you can do is perform to your very best and forget about the lads who are challenging for your position.'

But nothing could compare to the fairy tale of Old Belvedere's Ollie Campbell. Enid Blyton couldn't have emulated his story. The 25-year-old's international career had been launched and almost abandoned courtesy of one shattering appearance at Lansdowne Road against Australia three years earlier. He missed four penalties and was immediately written off by many who claimed to be judges of international players. Despite injury problems, having been out of rugby the previous season from September to February with ligament trouble, he had shown good club form and justified his recall to the Irish squad as cover for the out-half position. In the greatest selection shock in living memory, he displaced the greatest superstar in Irish rugby. Ollie's subsequent textbook performances were a revelation and he kicked Ireland to victory in both Tests. For Campbell, all his Christmases had come at once, but his dream was Tony Ward's nightmare.

For the next thirty-nine years both men would be inextricably linked in the public consciousness, and in the lead-up to Ireland's tour to Australia in 2018, the story was inevitably recycled in many media outlets. When Ireland won, both men breathed a sigh of relief, thinking they could finally put the story to bed. Campbell sent Ward a text which simply stated: 'It's over.'

The next day Campbell was out on a social engagement when a young lady asked him to pose for a selfie.

As he smiled for the camera, the lady said: 'This is for my dad. He's a massive fan of Tony Ward.'

'Sorry?'

'My dad is a huge fan of Tony Ward.'

'I see. And what's your name?'

'Toni.'

41

DOWN UNDER

Ireland Tour New Zealand in 1976

There is a great book to be written on Ireland's tour of New Zealand in 1976, albeit more for off-the-pitch activities than what happened on it. Mick Quinn's worst moment in rugby came on that tour:

'We were losing 15–3 to Canterbury. I was sub. From my point of view everything was going great. When you're a sub, you don't really want things to be going well for the team, because if it does, how else are you going to get your place back? Larry Moloney broke his arm so Tony Ensor replaced him. Then Wallace McMaster got injured and, with a sinking heart, I realised I would have to play on the wing. It was my first time ever to play in that position. I was petrified, and I can tell you I wished I was wearing brown shorts!

'As I walked on, one of their players, Alex "Grizz" Wyllie, came over to me and said: "You've come a long way to die, son."

'When I was in school in Newbridge, Father Heffernan had always drilled into me the belief that you should never let anybody intimidate you. At that stage I made the biggest mistake of my life. I said: "Listen, pal, if my dog had a face like yours, I would shave his arse and get him to walk backwards." Every chance he got after that he clobbered me. Even when the ball was somewhere else he kept coming at me. When I said the ball is over there, he answered, "I couldn't give a f**k where the ball is. I'm going to kill you."

'Mike Gibson had a great temperament. The only time I ever saw him rattled was on the tour to New Zealand in 1976. We were really up against it in some of the matches. I remember Tom Grace saying at breakfast: "Quinner, do you think we'll get out of the place before they realise we're afraid of them." We laughed at the time but I wonder! Barry McGann didn't share the general concern. He was playing at out-half that day and was kicking everything – and I mean everything. At one stage, Mike Gibson yelled for a pass but Barry said: "Listen, Mike when I meet a player who can run as fast as I can kick it then I'll think about passing it!"'

Phil O'Callaghan had been recalled for the tour of New Zealand. The Dolphin player was capped twenty-one times for Ireland over a ten-year period between 1967 and 1976, although he won no caps from 1971 through to 1975.

'Phil had really established his credentials when Ireland went to Australia for a six-match tour in 1967, but he looked a bit older than the rest of us in '76. A journalist asked him who he was. Philo answered: "I'm Ireland's secret weapon." There was a lot of surprise that he was selected, but he played a very significant role on that tour. He earned his cap on merit. I would describe him as the traditional Irish rugby tourist. When we were being intimidated on the pitch, he wasn't found wanting.'

John Robbie was chosen to tour New Zealand in 1976.

'The tour was a marvellous experience. I was the youngest in the party and looked it. On one boat trip during the tour, some New Zealander glanced at me and remarked in all seriousness that it was nice of the New Zealand rugby union to allow the Irish manager to bring his son along on tour.

'It was all rugby at the start but loosened up a little at the end. On the way home, we stopped in Fiji for a few days. We travelled throughout the island in an old bus with no windows. I'd got a bit drunk in Auckland. I had told the team about the current craze of "lobbing moons" – pulling one's trousers down, bending over and displaying the bare backside to all and sundry. The trick was to choose the time and the place with the most care to get the greatest effect. The Fijian bus without windows was too much of a temptation, and so I lobbed a moon out at a village through which we were passing. The locals were totally amazed, and we all had a great laugh until I couldn't find my wallet. It looked like I'd lobbed all my travellers' cheques out of the window. In the end, we discovered that they'd just fallen down the side of the seat – but it was a close call.'

The last word about the tour goes to Mick Quinn.

'On that tour, Jimmy Davidson was called into the Irish side as a replacement. He was so happy to be selected that he jumped for joy when he got on the team bus for the first time. He jumped so high that he smashed his head against the roof and needed six stitches.

'For his first game on the tour, we were worried about things getting out of hand on the pitch. At one stage, there was a melee in the ruck and Pa Whelan mistakenly stamped Davidson on the head. Initially the lads thought one of the New Zealand guys had done it and there was bedlam for two minutes. When order was restored, the first thing we heard was Davidson shouting: "You f**king idiot, Whelan." After the game, he needed plenty of stitches.'

42

THE PASSION MACHINE

Kennedy's Lions Tour, 1974

While the Lions tour to South Africa was a great success on the pitch for Irish hooker Dr Ken Kennedy, it was also a great success off the pitch – also largely because of the friendship he formed with Welsh legend Bobby Windsor, one of the game's great raconteurs. One of his favourite stories was about a Welsh Valleys rugby club on tour in America.

On coming back from a night on the town, two of the players couldn't find their rooms. They decided to check for their teammates by looking through the keyholes and at one stage, they came on an astonishing sight. There in her birthday suit was a Marilyn Monroe lookalike. Close by was a man who was chanting with great conviction: 'Your face is so beautiful that I'll have it painted in gold. Your breasts are so magnificent that I'll have them painted in silver. Your legs are so shapely that I'll have them painted in platinum.'

Outside, the two Welsh men were getting very aroused and began jostling each other for the right of the keyhole. The man inside, hearing the racket, shouted out: 'Who the hell is out there?'

The two Welsh men replied: 'We're two painters from Pontypool.'

Bobby had some great exchanges with waiters during the '74 Lions tour. One went as follows:

Windsor: 'I want one egg boiled for exactly twenty-six seconds and I want another one boiled for twenty-five minutes and fourteen seconds. And I want three slices of toast which are pale gold on one side and burned pure black on the other.'

Waiter: 'But, sir, that's simply not possible. We can't go to all the trouble to fill an order like that.'

Windsor: 'Oh yes you can, sonny boy. That's exactly what you dished up to me yesterday!'

At another meal, the players were tucking in to a big steak dinner. Bobby was feeling a bit under the weather and just asked for an omelette. The waiter asked, 'What kind of omelette would you like, sir?' Bobby just looked up at him and barked, 'A f**king egg omelette!'

In the golden age of amateurism, the manager of the Lions 1974 tour was Alan Thomas. He tended to lose things, especially room keys. He had a phone in his room but each player on the team was only allowed one phone call a week. Bobby Windsor spotted Alan's key and held on to it. Every evening he used it to sneak into Alan's room and phone his wife. As the tour concluded and the team were leaving the hotel, Alan came into the foyer and addressed the entire squad in a crestfallen voice: 'I'm very disappointed. I have been handed a phone bill for a thousand rand. One of you guys has been using the phone every night behind my back. The Lions are supposed to be the cream of rugby, but one of you has let the side down in this way and sadly, the guy who did this is a countryman of my own. He's been ringing Pontypridd.'

At this point Bobby Windsor jumped up from his seat and

started waving his fists menacingly as he said, 'Which of you bastards has been phoning my wife?'

On the Lions' flight to South Africa in 1974, Windsor was taken ill with food poisoning. He was so ill that he was taken to the back of the plane and told to suck ice cubes to help him cool down. The team doctor, Irish international Ken Kennedy, came to take his temperature without knowing about the ice cubes. When he looked at the thermometer, he shouted out, 'Jaysus, Bobby, you died twenty-four hours ago!'

43

THE LYNCH MOB

Seán Lynch Stars for the Lions

In 1971, Colin Meads prematurely dismissed the Lions forwards as 'too many sweat bands, not enough sweat'. Seán Lynch was one of the men who made Meads eat his words. Capped seventeen times for his country, Lynch is not a player to take himself too seriously. Success at club level provided the platform Lynch needed to step on to the international stage.

'Denis Hickie and I were capped for the first time against France in 1971, becoming the first current Mary's players to play for Ireland. Jimmy Kelly and George Norton had played for St Mary's and Ireland but weren't Mary's players during their international careers. It was a wonderful achievement for the club. When the side was announced there was a great club celebration.'

After just one season at international level, Lynch was chosen by the Lions for the historic tour to New Zealand. He was to play a more central role than anybody could have foreseen at the start of the tour. The week before the first Test in Dunedin, the Lions had lost their two first-choice props, Ray McLoughlin and Sandy Carmichael, with long-term injuries in the infamous 'battle of Christchurch'. The match confirmed an old adage: 'New Zealand rugby is a colourful game – you get all black and blue.'

Willie John McBride warned his fellow forwards after this bruising encounter: 'You haven't seen anything yet. They'll throw everything at you, even the kitchen sink.'

Lynchie's prop partner was the squat Scot, Ian McLauchlan, nicknamed 'Mighty Mouse'. One of his opponents scornfully dismissed him with the words: 'You'll be Mickey Mouse by the time I've finished with you.' Yet it was the Lions who had the last laugh, winning 9–3. The crowd's silence after the game bore eloquent testimony to the scale of the shock. From that moment, a win in the series was a distinct possibility, though the All Blacks restored parity in the second Test.

The Lions won the third Test 13–3 in Wellington, thanks in no small measure to a vintage display by Barry John. The final Test at Eden Park, Auckland, ended in a 14–14 draw. For Lynch, it was do-or-die.

'We were getting very tired at that stage and were anxious to return home, but at the same time we didn't want to squander a 2–1 lead. We were determined to prove that we were the best. Our mood had changed during the tour. When we arrived, we probably believed deep down that the All Blacks were invincible. By the finish it was us who thought we were almost invincible.'

Before the match, the captain, John Dawes, simply said to the players: 'We've come this far. We're not going to throw it away now.' Dawes looked each player in the eye. Further words were superfluous. Each one knew what they had to do. The joke later among the players was: 'We were so fired up, when the referee ran on to the pitch, three of us tackled him.'

Spurred on like a wounded animal by the ire of a fanatical nation, the All Blacks started like a whirlwind, taking the lead after just four minutes, courtesy of a soft try from Wayne Cottrell. The tension got to the Lions and they underperformed. However, when they were trailing 14–11, J.P.R. Williams dropped a goal from about forty yards to tie the match.

Lynch is perpetually grateful for the two coaches who had a big impact on his development into a top-class player.

'Carwyn James, the Lions' coach in 1971, was one of the great visionaries of the game. Ronnie Dawson was Ireland's first coach and was very instrumental in bringing Ireland into the modern era.

'On the non-playing side, my greatest memory of the Lions' tour is of visiting a vineyard – I think it was run by a religious order. I had red wine, white wine, blue wine and everything that was going. At the end, I didn't know where I was or who I was! I wasn't moving very sprightly the next morning.'

44

THE LIFE OF O'REILLY

Tony O'Reilly Stars on the Lions Tour in 1955

After listening to Tony O'Reilly give a lengthy speech in his alma mater, the then Taoiseach, Bertie Ahern said, 'I'd like to congratulate Belvedere College on the great job dey did in teaching Tony O'Reilly to speak so well. A pity dey didn't teach him to stop!'

Such is O'Reilly's flair with words it's difficult to imagine that he was once outquipped – but miracles do happen. England beat Ireland 20–0. As he walked off the pitch, O'Reilly turned to Tom Reid and said: '20–0! That was dreadful!'

Reid responded: 'Sure, weren't we lucky to get the nil!'

O'Reilly held the distinction of having the records for the most tries ever scored by a Lion and the most tries ever scored by a Barbarian. Coached at Belvedere College by the legendary Karl Mullen, he played his first match when he was six years of age. His mother asked the priest what he thought of the small players on show. The Jesuit, who had no idea who she was, answered: 'The red fellow's the best.' She glowed with pride. The red fellow was her son.

O'Reilly is very much the Roy of the Rovers of Irish rugby. Having first been capped against France as an eighteen-year-old in 1955, he was the undisputed star of the Lions' tour to South Africa in the same year. The Lions were captained and managed by Irishmen, Robin Thompson and Jack Siggins respectively. The squad featured five Irish players, Thompson, Tom Reid, and Robin Roe in the forwards and O'Reilly and Cecil Pedlow among the backs. O'Reilly scored no less than sixteen tries, a record number, and emerged as top scorer.

In 1959, O'Reilly did even better on the Lions tour to New Zealand and Australia, amassing a staggering twenty-two tries. It is probably a testimony to his importance to the team that he played in more matches than any other player, twenty-four in all. However, this time it was another Irish player, David Hewitt, who was top scorer, with 106 points.

O'Reilly celebrated his nineteenth birthday on the Lions tour to South Africa in 1955. In the opening Test, the Lions won 23–22 in Johannesburg. It was the biggest attendance ever seen at a rugby game. The Springboks led 11–3, and to compound their misfortune, the Lions lost their flanker, Reg Higgins, with a broken leg. At the time no replacements were allowed, so they had to play with fourteen men in front of over 100,000 partisan South Africans. Then three tries from Cliff Morgan, Cecil Pedlow and Tony O'Reilly gave the Lions a 23–11 lead. The Afrikaners replied with a vengeance. In the final minute, Chris Koch crashed over for a try to cut the deficit to just one point. As van der Schyff faced a relatively easy kick to give the South Africans victory, the Irish members on the team turned to religion. The Limerick lock Tom Reid said, 'Jesus, if he kicks this, I'm turning Protestant.'

To the horror of the home fans, van der Schyff pushed his kick left of the post.

O'Reilly's achievements on the field don't seem to square with his own assessment of his playing style: 'I suppose you could say I was a slightly furtive player. I hung back waiting for the game to show itself to me rather than showing myself to the game.'

O'Reilly could have been a film star. The late Noel Purcell recommended him to Al Corfino, the casting director of the film *Ben Hur*, for the role that was eventually played by Charlton Heston. O'Reilly's physique made him ideal for the scenes in the galleys. Purcell arranged for a meeting between the director and O'Reilly, but the rugby player never showed up. The story of O'Reilly's possible role in the film made headlines in places as far away as South Africa.

The late Tom Reid toured with O'Reilly to South Africa. Reid suffered from bad eyesight and went to live in Canada after that tour. In 1959, he memorably linked up with O'Reilly again. After the Lions tour in New Zealand, the Lions stopped off to play a Test in Canada. O'Reilly was standing in line before the match when he heard a loud Limerick accent booming out over the ground: 'Hello, O'Reilly, I know you're there. I can't see you but I can hear you all right!'

In May 2019, Old Belvedere marked their centenary with a dinner in the RDS. They are one of the handful of clubs that produced a truly iconic name in world rugby – I of course refer to Sir Anthony himself.

Ollie Campbell's most vivid memory of O'Reilly goes back to 1982. He was practising his penalties with great diligence. Sir Anthony walked over to him and told him that he was a perfectionist. Campbell felt not ten foot tall but 110 foot tall. Then, just as Tony was walking away, he turned around to Ollie and said: 'A perfectionist is someone who takes great pains – and gives them to everybody else.'

45

BIG TOM

Tom Clifford Becomes a Lions Legend in 1950

No one encapsulates the passion for rugby better than Tom Clifford. He was first capped for Ireland against France in 1949 and won the last of his fourteen caps against France in 1952, a match that also saw the end of the international careers of Karl Mullen, Des O'Brien and Bill McKay. Clifford was a key part of the '49 Triple Crown victory and toured with the Lions to New Zealand in 1950. He was one of nine Irish players to make the tour with Karl Mullen, George Norton, Michael Lane, Noel Henderson, Jack Kyle, Jimmy Nelson, Billy McKay and Jim McCarthy. Clifford was famous on the tour for his singing. One of his favourite ditties was: 'When I was a wee wee tot, they put me on a wee wee pot, to see if I could wee or not.'

For Jim McCarthy, Clifford was not only one of the great props but perhaps the greatest character in Irish rugby.

'When I look back, it's the matches with Munster that stand out for me. Bill Shankly's famous saying that football is not a matter of life or death but more important applies to rugby in Munster, especially in Limerick. For me, the person that encapsulated that feeling was the late, great Tom Clifford. He was the character among characters. I'll never forget his funeral. The church was teeming with rugby folk. The priest giving the homily had been a lifelong friend of Tom's and told us how he had invited the legend of Irish rugby to his ordination Mass. After the ceremony, he'd asked Tom what he thought of it. Tom replied: "You spoke too long. The next time, if you go on for longer than ten minutes I'll set off an alarm clock in the church." The next Sunday the priest saw Tom arriving at the church and noticed he had a bulge in his overcoat. When Tom caught his eye, he pulled out an alarm clock!

'I was on the Lions tour with Tom in 1950. Tom was a larger-than-life figure, especially when he sang his party piece, "O'Reilly's Daughter". His only rival in the character stakes was probably Cliff Davies, a Welsh coalminer. Cliff was greeted by the New Zealand Prime Minister, S. G. Holland, who said: "Glad to meet you, Cliff." Cliff retorted: "Glad to meet you, Sid."

'Another typical Munster forward was Starry Crowley, a hooker. At one stage, we were playing in a ferocious match when he "made contact" with a player. He explained his motivation to me afterwards: "I was running across the pitch and I saw a head lying on the ground and I kicked not to maim but to kill."'

Jack Kyle also had reason to remember Tom fondly from the Lions tour in 1950.

'We were given two blazers and our jerseys and two pounds, ten shillings a week for expenses. If you adjusted that figure to allow for inflation I can't see chaps playing international rugby accepting that today! But from our point of view, the trip was a very enriching experience.

'We were gone for six months. Although we had journeyed to France to play an international, it was our first real experience of travel. We went out via the Panama Canal and home by the Suez Canal, so it was really a round-the-world trip. We kept fit by running around the ship. Every afternoon we had great discussions about rugby. I learned more about the game in those conversations than I ever had before or since.

'Our champion was Tom Clifford. Apart from the normal luggage, Tom brought a massive trunk on to the ship. We were all puzzled about what he could have in it. As cabins were shared, players were instructed to only store essential items there, but Tom insisted on bringing in his trunk, which immediately caused a lot of grumbles from his roommates, who were complaining about the clutter. They changed their tune the first night though when some of us said we were feeling peckish. Tom brought us into his cabin and opened his trunk, which was crammed with food which his mother had cooked. So every night we dined royally in Tom's cabin. Someone said that we should all write a letter to Mrs Clifford because she fed us so well on that trip!

'Tom had a very healthy appetite. To break the monotony of the journey, we had all kinds of competitions. One night we had an eating competition. Tom won hands down because he got through all thirty courses that were on the menu!'

Rugby was a much more physically dangerous game in times gone by. I remember one of my first conversations with Karl Mullen. He told me about a game he played in Limerick against Young Munster. Old Belvedere were on fire and had built a big lead when Tom Clifford uttered the immortal words: 'Kick a head, kick any bloody head.'

The Young Munster lads responded so enthusiastically to his battle cry that within two minutes everybody ended up in the next field!

Tom Clifford grabbed Karl forcefully by the jersey and shouted at him: 'Come here for a laugh and you'll end up in stitches.'

PART III
The Brave Ones

Rugby has produced many moments of courage. In the 2019 Six Nations, an injury-ravaged Scotland trailed England 31–0 at Twickenham but the gutsy Scots not only pulled back the deficit, it took a try from George Ford in the last play of the game to salvage a 38–38 draw for the English.

Courage is part of the fabric of the Irish rugby story. In the 2019 Six Nations, C. J. Stander played sixty-two minutes against the English, despite fracturing a cheekbone and eye socket in the first twenty minutes.

Today's generation of Irish rugby players do not conform to the traditional stereotypes. A case in point is Robbie Henshaw. He is a wonderful accordion player and a keen fan of traditional music. In his native Athlone, his family are renowned for their prowess in the genre. In 2018, they teamed up with Sharon Shannon to make a very successful fundraising CD for the South Westmeath Hospice called *The Secret Sessions*.

Shay Deering, Willie Duggan, Axel Foley and John Muldoon are just some examples of the many legendary Irish players who were famous for their bravery on the pitch. However, Irish rugby has also produced many moments where players have shown remarkable moral courage off the field. This section celebrates some of the bravest people in Irish rugby. It is indeed right and fitting therefore that this section begins with Jack McGrath.

46

YOU DON'T KNOW JACK

Jack McGrath Shows His Mettle

Jack McGrath is always a ferocious presence who would never flinch from a tackle for province, country or the Lions. However, he perhaps showed even more moral courage when he spoke out publicly about his brother's death by suicide to raise awareness about mental-health issues. It was a dark chapter in his life as he explained to me:

'I suffered in silence for five and a half years following my brother's tragic death. I struggled to talk about it. I told myself, "Don't cry. You need to be strong," but when it came to a head I had to speak out.

'I had used rugby as a way of coping with my struggle. I had a very macho approach initially, which was to show no weakness. Eventually it began to affect my rugby and my relationships. I needed to talk about it. When I finally did, it was a huge weight off my shoulders. It was like a gas valve had been released.

'What had held me back for so long was that I was afraid what people might think of me and, I confess, that they'd think a bit less of me. We live in a very judgemental society. You only have to look at social media for the proof of that. However, when I did speak out and when I went public, everybody was very supportive. My friends, my family and my rugby teammates were all there for me.'

Joe Schmidt is a keen fan.

'As someone who does enjoy a real privileged position and the opportunity to work with elite people, to help people a bit I think is incredibly important.

'I think it's important that the Irish team has a social conscience and does some community service. The first year we had our Christmas camp we had a Kris Kindle. We put Rala (Patrick O'Reilly, the team's baggage manager) in charge of it and it was after our Christmas dinner. The only problem was that he talked so long it felt like we were there 'til New Year's Day! Rala is a great character but brevity is not his forte. He did his own book and I asked him how many words he would need. He said 70,000. I said that was a lot of words and asked him how many were his. He answered: "130,000."

'The second year I wanted to do something more substantial. I spoke to the team captain at the time, Paul O'Connell. He agreed to my suggestion that we should visit the Capuchin Centre. We spent three hours there and I know it was a very positive experience for all of us.

'I think it's great when players get involved in serious issues. I do a lot of visits to schools, and I am very aware of the importance of mental-health issues in Irish society. Jack McGrath led the way in the Irish camp in the way he headed the "Tackle Your Feelings" campaign, and he deserves great credit for that. It would make you proud to see how well the squad responded to him. He's a great guy.'

47

SUPERMC

Ian McKinley Redefines the Face of Rugby

Ian McKinley has literally changed the face of international rugby.

He played rugby at school for St Columba's College in south Dublin. From playing with them, he was selected for various representative teams with Leinster and Ireland to under-19 level. His performances were deemed good enough that he was selected to enter the Academy in Leinster. The day after his final exam for the Leaving Cert, he started training with the province, aged eighteen.

'Coming from a non-rugby school to a full professional environment was certainly a massive challenge. My first memories would be meeting Dan Tobin (strength and conditioning coach) and him trying to get me up to speed with all the important lifts, e.g. squat, clean, deadlift. On the field, it was very much about integrating with other Academy members, like Felix Jones and Dave Kearney. We played a lot of fitness games, and in particular I remember a gruelling boxing circuit of fifteen rounds with Michael Cheika. I trained a lot with the first team as the season went on and I played my first game against the Dragons the week before the 2009 Heineken Cup Final. I just remember Felix Jones being so professional in all aspects. He was, though, quite light and Dan, our fitness coach, would make him eat a lot to gain weight. One time he made him eat so much that Felix had to throw up.'

McKinley found himself battling with Ian Madigan to see who would be understudy as Leinster out-half to Johnny Sexton.

'Myself and Ian had a good rivalry from under-20s. We both have different strengths, but I just remember he was very gifted with his handling and passing. Johnny was very much a dominant figure and you needed to be on point with everything. Cheika demanded work rate and the things that you didn't necessarily need to be skilful at (ruthlessness, physicality, defensively strong).

'Then Cheika moved on and Joe (Schmidt) replaced him as Leinster coach. Joe just demanded the utmost in concentration, both in training and games. His attention to detail is incredible. I remember I was going to be picked for a game against Cardiff and I went into his office to point out where we could attack. I gave him an example, via video, and he just turned and said, "Good work but go look at these clips and tell me what you see." In those you saw different spaces to attack. He was always one step ahead.'

Then came the moment that would redefine McKinley's career.

'It was an AIL top-of-the-table league game (UCD v Lansdowne) in Belfield. I was dropped to the pitch by my dad as I didn't drive at the time. It was always my mum bringing me, but she had to miss the game. It was a normal build-up. I did my usual preparation and the weather was fantastic.

'About two minutes into the game, I was at the bottom of a

© INPHO / James Crombie

The Hands of BOD: Brian O'Driscoll touches down for a try against Wales in 2013.

For Whom the Bell Tolls:
Ulster's Jonathan Bell gathers the ball under pressure in the 1999 European Cup final.

© INPHO / Billy Stickland

© INPHO / Dan Sheridan

My Ball:
Rob Kearney and Scotland's Greig
Laidlaw fight for possession in 2019.

© INPHO / Dan Sheridan

The Line(out) King:
Paul O'Connell soars like an eagle in
the 2008 Heineken Cup final.

© INPHO / James Crombie

But, Hark! Some Voice Like Thunder Spake, The West's Awake: Connacht celebrate their historic 2016 Pro 12 final victory.

We Are the Champions: Leinster celebrate beating Ulster in the Heineken Cup final.

© INPHO / Dan Sheridan

Paused to Pounce:
CJ Stander surveys the gain line against Wales with Jamie Heaslip in support.

King Rog: Ronan O'Gara
eyes his options with Cian Healy on hand.

The Best of the West: Connacht'
John Muldoon claims a lineout.

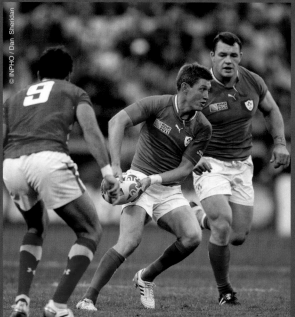

© INPHO / Morgan Treacy

The Fab Four: Conor Murray, Jonathan Sexton, Seán O'Brien and Rory Best eye the ball against Wales in 2019.

Charging Forward: Iain Henderson breaks the gain line against Wales.

Gone But Not Forgotten: The late, great Nevin Spence in characteristic all action style against Scarlets.

© INPHO / Billy Stickland

© INPHO / Darren Kidd

© INPHO / Gary Carr

Centre of Excellence:
Robbie Henshaw evades England's Ben Youngs in the 2019 Six Nations.

Flying High: Ireland's Marie Louise Reilly competes with
Justine Lavea of New Zealand at the 2014 Women's Rugby World Cup.

© INPHO / Dan Sheridan

© INPHO / Dan Sheridan

Sophie's Choice: Sophie Spence makes a break against Italy in the 2013 Six Nations.

Setting the Tone:
Devon Toner beats Kieran Read to the ball against New Zealand in 2018.

© INPHO / Billy Stickland

© INPHO / Bryan Keane

Slamtastic: The Irish team celebrate winning the Grand Slam in 2018.

Bundee Brillance:
Bundee Aki breaks the English line in 2018 with typical true grit.

Catch of the Day: The peerless Peter O'Mahony wins a decisive ball against England's Maro Itoje in 2018.

© INPHO / Billy Stickland

© INPHO / James Crombie

ruck, wrestling for possession. I went for one big rip and found myself on my back. In that moment, a teammate accidentally stood on my face and his stud went straight into my left eyeball and it burst.

'There was actually no pain. My vision went straight away, so I knew it was serious. The medical staff of UCD rushed on to the field and they knew it was serious as my eye was out of place.

'I suppose I didn't realise how serious it was until I was in the A&E in the Royal Eye and Ear. There, after seeing me, they left me for a while in the room to try and get a senior surgeon to perform emergency surgery. That was actually quite a lonely time as I didn't really know what was happening.'

Thoughts about never playing again were initially not part of his subconscious.

'It never entered my mind. I just knew if my recovery was good I could get back on the field as soon as possible.'

There were some particularly low points to be faced though.

'The first was when my retina detached and I didn't fully process it, and it just hit me on a night out with friends. The second was when I was in Udine and my girlfriend, Julie, had moved back to London to work. Even though I was surrounded by such good people, I felt alone and underachieving.'

In 2011, he was forced to announce his retirement. Then, when things were looking bleak, the rugby authorities threw him a lifeline.

'I found out that the IRB were looking at introducing eye protection for players worldwide. We got in contact with them and we found out that this was true. They were going to test the product on a trial basis. The goggles became available in January 2014 and I managed to get a pair. From there I managed to play my first game back, three years after I initially retired, in Italy's Serie C with a team called Leonorso Rugby Udine in March 2014.

'Because it was a trial, every nation had a choice whether to participate in it or not. Ireland, England and France chose not to take part. As I climbed up the ladder with the quality of teams, I wasn't allowed to play in these countries. After many months of battling and campaigning, we managed to change this decision and now everyone who wears these goggles can play freely.'

Italy offered a new beginning for Ian.

'The opportunity came to go and work there as a coach originally. I had never been but I'd always had a fascination with it. I also just wanted to get out of Ireland and go somewhere that was completely out of my comfort zone in the role that I would develop.'

There had to be a period of adjustment for him.

'It certainly took a while! To learn a new language, culture and to meet new people is challenging. I remember Julie went into the supermarket to ask for stock cubes. She looked up the direct translation in the dictionary and asked an assistant, "Where is the livestock?". The assistant, as you can imagine, laughed and laughed. So things like that happened all the time.

'After playing in Serie C, I moved to Viadana, who play in the main league for club teams, which is called Eccellenza. I played there for two years. In those two years, I was a permit player for Zebre, which meant I could cover for them during the Six Nations and World Cup. I managed to play three games with them. One was against my old team Leinster and the other against Ulster in Belfast (my first game back in Ireland). Benetton must have been happy with me so they signed me up.'

Then came the fulfilment of a dream in autumn 2017 when he won his first cap for Italy, having qualified on the residency rule.

'It was a day filled with lots of different emotions. There was a job to do, but at the same time I was going to play international rugby. There was a fair bit of media interest during the week, so I had to block that out and just concentrate on the job at hand. The national anthems was an emotional moment as I had my whole family in front of me in the stand and there were many tears. When I got on in the 60th minute, the game (against Fiji) was very much in the balance at 16–10 so I had to be spot on with things. I remember we got a penalty to close out the game and certainly my heart was pounding out of my shirt as I stood up to take it. When it went over, there was a lot of relief. I was just happy that we won, to be honest.'

Ian is a big admirer of Italy's Irish coach Conor O'Shea. 'He definitely has the right vision for us and his work rate is unquestionable.'

There was a lot of speculation that McKinley would be in the Italy squad when they played Ireland in the Aviva in 2018. It was not to be.

'Of course, I would have loved to have played but the great thing about rugby is that it's not about the individual but the team. Thankfully I was lucky enough to play for Italy against Ireland in Chicago in the Autumn Internationals later that year.'

McKinley is philosophical about his injury.

'My experience has taught me never to try and predict the future but just be as prepared as you can. Most people are lucky to call one place home but I'm lucky to have two.'

48

I WILL WALK ALONE

Ciarán McCarthy's Story of Hope

Sometimes we need to be jolted out of our normal routine to really appreciate the magic of Christmas. In 2002, Ciarán McCarthy had such an experience.

'It was time for the Vigil Mass on Christmas Eve; as a family, we were ready to go to the chapel. I had not been to a Christmas Eve Mass in many years. Instead, the dawn Mass on Christmas Day in a different parish was my preferred option. However, that year, such an option wasn't available, the reason being I wasn't sure if I had direct access to that church. For the first time in my life, access to buildings had become a personal issue. It was my first Christmas in a wheelchair.'

Earlier that year Ciarán had been paralysed in a freak rugby accident while playing for CYM Terenure. The match was played in atrocious conditions, and had the weather not been so inclement, the accident wouldn't in all likelihood ever have taken place. The medical diagnosis was emphatic: 'You will never walk again.' Nine months of rehabilitation left him as strong as possible in the circumstances. But the wounds of the body can sometimes heal much quicker than those of the mind and spirit.

'We arrived at the Vigil Mass in plenty of time. The chapel is located on the grounds of my old school. Memories came to mind of time spent playing rugby and winning championships on the running track – physicality once vibrant now morbid. Sitting there in the chapel, did I feel broken at a time when the Christian message to the world is one of great joy and universal peace? No, I did not feel broken; I felt relaxed with the divine Spirit within me and at one with my family. Did I feel anguished, bitter or resentful this first Christmas wheeling rather than walking? No, I had none of these feelings. So at an emotional level this particular Christmas wasn't any different from any other that preceded it. Something that may not be readily believable but nevertheless remains true. The meaning of Christmas for me is unchanged – living through love to experience both joy and peace.

'After Mass, I was making my way to the exit when something unique took place. A few old teachers of mine said hello, shared season's greetings and cried for me. It was the first time they'd seen me in my paralysed state. I could see the sadness and sympathy in their eyes. These people were moved to tears. Not floods of tears but reluctant tears – reluctant to show how upset they were in case they upset me. Caring, thoughtful teachers touched in a way that elevated their humanity.

'I left the chapel, got into my car and drove us all home. With my adapted car, driving has become a more enjoyable activity than ever before, possibly because such issues as getting around and gaining access to places are not so urgent behind the wheel. I had relearned to drive during my nine-month stay at the National Rehabilitation Hospital.'

Although he has had a lot of reason to feel despair, Ciarán

shows anything but. Although the medical advice was that he would never walk again, Ciarán has not accepted that, and with intensive physiotherapy he has made some progress. He firmly believes that someday he will walk again. Positive thinking is his hallmark.

'The one thing I've learned is that there is always someone worse off than you. During my stay in rehab, I was learning to get the most from my broken body, while at the same time retaining an unbroken spirit. One of the lessons learned was to be patient with my condition and have the discipline to remove my urgent desire for an immediate restoration of my physical state. Thankfully that Christmas lacked any urgency; instead it provided me with a belief that life beyond rehabilitation was worth living.'

Ollie Campbell is a big fan: 'Sometimes when I think of Ciarán I think of that colossal and regal seated statue of Abraham Lincoln in Washington DC. Lincoln once said, "To remain as I am is impossible; I must improve or die." As far as I'm aware, Ciarán has never given up hope since that day, despite the many setbacks and the many hurdles he's had to overcome.

'Another man I sometimes think of when I think of Ciarán is Richie McCaw, the All Black double World Cup-winning captain who once said that in his life he has no rear-view mirror. Ciarán has that same philosophy and only ever seems to think about the future, and what might yet be. Like McCaw, Ciarán is a rare gem.'

49

'THE GEORGE BEST OF RUGBY'

Geordan Murphy Overcomes Crushing Disappointment

In the build-up to the 2003 World Cup, rugby pundits around the world predicted that Geordan Murphy was destined to become one of the stars of the tournament and one of the giants of world rugby. Tragically, injury intervened and Geordan missed out on the world stage his rich talents deserved, having emerged as the star of the previous Six Nations. It was a catastrophic setback to Ireland's chances for glory. With Murphy in the side, Brian O'Driscoll would have had extra space, because opposition defences would have had to work out which one of Ireland's two big threats was going to make the break.

The Kildare man is one of the many rugby players who owed a great debt to his teacher.

'My mentor in Newbridge, Kevin West, arranged for Jim Ferris and myself to have a three-week trial at Leicester. It was very intimidating going over to play with one of the biggest clubs in Europe. Most people told me it would be a brilliant experience and I went over there just to enjoy it, never expecting anything to come out of it. The 1997 Lions tour to South Africa had just happened and many of the stars for the Lions team, like Martin Johnson, Will Greenwood and Eric Miller, played for Leicester. There were about fifty in the squad, and Jim and myself were thrown into the action pretty much straight away. I was pretty overawed looking around the dressing room with rugby legends like Dean Richards all around me.'

Geordan cringes at one of his earliest memories from his time in Leicester.

'I had a real Homer Simpson moment standing beside this guy at the club one day. I didn't recognise him from Adam and I asked him if he got a chance to play much rugby at the club. I knew immediately from the way he looked at me that I'd said something incredibly stupid. It was the Scottish international Craig Joiner! To complete my shame, when he turned around I saw on the back of his jersey the word "Joiner"!

'The legendary Bob Dwyer was in charge of Leicester during my trial. In my second week I was playing in the second team and I had six full internationals in the side with me, like Niall Malone and Dean Richards. It was just jaw-dropping. Bob said he wanted me to stay after the trial. I got a few games with the first team in my first season and played four games in a row after Christmas, but shortly after that Bob got the sack and Dean Richards replaced him. I got on well enough with Dean and he was decent enough to me. He had a tough job trying to rotate the squad to keep everybody happy. When a new coach like that comes in, the key thing is to find out which buttons to push to make them rate you. If you discover that what they want you to do is kick the ball fifty yards, you kick the ball fifty yards. In my first couple of seasons, most of my appearances were coming on as sub as a utility back.'

With typical modesty, Geordan makes no mention of the fact that Dean Richards christened him 'the George Best of rugby' because of his exquisite skills. He is happier singing other people's praises rather than his own.

'With Leicester, there were also great characters and practical jokers. We had a decent spread of them throughout the squad, but it comes as no surprise that Austin Healey was the tops in this respect. He was always willing to get a laugh, and it's great to have someone like him in the squad because he keeps morale up. Of course, he can rub people up the wrong way and often has done so! He did the craziest things. To give a typical example of an Austin activity, when he was away with the English squad, he was bored and decided to liven things up by having a game with the English forward Lewis Moody. They sat about ten feet away from each other with their legs apart and the idea was to throw an orange at each other's groin. The problem for Austin was that he wasn't very good, but Lewis was the world champion!

'One of the funniest episodes came before playing a European Cup Final with Leicester. In the warm-up before the game, I was throwing the ball around. I tried to do a clever dummy pass and ended up firing the ball into my teammate's groin. It made me laugh. It made him cry!'

There was a general perception that, given Geordan's status in English rugby, he should have cemented his place on the Irish team much sooner. Is this a view he shares?

'I'm not sure. I think that perhaps being over here in Leicester was initially detrimental to my international career by virtue of the fact that the selectors didn't see me that often. All I will say is that I was delighted to win my first cap on tour against USA on 6 June 2000. The previous week I had played in a friendly against the Barbarians and I'd damaged some ligaments. As a result, I was forced to miss Ireland's trip to Argentina, but the then coach Warren Gatland told me they would consider me for the game against USA if I was fit. I spent most of the next week in an ice bath. I got myself into good-enough shape to bluff passing a fitness test and played in Boston, which was great because my older brother was living there. To cap it all I got two tries.

'I came on as a sub for the injured Justin Bishop on the final game of that tour against Canada, but it wasn't such a happy occasion for me. To win your first cap is great, but to play your first game in a home international is also a highlight. My induction was in a friendly against Fiji. Although we won easily, I felt the game didn't go as well for me as I would have liked. I probably tried to do too much to convince people I should be on the team. I suspect, though, there was an element of people looking at me as a little guy and they had doubts if I had it physically in me to hack it at the very highest level, and as a result I didn't find myself on the Irish team for a while. You also have to remember that it takes a while to settle into international rugby, just as it took me time to settle at Leicester.

'Things really came together for me in the Six Nations in 2003. It didn't start off like that. I remember flying over for the first match of the season and at the back of the plane I could hear a few lads from Terenure having an in-depth discussion on the "Girvan (Dempsey) vs Geordan" debate for the full-back position. As they were from Girvan's alma mater, you can guess where their biases lay! It was very interesting, though, to hear them going through the pros and cons. When the plane landed and I stood up, I think they were a little embarrassed that I might have heard them, but they graciously wished me well. In fact, when Girvan got injured against Italy, I replaced him and held that spot for the rest of the season. Although we lost the Grand Slam decider against England, it was a good season for me, and I was so looking forward to taking it on one step further at the World Cup, but it wasn't to be.'

In one of the warm-up games against Scotland, Geordan broke his leg. How did he react to this calamity?

'When I woke up in the hospital in Scotland, I was devastated. Although I was morphined out, I couldn't believe it. There were a few tears shed. It was very tough to deal with. I can smile and laugh when I think about it now, but as I never made it on the plane, I learned the lesson that you should never count your chickens. To be honest, there's still the odd day when I think: *Bugger it, I can't believe I missed out on that opportunity.*

'The specialist carried out the operation in such a way as to ensure that I got back on my feet as quickly as possible. Everything I was asked to do I did, and I played again in under six months, which was great. Of course, I was a bit rusty in the first few games back, but it was great to play some part in Ireland's Triple Crown win. I felt it was a reward for the fact that I'd worked so hard to get back to fitness. As the season started so badly for me, I'd hoped it would finish well on the tour to South Africa, but I picked up a dreadful viral flu in Cape Town and missed out on the second Test. Happily there were great days down the road for me in the green jersey, and winning the Grand Slam in 2009 was the high point.'

50

THE RAINBOW NATION

John Robbie Switches from Ireland to the Springboks

Q: Which Lions player who never played on a losing Lions
side had a record of played nine, lost nine for Ireland?
A: John Robbie

John Robbie is unique in Irish rugby history. He turned his back
on playing for Ireland and took the gutsy decision to take his
young family to South Africa to seek a career playing with the
Springboks.

Although he was substitute to Colin Patterson on the Irish
team, Robbie was chosen as Terry Holmes's replacement on the
Lions tour to South Africa in 1980. The Lions lost the series 3–1.
Why?

'One day, I think it was before the third Test, we were training
in Port Elizabeth. The Lions side was practising winning the
ball from a set phase, moving it to first centre, when it was
then hoofed up in the air. This was a main tactic to draw up
the defending line and then turn them. I noticed that sitting
on the grandstand, deep in conversation, were Carwyn James,

Chalkie White and Ian Robertson. They were three of the best backline coaches ever produced by British rugby, watching the cream of the current players practising booting the ball up in the air. I must say I felt a little ashamed.

'One of the problems, I believe, was that all the big guns on the tour – Syd Millar, Noel Murphy and captain Bill Beaumont – were all forwards, and the senior players on the tour – Graham Price, Peter Wheeler, Jeff Squire and Derek Quinnell – were all forwards. I've read books on the tour where the backline was blamed, but I blame the decision-makers who framed our tactics. We had backs of the calibre of Colin Patterson, Ollie Campbell, Dai Richards, Ray Gravell, John Carleton, Clive Woodward and Andy Irvine. To say that with the amount of ball being won by the pack that this backline, or one with a few other players, was incapable of using it is nonsense. Instead of moving all balls early in the tour, thus developing a pattern of movement and support, the team kicked for position and drove excessively with the pack. It was good enough against the provinces, but in the Tests, it was different.'

Robbie retains many memories from that time.

'At one stage, quite near the end, we were all called into a special meeting. Syd Millar addressed us and asked if we were unhappy, as he'd read reports to that effect. We all said we were having a whale of a time. He then asked us if we would all return to tour South Africa if selected. Ironically enough, I was the only player who indicated that I would have to think about it; everyone else said they would. In fact, Peter Morgan, the young Welsh utility player who had played in only a few games on the tour, brought the house down by saying that he'd love to come back again as next time they might let him have a game!'

The tour opened Robbie's eyes to the sham amateurism that operated in rugby at the time.

'Almost all the Lions were sponsored with kit from their local agents of a major footwear firm, the Irish players as well as those from Britain. Well, we heard that the British guys had actually received some cash as well. It now seems a very small amount – £300 each, I think. The Irish convened a meeting one evening in one of the player's rooms. We were all there: Ollie Campbell, Tony Ward, Colin Patterson, Phil Orr, Rodney O'Donnell, Colm Tucker, John O'Driscoll and myself. The meeting was to decide whether we would contact the firm and insist on our cash. Despite two players wanting to do so, the rest of us felt that this would infringe on our amateur status, and so the motion carried was to say nothing. We actually threw away £300!

'Another time, Ollie and I were approached by a sports firm in South Africa; they offered us a four-figure rand fee if we would wear their make of boots in a game for the Lions. We explained that we were amateurs – but as a favour we wore their boots in many practices. Can you believe it! The tour was generating millions, the players were making money on the normal team pool arrangement, against the amateur laws but as much a part of major touring as team courts or duty boys, and here we were chucking it away.

'I was also approached by a senior Lions player, a Scot, who said that the boot firm sponsoring him wanted me to sign for them the following season. He started talking cash that I couldn't believe, and I said no. Although I had never received a penny for wearing kit, I was very grateful to my sponsors, who always gave me free boots. I can still remember the look of disbelief on his face, and he told me that one day I would look back and laugh at my attitude. He was wrong – I now look back and cry.

'When I moved to South Africa, I discovered that one of the benefits of being a high-profile sportsman there was sponsorship. I was given a car at a time when I was dropped by Transvaal. The panel on the door read: "Opel supports John Robbie". Some wit suggested that the lower panel should read: "Transvaal doesn't".'

Colin Patterson's international career ended on the Lions tour and Robbie was back as Ireland's number nine. Given his record as a captain, some suggested that he would become Irish captain, but he had equivocated in an interview with Edmund Van Esbeck in *The Irish Times* when asked if he would tour with Ireland in the forthcoming South African tour in the summer of 1981; and Fergus Slattery retained the captaincy.

'In the run-up to the tour I met Eamon Dunphy, by chance, in a Dublin pub. I had admired his writing, but as soon as we met he informed me that, in his mind, rugby had done more to harm Ireland than anything else in history, including the crown of England. I was a bit stunned and said nothing. Eamon was like an opened tap and went on to give his views about the tour, interspersed with his own hatred of rugby as an elitist sport.

'The Irish soccer team had recently played in Argentina, and this had coincided with a lot of his articles about human-rights abuses there. I asked him his views on this, and the question seemed to throw him a bit. He didn't answer, and then launched an attack on me because as a university graduate I was automatically a member of the oppressing upper classes, etc. I started to get annoyed, and I thought Eamon was a pain. I told him that my father had started his working life labouring in a coal yard after the Great Depression and through his hard work at sea, his after-hours study and later his work as a marine engineer, he made enough for his kids to have the chance of a university education. I told him that, far from feeling guilty about this, I was extremely proud. Then I realised that Eamon had a few drinks on board, and he disappeared somewhere.

I enjoyed reading Eamon's articles subsequently, but he took himself extremely seriously. Our meeting must have done something because the next weekend he wrote a rambling article castigating everything to do with rugby.'

Before the tour to South Africa, Robbie was called into his bosses' office (he worked for Guinness) and told that he was not allowed to go. Robbie resigned, although he was married with a young child to support. He did retain his sense of humour through this difficult time:

'The great departure day arrived, and then we learnt about the cloak-and-dagger methods that we were going to use to get to South Africa. I suppose it was necessary, and we were getting worried about running the gauntlet at Dublin airport, as we'd heard that a massive demonstration had been planned. I rang one of my fellow players, Terry "The Rat" Kennedy, and in my best Peter Sellers Indian accent I told him that I was Kader Asmal, the high-profile leader of the Irish anti-apartheid movement, and could I talk to him? Terry was very worried and when I asked him to confirm some secret arrangements for our departure, I could almost see the beads of sweat pouring from his brow. He was gibbering like an idiot and nearly collapsed in relief when I told him it was me.

'I was super fit because of my extra training when I was on the dole; remembering how I had played with the Lions, I was confident that I could play the best rugby of my life. As things turned out, it was a disaster. I got sick and only played a game and a half in the month or so we were away. However, by the time I returned to Ireland, I had decided along with Jennie that we were off to live in South Africa, a decision that would have seemed ridiculous three months earlier.'

After making the momentous decision to take his family to strike out for the shores of the promised land in South Africa,

Robbie's introduction to provincial rugby was not what he expected.

'I made my debut for Transvaal away to Griqualand West. We won well and I assumed it was drinks and bed, just like at home. But I was told that all new caps had to wait outside the team room until summoned. I got called in. The room had been altered and for all the world it was like a courtroom. All the players were dressed immaculately in their number-one blazers, ties and pants and there were three "judges" sitting at the front. Everyone was deadly serious and there wasn't a sound. I made some wisecrack as I walked in, and I was quickly told to shut up. It was all serious and I got nervous. I had to remove my shoes and stand on a chair in front of the dock. I was asked what I thought of playing for the team. Again, I made a joke but no one laughed. I was asked to sing a song, which I did; no one clapped or did anything. Suddenly I was grabbed, turned upside down across one of the lock's shoulders with my backside up, and each member of the team with the flat of his hand gave me, in turn, a real smack across my bum. I couldn't believe it. The pain was excruciating. After they stopped I was angry and nearly lost my temper. Luckily the judge told me this was just tradition, and to say nothing. Then I was turned up and hit again. I was actually crying in pain and anger. But when it stopped, the judge made a genuine speech of welcome, I was told that now I was a true Transvaal player and each player shook my hand. During this escapade, I also had to drink four or five glasses of beer. At the end, it was actually quite emotional. I gather it was a fairly tame initiation, known as the *borsel* (brush), by some provincial standards, but I must say I still hated it.'

After his rugby career ended, Robbie carved out a new career in radio, working for Radio 702, and became South Africa's answer to Joe Duffy. By 1995, with his unique insight into the host country he was ideally placed to observe the World Cup as a commentator for RTÉ. This was reflected in the accuracy of his predictions, particularly when the host nation was involved. Against the weight of popular opinion, he called the fairy-tale ending that saw Nelson Mandela's rainbow nation upset the favourites on their World Cup debut, leaving the All Blacks to blame food poisoning.

'To be here was marvellous – that and South Africa winning the African Nations Cup in soccer for the first time the following year had a hugely bonding effect on the country.'

51

WHEN CONSCIENCE DOES NOT MAKE COWARDS OF US ALL

Tony Ward Boycotts Ireland's Tour to South Africa

Tony Ward made a decision to tour South Africa.

'I first recall my own experiences of life in South Africa on the Lions tour in 1980. I candidly confess that I had no hesitation about going to South Africa, despite the apartheid regime at the time, once the call came. I wanted to be a Lion, and it was really as simple and selfish as that – I don't deny it. Donning that red jersey of Wales, those white shorts of England and the Irish and Scottish green-and-navy socks represented the be all and end all of my very existence at that time. I offer no justification. I didn't even think; I simply went. However, was I in for a rude awakening?

'I have never forgotten my first few minutes in South Africa. As I walked through customs I spotted those toilet signs, "black-only toilets" and "white-only toilets". From the moment I entered the baggage area of Jan Smuts Airport in Johannesburg, I was confronted by apartheid. To see this on television is akin to watching *The Simpsons* or *The Sopranos*. You say to yourself, "This can't really happen." But when the stark reality is but feet away from you, believe me, it's frightening in the extreme.

'Although rugby preoccupied my attention, I was not immune to the sociopolitical environment. My first glimpse of how many of South Africa's blacks lived was gleaned from a visit with Colin Patterson and some friends to a black township outside Bloemfontein. We drove around slowly in the car with Colin snapping pictures from the back seat. We were afraid even to stop and get out. I found it absolutely horrific. The shacks were made of tin; there seemed to be thousands upon thousands of them. If they had toilets it was just a barrel at the back, and one thing that struck me was the number of cars they had – old bangers, mind you. I understand under law they couldn't buy their houses so they bought these cars instead. It was a real horror story. I was sickened.

'At a later stage in the tour, I and a group of players and journalists tried to visit the New Brighton black township close to Port Elizabeth. The authorities had been gravely upset by the reporting on other townships earlier in the tour. They decided to make a pre-emptive strike in Port Elizabeth because there was a huge international press corps in attendance for the third Test. All eleven entrances to the township were sealed off by armed police with a convoy of Land Rovers. We were warned off and told that there was rioting going on. Quite clearly, the place was totally quiet. We could see right down into it.

'All the Lions players were puzzled by the attitude of the blacks to them. They all wanted them to win. We found this quite extraordinary. After all, they were South Africans too. Yet everywhere we went we met blacks who told us, "Go, man, beat the Boks."'

The agonising plight of the majority struck Ward most

forcefully on a visit to the paradisal world of a golf course in Bloemfontein on an excursion with John Robbie, Paul Dodge and Clive Woodward. 'On the course, we were surrounded by about thirty black youngsters – about late teens and all literally dressed in rags. They wanted to caddy for us. "Masta... Masta" they called me. This was the bit I could never take – people calling me master. We selected two kids and I took them aside and I said, "This is John and Paul, and I'm Tony," but after that they didn't call us anything at all. It really confused them. They explained that they were allowed to play golf only on a Monday morning and had to pay handsomely for the privilege. The cost was way beyond the two rand they received for the average two- or three-hour caddy. Tipping was forbidden, but we left them thinking they were millionaires. But all these little inequalities, they were simply everywhere.

'The incident, all the more powerful for its stunning simplicity, which sums up the treatment of blacks for me came in the hotel lift in Bloemfontein Hotel, smack bang in the centre of the town. A group of us were coming down for breakfast. A black chambermaid entered the lift laden down with a huge tray of glasses. Seeing her, the manager roared at her to get out and walk down. We were all deeply affected.

'Another disquieting experience for me was visiting a white school with Clive Woodward and Billy Beaumont. What particularly distressed me was their assembly song, a German marching song. It was sung in Afrikaans, which is a very intimidating language, and was pumped out with gusto. Obviously, I didn't understand the words but I vividly recall the effect it had on me. I can still hear the voices now and it inspired nothing in me but terror.'

Then Ward had an encounter with a remarkable man.

'Without a shadow of a doubt, the most formative influence on my subsequent attitude to tours in South Africa occurred when I, Bill Beaumont, Colin Patterson and some other players went to visit the Watson brothers. Both Cheeky (Daniel) Watson and his brother, Valence, who lived in Port Elizabeth, had decided some years previously to play rugby with a non-racial team in the New Brighton township, Kwaru, rather than continuing to play with a whites-only club. Cheeky was a top-class rugby player and had even won a Springboks trial. I have never forgotten Cheeky telling me his story: "By 1979 we had developed into a brilliant side, playing superb rugby. However, we went into it unaware of what we were up against. You couldn't go and play against the blacks just like that. We were arrested and fined countless times. Military intelligence was actively trying to destabilise non-racial sport in South Africa, and we had been singled out as enemies."

'Back in 1976, Cheeky was approached by South African coach and selector Ian Kirkpatrick, who informed the very promising winger that he was prepared to give him written guarantees that he was going to be on the following year's Springbok team to France, on condition he stopped playing for Kwaru. The then twenty-year-old refused to compromise and became the only player in rugby history to have spurned the hallowed Springbok jersey on ethical grounds.

'Cheeky was renounced by his white friends because he was playing with a black club. Naturally enough, the authorities didn't rejoice in the Watsons' principled stand. The clandestine repressive regime went into action, with the family house being burned down by "unknown assailants". To rub salt into their wounds, the Watson brothers were accused of deliberately burning down the house in order to cash in on the insurance and were arrested. The evidence against the government case was overwhelming and the court action collapsed. The trial, though, left the Watsons nearly destitute. The harassment continued and even intensified with the disinformation department of military intelligence spreading rumours about them. The brothers received phone calls threatening them and their children. Cheeky couldn't find work. One of his brothers, Gavin, was stabbed in the family shop, and there were two attempts on the life of another brother, Ronnie.

'Cheeky joined an action group "Concerned Citizens", whose aim was to explain to the white community the profound injustice of the system and to expose the whites to the real situation in the townships. In a bid to combat that threat, the infamous Colonel Kaletski of military intelligence offered Cheeky the opportunity of becoming an informer, with all the advantages that would have brought him. Cheeky typically acted against his own self-interest and declined the offer. As a result, there were endless intimidating calls to his home, police were constantly breaking the door down to enter the house and Cheeky was arrested numerous times for breaking the law by entering the black township without a permit.'

It is a symbol of the profound changes that have taken place in South African rugby and society that Cheeky's son, Luke, became famous as flanker with the Natal Sharks.

'When I spoke with the Watson brothers in 1980, none of us could have envisaged the transformation that would take place in the 1990s. The brothers explained in great depth the set-up in South African rugby, and they told us in unequivocal terms that we shouldn't have come at all. Looking back now, I guess that afternoon was in many ways a unique occasion, a debate about South African rugby among rugby players only.

'They made no bones about the damage we were doing just by being there, and I remember that this seemed to have a strong effect on Bill Beaumont. As Lions captain, he was of course in a difficult position, but as we drove back in the car, I spoke to him about it and he seemed both deeply impressed and depressed at what he had heard.'

As the Lions tour progressed, the players became more sensitive to the racial mix that was going on all around them – the factional and racial closenesses and distances which were the reality of South Africa. However, events approached boiling point after the game against Transvaal in Johannesburg.

'We noticed that among the huge crowd of people there was not one person of colour to be seen. Then, for some strange reason, we were refused entry into the members-only bar at the Springboks ground. To add insult to injury, in his after-dinner speech, the local dignitary cracked a most inappropriate joke. Its punchline had to do with a coloured television. I can't remember the actual joke but it was clearly a racist one, and all the Lions in the room felt very uneasy.

'If I ever needed further demystification and dismantling of the idealising message I had been given about the position of blacks in South Africa and of the dangerous Messianic arrogance of some whites, it was provided by an acutely suggestive discussion with a number of wealthy women after the Orange Free State match in Bloemfontein. This was a real eye-opener for me in terms of the attitudes of whites to blacks. The women talked about the "black problem" and boasted about the number of servants they had. The way they were talking about them, you would think these people were the scum of the earth. They really believed this, but I couldn't figure out where this attitude came from. It just sickened me.

'The best analogy I can find for the Lions 1980 tour is a war. The pressure from the Afrikaners to beat us was enormous. They even cheated by loading the midweek teams. The day they won the Test series I remember seeing in the papers "Springboks –

World Champions". There was an awful lot more than rugby at stake in that tour for the South Africans. For them it was a vindication of their way of life.

'I was one of a number of players brought to visit a children's hospital by former Irish scrum-half, Dr Roger Young, in Cape Town. It was a harrowing experience to see so many seriously disabled children, but for me what compounded their tragedy was that even in the wards there was segregation between whites, blacks and those of mixed race. It was a hospital similar to Crumlin, full of sick children. Some very serious, some not so serious, yet within that children's hospital there was the black children's wing and one for the whites. It was unbelievable. I found it the saddest sight I had ever seen. For me, that was as much as I could take, and the sad feeling of that moment will stay with me forever.'

A year later, Ward would make a very different decision. 'With an Irish tour to South Africa in the offing for the following summer, I decided I wouldn't travel on the day I returned from the Lions tour. When I left South Africa in June of that year, I did so certainly enriched for my rugby experiences, certainly content to have achieved the personal honour of Lions status, but overall, I was deflated and deeply hurt by what I had seen, heard and experienced. So when, twelve months later, Ireland were to tour South Africa I had no decision to make. My mind – no, my conscience – said *no – never again.*

'I had no doubt whatsoever that politics and sport were one and the same in South Africa. To my mind, rugby was used as a political weapon, and that's why I refused to go on the tour. My view was that rugby was so important to the Afrikaners that if we refused to tour, they would be forced to confront the question: "Why is this happening?" Of course, the opposite view was the "building bridges" argument, which was widely proffered by rugby people in both Ireland and the UK at the time.

'I felt I owed something to those black players in South Africa. I love the game and felt that everyone must have the opportunity, at the very least, to develop their own game to the best of their ability. The South Africans were arguing that the blacks weren't good enough to play at all levels, but that was a catch-22 situation. How could they be good enough if they weren't given an equal opportunity? And responsibility lay on the shoulders of all rugby players to ensure that it came about.

'When I played a game anywhere else in the world, we all went for a drink afterwards. If I played a game with a black player in South Africa, that was not possible. I could go to the bar and he would have to go home to his township. That is neither rugby nor sport.

'It was a great place to tour from a number of points of view – the rugby is so hard, the pitches are perfect, the quality of stadia and training facilities are fantastic and there is so much beauty in the country. I certainly have visited no more beautiful city than Cape Town, and Durban wouldn't have been far behind it. Turning down an invitation to tour there wasn't easy, particularly in 1981 when I was turning my back on two possible caps. However, when all is said and done, for me it came down to the fundamental issue as to what do those most sinned against want? How could we best help those deprived of the most basic human right by this vile system? They told us not to come. That said it all for me. It was the bottom line.'

52

FORTUNE FAVOURS THE BRAVE

Willie Duggan Shows His Bravery

Like Moss Keane, Willie Duggan was famous for his fondness for a party, and only he could have planned that his funeral be a party. Before the funeral itself, mourners were instructed not to wear black at Willie's request.

For the social aspect, Welsh legend Phil Bennett always enjoyed his trips to Dublin. After one post-match dinner, some of the Irish players were intent on stretching the evening a bit further with the Welsh team and hit a local nightclub. After entering the premises, Moss Keane beckoned to Willie Duggan. 'What'll ye have, Willie?'

Duggan replied, 'Moss, I'll have a creamy pint of stout, from the middle of the barrel.'

After a brief exchange at the bar Moss returned and said sadly, 'They've no beer here at all, Willie, only wine.'

'Oh,' replied Duggan. 'I'll have a pint of wine, so.'

Later that night, Bennett said to Gareth Edwards: 'Moss Keane has legs on him like a drinks cabinet.'

Gareth replied: 'That's very appropriate considering the amount he drinks.'

Getting in on the act, Bennett said, 'Moss and Willie read that drink was bad for you. They gave up reading. Throughout their career they lived by the adage that moderate drinkers live longer and it served them right.'

Duggan, though, will always be celebrated for both his talent and bravery. As captain of the Lions team that toured New Zealand in 1977, Phil Bennett needed players willing to shed blood for the cause. He found one in Willie Duggan.

During one match, Willie was so battered and bloodied that he went off for stitches just before half-time. When the rest of the team came into the dressing room, they saw him sitting there with a fag in one hand and a bottle of beer in the other as they stitched up his face. 'Bad luck, Willie. Well played,' the Lions captain Bennett said.

'What do you mean?' Willie demanded. 'As soon as the f**ker sorts my face out I'll be back on.'

On the tour, Willie played for the Lions against a Maori team in a very physical contest. At one stage, he was trapped at the bottom of a ruck when a few players kicked him on the head. True to form, he got up and carried on. After the game, Bennett asked him if he remembered the pounding on his head. His reply was vintage Dugganesque: 'I do. I heard it.'

53

A GIANT AMONG MEN

Shay Deering's Career

Talk to anybody who played international rugby for Ireland in the 1970s and two constants emerge. Firstly, at the very top of the players they most admired will be the late Shay Deering. Second will be their total bemusement that such a talented player with so many great attributes as a player and as a man should have, relatively speaking, so few caps. In the past, such blunders from the Irish selectors were even easier to predict than Keith Wood's latest hairdo.

When Ireland drew 9–9 with Wales in 1974, Shay Deering ('Deero') made his international debut. His selection continued a great family tradition. His father Seamus was a distinguished Irish forward of the 1930s, and his uncle Mark also played for Ireland. Deero was a colossus of a forward with awesome power who had the honour of captaining his country. Deering had the knack of leading a team with a mixture of humour, charm and lordly aggression. Leadership by example and his special presence was matched by the loyalty and respect he inspired in others. A fiercely competitive, though well controlled, streak burned inside him. Few people have made a greater impression on and off the field on those who knew them.

The legendary Phil O'Callaghan was a huge fan.

'The best wing-forward I've ever seen was Shay Deering. He was such a wholehearted, committed player and one of the greatest characters I've ever met, on or off the field. I have a lot of great memories of Shay. One of my strongest memories is of an incident involving him. The night before an Irish squad session Barry McGann, Shay and I had frequented a few pubs. In fact, we were even thrown out of one of them! The squad session the next day started with some laps around the pitch. Shortly after we started off, I heard Barry shout at me: "Cal, don't leave me." I dropped back with him and we were lapped once or twice. The cruel irony of the situation was that after the session, McGann was selected and I was dropped!'

Former Irish hooker and later team manager Pa Whelan was also an ardent admirer of Shay Deering.

'I was fortunate in that my international days coincided with that of three of my Garryowen friends, Shay Dennison, Larry Moloney and Shay Deering. It's very difficult to talk about Shay Deering to somebody who never met him. Anyone who played with him or against him will never, ever forget him – as a rugby player or as a man. He was a breed apart – someone you would walk on water for. It's one of the great mysteries of Irish rugby that he didn't win scores of caps. I'd say most players of his era who were asked about the legends of Irish rugby would have him at the very top of their list. The four of us travelled up to Dublin together for squad sessions. On the way home, we had a number of stops for "light refreshments". We came home at all hours of the day and night. My wife could never understand how a training session could last twenty-four hours!'

For his part, another former Irish captain Tom Grace finds

it very difficult to talk about his great friend's death, but his respect for Shay both as a player and as a man knows no limits. 'We all know about his bravery on the field, but the way he dealt with his terminal illness right up to the very end showed bravery on an astonishing level. None of us who knew him as a player thought it was possible to admire him more than we did, but when he was dying, he took the fight to his illness to the very last breath and was an inspiration to us all. That type of heroism is just indescribable. If someone asked me for a definition of the player's player I would simply have two words to say – Shay Deering.'

54

THE MAYNE EVENT

Blair Mayne is a War Hero

Second-row forward Lieutenant Colonel Robert Blair Mayne won six caps for Ireland between 1937 and 1939. With his massive frame, gained from years of lifting weights, his finest hour was the Lions' tour of South Africa in 1938 in which he played twenty tour matches, including three Tests – though curiously he was the only member of the party not to score on the tour. He also became Irish Universities Boxing Champion. He was awarded three bars on the DSO and was made *Légion d'honneur* for his sterling service during the Second World War in North Africa.

Craving excitement, he had enlisted in the British army in 1940 and found himself deployed in the desert in North Africa under General Auchinleck and later General Bernard Montgomery in what was known as the Eighth Army. The opposition was formidable because the Germans were masterminded by 'The Desert Fox', Field Marshal Erwin Rommel, and his African Korps wreaked havoc on the British forces before the decisive battle of El Alamein on 23 October 1942. At one point, Mayne had come very close to capturing Rommel. The incident subsequently was the basis of a lengthy conversation with his international teammate Con Murphy.

'I asked him what he would have done if he'd caught Rommel. He told me without blinking an eye: "I would have slit his throat." The way he said it, I don't think he was joking. After joining the SAS, his specialty was in night raids behind enemy lines where he destroyed 130 enemy aircraft all by himself. No less a person than Field Marshal Montgomery recommended Blair for the Victoria Cross after he saved a squadron of troops pegged down by heavy gunfire. He was some man because he lifted the wounded one by one and put them in his jeep. At the same time, he was mowing down the enemy.

'He was fond of a drink, and it was so sad that he died so young, at just forty, after he drove his sports car into a lorry after having a few drinks too many.'

PART IV

When the Winner Doesn't Take It All

Sometimes winning is not positive in the long term. Brian O'Driscoll claims that beating Munster in the 2001 Celtic League Final was a disaster for the Leinster team because of the complacency it created and the delusion that talent alone was enough and a strong work ethic was unnecessary. He believes the win was indirectly responsible for the province not achieving its potential for a number of years, despite the fact that they had many great players, particularly in the backline – meanwhile Munster were becoming big beasts in European rugby.

This section is about losses. At first glance losses have no place in a book of great moments, particularly since Irish rugby has long since rightly consigned the days of taking pride in moral victories to the dustbin of history. However, there have been times when defeats have paved the way for greater glory. This section presents the evidence to support this claim.

55

SO NEAR YET SO FAR

Ireland v New Zealand, 2013

At first glance, it was all too reminiscent of the 1991 Rugby World Cup quarter-final at the old Lansdowne Road when Australia's Michael Lynagh broke Irish hearts with a last-gasp try. But this was the All Blacks, which made it an even more bitter pill for the golden generation of Brian O'Driscoll, Paul O'Connell and Gordon D'Arcy, whose best chance of beating the mighty New Zealanders was snatched at the death.

The record books will forever acclaim New Zealand as the first side in the professional era to win all their Tests in a calendar year, a fourteenth win from fourteen games in 2013, an achievement which makes a powerful statement. To the outside eye, Ireland, as they had done for the previous 108 years against these opponents, could only settle for what might have been.

Neutrals watching this match will remember it as one of the great modern internationals, a contest good enough to restore faith in those who believe that it's rugby that's really the beautiful game. With fewer than thirty seconds remaining, Ireland were ahead 22–17 and seemingly on course for their own page of rugby immortality. Had it stayed like that, not a single All Black could have called it a miscarriage of justice.

Instead the All Blacks 'survived a sh*t storm', as their coach Steve Hansen bluntly described it. To quote Charles Dickens: 'It was the best of times. It was the worst of times.' As Joe Schmidt, himself a Kiwi, noted: 'To be a minute away from history and have the ball in your hands on their ten-metre line … it's devastating.'

The nation sat up and took notice when Ireland led 19–0 after eighteen minutes. The prolonged spell of early pressure yielded a fifth-minute try for Conor Murray. More frenzied approach work from the dynamic Seán O'Brien helped stretch the All Black defence and Rory Best, who later broke a bone in his arm, dummied his way over on the right. By the time Rob Kearney grabbed an interception to race eighty metres, the crowd were going wild with anticipation.

Julian Savea collected a smart diagonal cross kick from Aaron Cruden to score a try, but a further Jonathan Sexton penalty still ensured Ireland led 22–7 at the interval. Could they hang on? There was a further bonus for Ireland when Israel Dagg was held up over the try line in the third quarter.

A missed Cruden penalty with twenty-five minutes left also did them no favours, but Ireland lost Brian O'Driscoll with a blow to the head and a sixty-fifth-minute try for Ben Franks set up a frantically tense finale. Had Sexton not uncharacteristically sent a kickable penalty wide with six minutes to go, the outcome might have been different.

Even after the home side had been penalised deep into the 80th minute, the All Blacks were still a long way from victory. 'We were sixty metres from our line and I'd have been confident of holding them out the way we'd defended for the rest of the game,' said team captain Paul O'Connell. Instead the world champions, with Ben Smith and Ma'a Nonu both making critical yardage, gradually wore down the defensive line, and Cruden and Dane Coles worked the replacement Ryan Crotty over on the left, with the score confirmed after a very tense TMO referral.

If the prospect of a draw was enough of a downer in the circumstances, worse was to come. Cruden's first conversion trailed left, but the referee Nigel Owens ordered a retake after several Irish players, headed by Luke Fitzgerald, rushed out prematurely. As if to rub salt into the wounds, Cruden's second attempt flew straight through to clinch his team's uniquely successful status. 'It's not particularly relevant to us,' replied a phlegmatic Joe Schmidt, declining the invitation to start a controversy. 'A draw would have been as good as a loss to us. We haven't won in 108 years against these guys. We didn't want to do what we'd done before.'

With the benefit of hindsight, how does Schmidt look back on the game? When asked about the difference between the performance versus the Aussies – when Ireland suffered a crushing defeat – and the All Blacks, which appeared to many casual fans as the difference between chalk and cheese, he replied that it was not as big as it might have looked. He places a big emphasis on KPIs: key performance indicators. A lot of the KPIs were better in the Aussie game and they actually made less system errors, but there were some incidents which completely changed the game.

In the first half, Ireland were in a really strong position until Johnny Sexton's injury. The timing of it ruined a great attacking opportunity. However, even after that, Ireland were well in the game at half-time. Then in the second half, two poor errors were made and capitalised on by the Aussies, and it was game over.

Schmidt thinks that any of the positive aspects from the Aussie game seemed to be completely ignored by the media. He felt that Fergus McFadden in particular had a superb game on the wing and made five clean line breaks, which is a rare feat in top-level international rugby. He recalls that the players were gutted afterwards, and there was a monumental effort to make sure no stone was unturned in their efforts to beat the All Blacks.

Schmidt is more animated than normal when asked if New Zealand have got a mental edge – when critical moments arrive in matches, they always step up to the plate, are always mentally strong, always make the right decisions.

Joe replies, 'That's a load of rubbish. With our game, Johnny's penalty miss was a big moment. He was sure it was over as it left his boot, and the feeling a kicker has at the moment is right ninety-five per cent of the time. That time it didn't go over, and these things happen. But if it had, it wouldn't have mattered how psychologically strong the All Blacks were – they were beaten. Not that I believe they are mentally stronger. Late on, Cruden hit a terrible kick from his own twenty-two that showed clear signs of panic. They handed possession right back to us and gave us a chance to kill the game. But then we must talk about the crucial late penalty given to New Zealand. I had a good long chat with the referees' assessor, and he agreed completely that there were two clear penalty infringements by New Zealand players in the moments before Ireland were penalised. If the ref had picked up either of those, as he should have, then Ireland had the game won, and nobody would have been talking about New Zealand's supposed amazing mental strength.

'Even after that, we made seven system errors, for example wrong body shape in the tackle, and that really frustrated me. It can be the difference between turning the ball over, at least stopping the yards being gained.'

Schmidt warms to the theme.

'I think back to all the stuff I read about the All Blacks in 2007 versus 2011. In 2007, they were supposed to be the best team in the world, but they let the pressure get to them once again in the World Cup and bottled it. But in 2011, being at home and post the earthquake, there was no way they were going to let that one go, and mentally, physically and every other way they wouldn't be beaten. So the story goes. But it's utter bollocks!

'The main reason they lost to France in 2007 was Wayne Barnes. New Zealand had seventy per cent possession and couldn't get a penalty. All the big decisions went France's way and the crucial try had a clear and obvious forward pass.

'Again, in the 2011 final, it was the referee who decided the outcome of the game. I think (Craig) Joubert is a superb ref, probably the best around, but he had a very bad day. New Zealand cheated throughout the game and got clean away with it. I've talked to some of the players since then and they could hardly believe it was happening. In my opinion, the All Blacks completely bottled it in the second half of that final; they were awful, but because of Joubert they got away with it. At the end of the day, it's the old story: whoever wins the war writes the history, regardless of what the actual facts are.

'In my opinion, those Irish lads were mentally tough, and I had no doubt they were a very resilient bunch. One area that I will admit to being behind the likes of New Zealand then was the quality of their bench. If I list off all the guys who came on as a sub against us, they would have started for pretty much every other team in the world. I resolved to try to have a squad of thirty to thirty-five players, where one could replace another seamlessly, without any weakness to the overall team. We hadn't reached that stage in 2013, but when we played them in Chicago, we were a lot further along on that journey, with young players like Joey Carbery slotting in, and that's one of the reasons why we finally beat them then.'

56

LEINSTER'S LOSING STREAK

Joe Schmidt's Initial Struggles at Leinster

Joe Schmidt worked in several coaching roles in New Zealand, including New Zealand Schools, Bay of Plenty and at Auckland as assistant coach. He was backs coach at Clermont Auvergne from 2007 to 2010 when the club captured the coveted Bouclier de Brennus Top 14 trophy. Joe took over as Leinster head coach for the 2010–11 season and guided the province to their second Heineken Cup title in his first season. Leinster won back-to-back European titles in 2012, and Schmidt signed off his tenure with Leinster by guiding them to a double in 2013, capturing the Amlin Challenge Cup and RaboDirect Pro12 titles. It's a very impressive record with Leinster, but his early days were far from auspicious.

When Schmidt was twenty-four, he opted to take a year overseas. He and his wife, Kellie, moved to Mullingar. He played for the local club and was persuaded to do some coaching at Wilson's Hospital School. That year, Wilson's Hospital made the A final of the Schools Cup for the first time. They won and scored five tries 'throwing the ball around'. Schmidt can still remember the names of the lads who got them. His brief to the players was the stuff of legend, including the instruction to one aspiring star, 'Don't smoke in the showers.'

Schmidt believes coaches are like magpies – they take 'shiny bits from wherever they've been and keep adding to the nest. I have no doubt some of the things I believe in now come from the time I spent in Westmeath.'

There were some cultural adjustments to be made. All these years later, the prevalence of the litigation culture in Ireland – which is in stark contrast to the New Zealand experience – still remains a source of bemusement.

Soon after Schmidt returned to New Zealand, he injured an Achilles tendon. His playing days were over, so he began to concentrate more on his coaching. In 2000, he was made assistant coach of the New Zealand Schools side, where he worked with players such as Joe Rokocoko and Luke McAlister. Soon afterwards, Schmidt made the decision to take up coaching full time. He got a job as assistant coach at Bay of Plenty, working under Vern Cotter. It turned out to be the beginning of a long and fruitful partnership.

In 2007, Schmidt was on the move again, this time to France, where he was reunited with Cotter at Clermont Auvergne. The experience has certainly enhanced Schmidt's sense of the importance of life outside rugby and his empathy when dealing with players with personal problems.

Schmidt took over at Leinster in 2010 almost by accident. He was talking to Leinster's Kiwi back Isa Nacewa, to see if he could tempt him to come and play at Clermont. Nacewa ended up persuading him to apply for the job at Leinster instead. Schmidt, though, lost three of his opening four games with Leinster and found himself under severe critical scrutiny. Rather than buckle under the pressure, he stuck to his principles.

Part of his philosophy was 'to take what you are good at and become exceptional at it, make it a real weapon'. As Ronan O'Gara has incisively observed, so many moves 'break down due to balls being passed to the hips, above the head, or at the feet. These basics were what Schmidt concentrated on with Leinster, and they became the best passing team around. That was no coincidence. He didn't give anyone an easy out, whoever they were.'

Part of the process were his infamous video sessions after games. He has no tolerance for those who don't work for the team. He insists that apart from mastering basic skills and their own individual roles, players must be constantly working on helping their teammates. No player wanted to be under the spotlight in those Monday-morning reviews and in particular to be seen to let their teammates down.

The Leinster squad found out very early on that nobody was above criticism. Some were taken aback by how critical Schmidt was. An early example was when he showed a clip of Brian O'Driscoll fumbling a poor pass from Gordon D'Arcy. When the coach asked Drico for his comment, he reluctantly said: 'It might not have been the best pass in the world.'

O'Driscoll, though, quickly realised it was him rather than D'Arcy that was the focus of the coach's ire. Schmidt asked, 'Should a world-class centre have been able to take that pass?'

O'Driscoll could only meekly agree that a world-class centre should have caught the pass.

O'Driscoll, though, does not disguise his admiration for Schmidt. 'He is a player's coach because he notices what you do. If you're a workhorse, doing your stuff unseen by almost everyone, he knows you've done the work. If there's a professional game of rugby going on, he's seen it. If you call him and tell him about a play you've seen, he'll know about it. He has a photographic memory about rugby. I've never seen a coach show such massive attention to detail, or one with such a smart rugby brain. He makes little tweaks and all of a sudden, an opposition defence opens up in front of you. And you look over at him and he's smiling.'

Coming up to a game, regardless of what went on the previous weekend or during the early part of the week, everything Schmidt says to the players on a Thursday and Friday is positive. On one instance in that early losing streak in Leinster where they had suffered a defeat, put in a poor performance and taken a hammering in the press, and had another big game the following weekend, morale was as low as he had seen it. Leo Cullen came up with an idea, or basically an order, where every player was assigned a player they had to send a text to. It had to be a positive text, about something the recipient did really well. Schmidt was initially unsure about the idea, but it worked wonders. The following day morale was back to sky high, and they put in a powerhouse performance that weekend.

After a Saturday game, the players would come in on Sunday morning at about 10 a.m. for any medical treatments, messages, general loosening up, etc. Usually two or three of them would take time to come into his office for a chat about a particular incident in the game, and he felt it was one of his jobs to know exactly what they were talking about, no matter when the incident happened during the game. Between the end of the game and the Sunday-morning chats, he would have spent six hours reviewing the video of the game, going through every incident in fine detail. This meant that a player knew that he could have a proper conversation with him about any incident and the coach would be able to answer it. Typically, it would be a player asking if he had made the right decision with a kick or pass.

Schmidt likes a controlled environment – so dealing with

the media doesn't fit into that construct. He doesn't pay much attention to what is said and respects everyone's right to have an opinion, and he especially respects their right to have the completely wrong opinion! One that sticks out for him, though, was George Hook's comments after his fourth match in charge of Leinster, when they had lost for the third time. Hook said that Schmidt had clearly lost the dressing room and that basically he should pack it in. 'This despite the fact that not only was he never in the dressing room, but he hadn't even spoken to one individual in there.'

The following morning Drico and Leo Cullen came to see him in his office. They said to completely ignore Hook or any other criticism, that they had 100 per cent faith in what he was trying to do and all the lads felt the same. They told him not to change anything regarding his approach and that they truly believed it would all come together.

Schmidt claims that while the pressure was on, he had never felt as good. He was still a newbie with the team, but having these two giants of men on his side, he knew it would come right.

That weekend they played Munster, and O'Driscoll scored a late try to win the match, and the team never looked back. Not for the last time Schmidt had turned adversity to triumph.

57

IN THE EYE OF A STORM

Ciaran Fitzgerald Captains the Lions

In 1983, Ciaran Fitzgerald was selected as captain of the Lions. It should have been a joyful occasion for him. It was anything but.

'It was like a whirlwind. I first heard about the captaincy when I got a call from a journalist. I was very surprised to hear the news because the strong rumour, coming from the English press, was that Peter Wheeler was getting the job. It was a tremendous honour and I didn't give a tuppenny damn about who was disappointed. There was so much media hype it was hard to focus. It was like getting a first cap multiplied by ten with all the receptions and media interest. I had to take ten days off in Mayo to regain my focus and kept in shape by training three times a day.

'I underestimated the ferocity of the campaign that would be waged against me. I couldn't influence what was said about me, so I just tried to do all I could to get the best possible performance out of the team. It's part of the psychological war that goes on when the Lions tour New Zealand that both media "talk up" their respective squads. In New Zealand, though, they were stunned to see that the British media were trying to outdo each other in terms of rubbishing me. By the time we arrived, everybody wanted to know: who is this fool of a hooker? It got to the stage where I expected the first question of every interview to be: "What kind of ape are you?" I was amazed that the New Zealanders knew everything about me. It shows how fanatical they were about the game.'

Things got worse – before they got even worse.

'The tour was a rollercoaster for me. As captain, I was asked to attend all kinds of receptions and press events, which I was determined to do because the PR aspect is so important. The result, though, was that I never got a day off and couldn't get away from the press. There was one day though I was determined to get away for a break. The Irish guys had arranged a game of golf so I decided to join them. We pulled a fast one by having our team car parked outside the front of the hotel as a decoy but arranged to have another car discreetly whisk us away. I'm not a golfer but was just managing to relax at last at the fourth hole when I heard a rumpus behind me. It was the media scrum!

'The press have to fill their columns. There were all kinds of stories about splits in the camp, which were absolutely untrue. There was a story about fights on the team bus, which was a blatant lie. At the end, the English players threw some of their journalists into the swimming pool, they were so disgusted by the untruths. As a result of all that was written about me, I developed a very tough skin. You are judged by your results, and at the end of the day, we didn't win our matches, which was a huge disappointment for me.'

The Lions got off to a bad start and never really recovered.

'The crucial Test was the first one. We had a few really good scoring opportunities which we didn't take, especially in the second half, when we dropped the ball a few times. If we had scored, we would have won the match, and had we won the match, the momentum would have been with us and they would have been forced to change what was a fairly seasoned team, because there was a lot of clamour down there to do that, and a loss would have added to the pressure. They had an element of doubt going into that game, but the Test win blew all that doubt away, and I suppose put doubt in our minds instead. That first Test was probably our best shot, but we didn't grasp it and ended up losing all four.

'They also had the advantage of having a more settled side throughout. They only had two changes in the backline in the whole series. Because we had so many injuries, we had to make a lot of changes, which is not what you want when you're trying to put patterns of play together and get cohesion into the side. We were particularly hard hit at scrum-half. Terry Holmes got injured. Then Roy Laidlaw got injured. Then Nigel Melville flew out and he got injured. Finally, Steve Smith had to fly out.

'I think we could have won the first Test, which would have changed the shape of the tour. I have to take part of the blame for that defeat because my throw-ins were poor. The only consolation for me was that the squad stuck together throughout, which isn't easy when you're losing. The controversy meant that we got off to a difficult start.'

There were other problems to be sorted out, including his relationship with the coach, Scotland's Jim Telfer.

'My style as a captain was more hands-on than other styles. I was always very used to the preparation side of it. Jim Telfer was different in that he would have been used to the captain playing a different role with Scotland, for example. They were just things that had to be accommodated.'

Some players would have crumbled with the vilification.

Fitzie, though, used the disappointment to drive himself forward and achieve more. His fortunes would be revived, and his redemption story was complete when he led Ireland to a second Triple Crown on 30 March 1985.

'Being successful with your country would always be the highlight of your career, and from my point of view, winning Triple Crowns would always be the high point, because they don't happen very often. Of course, on a personal level, the recognition of being selected as captain of the Lions was a lovely thing to happen, but doing well with Ireland meant the most to me.

'The best thing about '82 would have been the fact that we did it, even though up to '81 Ireland had lost nine matches on the trot. I took over the captaincy in '82 and it was the fact that we won the Triple Crown against that sort of backdrop that made me most proud. It was something similar in '85. In '84 I had been dropped and Ireland had lost their matches, and the next year, with a whole new team of young lads, Ireland won the Triple Crown against the odds. I think in sport it's the things you win when you're not expected to that are the great achievements.'

After the Lions tour, Fitzgerald's misfortunes accelerated when he was dropped from the Irish team against the English after the defeat to Wales in 1984. Was he a fall guy for Ireland's slide?

'I don't know why I was dropped. Nobody ever told me. Maybe I deserved to be axed. The one beef I had was the way the whole thing was handled. It was said that I wasn't available for selection because of injury, but in fact I played for St Mary's that day. I wish they had been straight about it and said I was dropped. The one thing, though, was that I was determined I would come back and play for Ireland in 1985, though I had no thoughts about the captaincy.

'When Mick Doyle took over in 1984, he brought me back as captain. Doyler made an enormous contribution to our Triple Crown win. He won the psychological war in terms of keeping all the media attention on him and away from the players. He was the crown prince of making edicts but was also very tactically astute. His chairman of selectors Mick Cuddy was a peculiar character. He was an insider in the IRFU but got on exceptionally well with Doyler and the players. His great gift was that he got things done. If we wanted new gear, he made the phone calls and got it for us. For my part, I got on exceptionally well with Doyler. Ours was much stronger than a rugby relationship. There was a deep friendship between us, and we complemented each other in lots of ways.

'I would say, though, Doyler's contribution was not nearly as positive the following season. There were some crazy selection decisions, e.g. dropping Phil Orr. Doyler's focus was not as clear. I'm not sure why that was, but I felt his heart wasn't in it as much. Having said that, I wasn't as focused myself because I had left the army and taken on a new challenging job with James Crean.'

In the end, business commitments led to Fitzgerald's premature retirement, forcing him to reluctantly forego the opportunity to play in the inaugural World Cup, but he was back at the heart of the action as coach to the Irish team in 1991.

'If I had the chance to do it differently I would, in terms of my time as coach. I was reluctant to take the position, but the IRFU pressed me. There was a good buzz early on in that we brought in a lot of new players and we played an exciting, expansive game. Although we played an attractive brand of rugby, we were always nearly winning. That's not good enough. Eventually you have to win, otherwise morale and confidence start to sap. The tour to New Zealand in 1992 was a bit of a disaster. We faced an impossible task because so many key players were unable to travel. For business reasons, I shouldn't have travelled, but out of loyalty I went, because there were so many defections. We made a superhuman effort and again nearly won the first Test, but it was downhill all the way after that. Later that year, I had to step down for business reasons. It wasn't the ideal time to go because I would have liked to go out on a winning note.'

58

FROM PARADISE LOST
TO PARADISE REGAINED

Ireland Tour South Africa in 1981

Like love and marriage, horse and carriage, rugby and nick-names go hand in hand. Perhaps one of the most surprising omissions from the Irish rugby landscape is that Fergus Slattery was not known as 'Tow Truck', as he was always first to the break down and first to the out-half.

Fergus Slattery won sixty-five caps for Ireland over four-teen years as an open-side wing forward (a world record for a flanker), between 1970 and 1984, scoring three international tries. He was part of a nineteen-match record back-row combi-nation with Willie Duggan and John O'Driscoll.

It is recognised worldwide that 'Slats' at his best was the best because of his presence on the field. His angles were so good that he always managed to put the opposition under pressure, forcing either the centre or out-half to release the ball. When this happens, it's the wing-forward who's dictating the game and not vice versa.

Although Slattery played his best rugby on the Lions tour of 1974 (when, with Roger Uttley and Mervyn Davies, he formed one of the finest back rows in Lions history), as he got older, he read the game so well. A master of mayhem, he put his body through extraordinary punishment. The great Phil Bennett famously said that he would rather play against any other open-side flanker than Slattery, and the doyen of rugby commentators Bill McLaren picked him on his all-time dream team.

Surprisingly, an apparent low point of his career elicits the greatest passion.

'The 1981 tour to South Africa was a landmark in the development of the Irish side. We played out of our skins. I had captained the Irish team to Australia in 1979, but that was an experienced, powerful squad that convincingly won the series. Those who went to South Africa were very young, as in only two years we had virtually changed the entire side. It was literally a B team, with twelve uncapped players in the party. And then we lost John Murphy, the full-back, and Ollie Campbell, whose loss was to prove very significant. Micky Quinn flew out the week before the first Test, and in mid-week we played a racially mixed team, scoring a lot of tries. I will always remember that we missed about seventeen kicks at goal. Still, it was the best investment in Irish rugby that could possibly have been made. We gave a number of young players a chance to show their wares.

'We played well in the first Test and lost 23–15, but we went into the second without two senior players of Campbell's and Murphy's calibre. In the first Test, they had out-played us in the line-out with three giants, Stofberg, Malan and de Klerk winning everything. All three were over six-foot-five, whereas our tallest men were only six-two and six-three. So we decided to revert to Plan B – in other words, play many three-man and four-man variations. We would play the line-out quickly and did all sorts of things, using every trick in the book. We said that if we won fifty per cent of the possession, we would be satisfied. We also realised that South Africa's immense forwards tend to kill you when they go forward, but if you turn them around, put the ball behind them and keep turning, they struggle. And we made every effort to disrupt their wheel and put-in to prevent them from getting quick ball. We were supposed to be very destructive on their ball and very creative on our own. And we certainly didn't go into the game without hope. Our loose forwards came out on top in both Tests. We knew that Rob Louw was their most potent loose forward, but we managed to keep him out of the game.

'In the end, it was Naas Botha who beat us. He was only the fourth man in history to drop three goals in a Test and we were out. We'd had no luck at all, missing a conversion and having a bloody good try disallowed. We were leading 10–9 when Botha got his last with a few minutes left. It left us too little time to do anything, and although we tried desperately, we just couldn't score. I really felt sorry for the guys – their achievement was spoilt at the very last moment.'

Ireland's fine performances on the tour tempted Slattery to engage in what was to be a lucrative speculation.

'When we left South Africa, Willie Duggan asked me: "Fancy a bet on the Triple Crown?" The odds were a generous 14–1 and it was the first time I had ever bet on myself. Of course, I was delighted to win.'

He relinquished the captaincy to Ciaran Fitzgerald before the 1981–2 season. What prompted the move and how did he evaluate his successor?

'We had lost seven matches on the trot and needed a change.

I was worried about Ciaran before the Australian tour in 1979 because he had a reputation for getting injured, but he held his own there and grew in stature from then on. He was made to lead, and his record as captain speaks for itself.

'The only disappointment I had in 1982 was the Paris game. We went there as favourites, but they hockeyed us. There was something wrong with the Irish psychological preparation. Our forwards in particular seemed to be too easily intimidated there.'

PART V
Symbolic Moments

I love the romance of rugby. Take the case of Joel Stransky. He was South Africa's third-choice out-half when the Springboks made their World Cup debut in 1995, yet he scored all his side's points in the final, including a drop goal in the second half of extra time to beat hot favourites New Zealand 15–12.

If Hollywood had been commissioned to write a script for the 1995 World Cup, they wouldn't have been able to come up with the fairy-tale ending that saw Nelson Mandela's rainbow nation upset the favourites on their World Cup debut. Sport is more than just mere games. When Mandela walked out to shake hands with the players of South Africa and New Zealand in the moments before the 1995 World Cup final, it was a reminder of how powerful sport can be in symbolising friendship and reconciliation in a public forum. As he presented the trophy to Francois Pienaar, Mandela wore his Springboks jersey. Here was a man who had spent twenty-seven years in a white man's jail, at a time when rugby had been the tuning fork which the white majority struck in order to conduct the whole orchestra of supremacy, but in his first opportunity to support a white man's game, he wore a white man's jersey. To witness him walk out there and shake hands with the black player Chester Williams, and all the white players in the Springbok team, bore eloquent testimony to sport's power to heal.

In this short section, we remember some moments that remind us that rugby is more than a game.

59

GONE BUT NEVER TO BE FORGOTTEN

Axel Foley's Funeral

Sometimes we think too much and feel too little.

Not on this day.

In 2017, Munster players wore the Irish Heart Foundation's logo on their jerseys when they played French side Racing 92 in an emotional rematch a year after the death of head coach Anthony Foley. The team were collaborating with the Irish Heart Foundation to leave a life-saving legacy in memory of Axel, whose death was related to a heart disorder, with the aim of highlighting the importance of cardiopulmonary resuscitation (CPR) training. 'This will hopefully help save lives, and if it's only one, it will be more than worth every effort made. It's an initiative that I know Anthony would really appreciate,' said Foley's widow, Olive.

The legendary number eight, who skippered Munster to the 2006 European Cup title, was found dead in his Paris hotel room on 16 October 2016, hours before a scheduled match against Racing 92. 'When I was in the Munster hotel (in Paris), they removed what I now know was Axel from the hotel. That was it, and unfortunately I can't get that image out of my head,' said the then Racing 92 defence coach Ronan O'Gara, himself one of Munster's greatest stars. The match was rescheduled, eventually being played in January with Racing 92 supporters offering free accommodation for Munster fans travelling to Paris for the European Champions Cup clash.

A statue of Foley with a ball clutched to his chest was unveiled on the banks of the River Shannon in Limerick in June 2017.

His funeral will never be forgotten. Munster flags and jerseys lined the back roads from Limerick city to Killaloe, where hundreds of community volunteers guided traffic down single-lane roads, into farmyards and across fields to park close to St Flannan's church. Some, like former coach Alan Gaffney and player John Langford, had travelled from Australia for the funeral.

Yet rugby was largely peripheral in Olive Foley's extraordinary fourteen-minute eulogy to her 'true soulmate' and husband of seventeen years. She spoke with extraordinary eloquence of his legacy and the people he had touched and for all those who had loved him for his indomitable spirit, loyalty and pride in his province. Not even the hardest heart could fail to have been moved when she described with raw emotion the stresses that 'the stones on the road knew about'; the 'very rough days' and 'pressure and the hurt' of his last two years as Munster head coach.

Just after midday, pallbearers – including Anthony's sister, Rosie – carried his coffin, topped with red roses and his eights Munster and Ireland caps, into the church. A rendition of 'Stand Up and Fight', the great Munster battle cry, was played.

Olive paused briefly and then, to a burst of laughter and applause, continued, 'He would absolutely have hated the fuss – but he would have been very proud.'

She recalled her last conversation with him on the previous Saturday evening. 'He'd been ringing all day. Because he was a ringer. He rang and rang and rang twenty times a day. I think if ever there was a little bit of a lull in what he was doing, he'd say, 'I'd better ring Olive.' He'd say nothing but, "Sure ..."' she said, raising a laugh among those who knew Axel as a man of few words.

In her brief reference to Anthony's last years with Munster rugby, she said how stressful they had been for him. 'But he took that journey with great hope. He took that job and gave it everything,' she said, 'with the same passion he brought when he put on the jersey and won two Heineken Cups ... They were very rough days in those last years, but despite the pressure and hurt during that time, he'd have an aul smile, knowing he gave it everything. He never held a grudge. When I found it stressful sometimes, his advice was always the same, the same line – "Olive, I was never as bad as they said I was, and I was never as good as they said I was. So read nothing."'

The ache of it filled the church, and friends felt sorry not for themselves but for the family Axel had loved so much. Even when they couldn't cry, the pain was evident behind the eyes, in the tautness in the throat and the tightening of the ribcage.

As Axel set off on his last journey, his pallbearers and escorts were drawn from his rugby brothers in arms: Keith Wood, Peter Clohessy, Mick Galwey, John Hayes, John Langford, Niall O'Donovan and Peter O'Mahony. His graveside farewell, inevitably, fittingly, included *There Is an Isle*, the anthem of Shannon RFC. As the coffin was lowered, the mourners exhaled deeply. Eyes began to moisten and a wave of sadness washed over the cemetery.

When Robert Kennedy was assassinated in 1968, his brother Ted said at the funeral that he 'need not be enlarged in death beyond what he was in life but to be remembered simply as a good and decent man.' The same is true of Axel.

To adapt George Bernard Shaw, rugby was not a brief candle to Axel but a splendid torch which he had got hold of and wanted to make burn as brightly as possible before handing it on to future generations.

For the Foley children, it has been a profound adjustment since their father died. He was their hero, their role model, their mentor, their friend, their idol, their teacher, sometimes their accomplice in mischief, the one who gave them their values. At first, they weren't sure if they could survive properly without him.

Their mother had lost not just a husband but a large part of her own self. Their tower of strength had crumbled. They briefly wondered if they could ever love again, but they soon learned that love can live long after death. It's a second-time love, like a summer shower, the leaves having retained the rain to fall on the unsuspecting head as though it had rained again.

It might have been a depressing story. In fact, it's quite the opposite. In sessions of sweet, silent thought, they have come to understand that Axel's love, like soft summer rain, can nourish from above, drenching his family with a soaking joy.

Death ends a life but not a relationship. Memory becomes your partner. You nurture it. You hold it. You dance with it.

To Munster fans in particular, Axel's absence has become a presence. Memory is our way of holding on to those we love. Axel will never be forgotten.

Neither will his funeral. It was a powerful reminder that, notwithstanding fierce and occasionally bitter rivalries, the Irish rugby community is, fundamentally, a family.

60

INITIATION RITES

Paul O'Connell Learns the Way of the World

One of the most striking things about spending an hour in Paul O'Connell's company is the amount of times he uses the word 'lucky' about himself. His all-informing, generous and humane sensibility is also indicated by the way the litany of coaches who helped him on the way are all mentioned by name and spoken of with genuine affection and respect. His towering frame and his fierce commitment on the pitch mask his gentle nature off it.

'I have had a huge amount of good luck to get where I am. To take one example, when I was playing in the trial for the Irish schools, I didn't play that well, but I was lucky because the guy who was lifting me lifted me by the legs, and the guy who was opposite me was getting lifted by the shorts, so I had two feet on him straight away. I robbed a few line-outs off him and so I got picked. If he had been picked it could be him doing this interview now and not me.'

Learning his craft in the second row, O'Connell couldn't have served his apprenticeship with a more skilled instructor beside him for both Munster and Ireland.

'I think every player on the Munster team has a bit of a Mick Galwey in him. Gallimh was very similar to Peter Clohessy in that he was old school. He likes his pints and wasn't very fond of training, but when it came to Saturday, there was nobody who put themselves on the line more or gave more on the pitch. He was a great guy to talk to players and to get them up for a match. When you saw a man who had accomplished so much get so emotional and be so committed for every Munster game, it did inspire you to give your best. He had a great ability to put his finger on the button for every occasion with every guy on the team in a way that got the best out of them.

'I saw his influence later in that respect in Anthony Foley. Frankie Sheahan was the same and so was Rog (Ronan O'Gara). When we went scrummaging, Frankie would pull us in together and say a few words to the forwards, and that was straight out of the Gallimh manual. Gallimh's legacy lives in all of us. When I played for Ireland under-21s, I was coached by Ciaran Fitzgerald and he was very Gallimh-like. Ciaran was very passionate and a great motivator.

'I learned a lot from Gallimh and The Claw because they knew every trick in the game and every shortcut there was to know. Gallimh had a very good tight game. He was clever, tactically astute and above all a great leader. When I first came into the Munster squad, Mick O'Driscoll was in the second row for Munster and he was brilliant in the line-out. I learned so much about line-out play from him. I was lucky enough to get his place on the Munster team and he was so helpful.

'Woodie (Keith Wood) was a great leader as well. When he pointed his finger at you and said he needed a big game from you, you wanted to give it to him because he was one of the greatest players in the world and had done it all himself.

'Drico (Brian O'Driscoll) had a different style of captaincy from either Gallimh or Woodie, but when he asked you to do something, you knew that anything he asked you to give, he himself would give more. Some players give a hundred per cent, but Drico gave a million per cent. He put his body on the line every time and I loved that about him. He was not a fancy Dan by any means.'

Paul made his debut for Ireland against Wales in the Six Nations in 2000 at Lansdowne Road. It was also Ireland's first match under Eddie O'Sullivan's tenure as Irish coach. O'Connell made an excellent start and thoroughly deserved his debut try but left the field injured and in tears after only half an hour.

'I think I scored the try after about twenty minutes, but I got concussed in about the fifth. I don't remember anything after that. I was basically on autopilot. It was a weird thing. I was doing everything I normally would, but I just can't remember any of it.

'There were seven Munster forwards in the pack with Simon Easterby, so I felt right at home. Normally after your first cap, everybody gets you a drink and you end up smashed. As I was concussed, that didn't happen to me. My parents were up for the game, and as my dad is such a massive rugby fan, it was a big day for him.'

There is one memory that will forever hold a special place in O'Connell's memory chest. Waking as a boy on Christmas morning was like this – the sleepy thrill before remembering its source. He loves the stories of the 'old school' before rugby went professional and the way players combined drinking and other 'extra-curricular' activities and playing. It was part of another time and place. The players from that era carry for O'Connell the aura of another life which is half secret and half open. He got a taste of it when he spent a week with Peter Clohessy.

'I used to travel up with The Claw for internationals because we were both Young Munster and both of us lived in Annacotty. Claw was such a legend at the time that he roomed alone, but as it was my first cap, he was asked to room with me for the week. It was a week I will never, ever forget!

'Later, I roomed with Anthony Foley and we knocked off at 11 p.m. and went to sleep. We ate a proper breakfast of muesli and scrambled eggs and drank lots of water. We also took protein shakes after training. We did our weights but went for a nap during the day to ensure that we were getting the proper rest. After having a proper dinner, we might do some video analysis, but then we were in bed early.

'My week with The Claw was very different! He was old school. On the way up to Dublin, we stopped off in a petrol station. I had a tuna sandwich with no butter and a pint of milk. The Claw had a sausage sandwich with plenty of butter and lashings of brown sauce and cups of tea with shovels of sugar.

'When we were in our hotel room, he was smoking fags the whole day. We'd be getting room service up all day, every day, with various not particularly healthy dishes, like mayonnaise sandwiches. I would go to sleep about eleven and he'd still be up watching the TV. I'd wake up about two to go the toilet. Claw wouldn't be one for bringing water into the room. The TV would still be on and I would knock it off. I'd wake back up at four and the TV would be back on! I'd knock it off again. Then I would wake up again at seven. The Claw would be sitting up in the bed, smoking a fag and watching the TV.

'On our afternoon off, the Dublin lads would go home to their families, but we didn't have that luxury because the journey was too far. We were staying in the Glenview Hotel and we drove up the Wicklow mountains and went to a cafe for a healthy diet of rhubarb tart, ice cream and custard!

'He did everything differently, and yet before the match he was the one with the tear in his eye. He would get more up for the game than anyone else. His understanding of professionalism was very different, but he had a bigger heart than everyone else, and that's why everybody loved him, and still loves him.'

61

ON AND OFF THE PITCH

Rob Henderson's Memories

My first meeting with Rob Henderson was memorable. On the eve of a Munster–Leinster Celtic League match, Rob invited me up to his hotel room. When I knocked at the door, he ushered me in. I was more than a little taken aback to discover that all he was 'wearing' was a small bath towel! Despite many hours of expensive therapy, I have never been able to erase that very disturbing image from the dark corners of my subconscious.

Henderson symbolises the characters that pervade Irish rugby. His accent immediately reveals that he was not born and bred on Irish soil.

'I'm one of the lucky ones that can play for Ireland with Irish parentage. My mother is a native of Wexford. My parents split when I was a young fella and I was living with my mum. Even though she wasn't throwing her Irishness at me, I picked it up from her, although my brother and sister didn't. As soon as I started playing rugby, I wanted to progress and play for Ireland, under-21s and exiles. I was always happy to put on the green shirt.'

During his playing days with London Irish, Rob came under

the stewardship of Clive Woodward. Apart from getting to know him as a coach, they also got to know each other socially.

'I've spent some time with him. I've even had Christmas dinner with him. I invited myself! We had a delightful Christmas. He's a lovely fella and he's very smart. He was as good at business as he was at organising the England team. The guy is focused to the nth degree. I expected that he would do a great job coaching the Lions. I told that to everyone I could think of who knew him before the tour in the hope he might pick me! He got the results he did with England because he got the best out of people. He did that by giving everything he had to it. He doesn't do anything unless he does it wholeheartedly.

'I played golf with him one day. I'd only started playing two or three months beforehand, but I'd got all the gear from a sponsor. We came to the first tee and I hit one down the middle, which was a miracle. I was really keyed up, but by the time I got to the eighth hole, I had lost all the balls in my bag and about fourteen of Clive's. He loves his golf and when I hit another ball into the woods, he just looked at me sadly and said: "I think we'd better go in now."

'I gave him the green jersey I wore when I won my first cap for Ireland. I presented it in a grand manner as befits Clive – in a Tesco bag. He wasn't there when I dropped it into his home so he wrote to me and said that when I eventually grew up, he would return it to me!'

Henderson took me by surprise when I suggested that the high point of his career must have been the Lions tour of 2001.

'No. Without question, the high point for me was when we beat France 27–25 in the Stade de France in 2000, the first time in twenty-eight years. It was an unbelievable atmosphere. It obviously helped that the fella next to me scored three tries. These are memories that I will never forget. Obviously, the Lions tour was also a real highlight. To make the trip in the first place was fantastic, but to play in all of the three Tests was wonderful.'

Hendo's awesome power was the perfect foil for Brian O'Driscoll's sublime skills, and they provided the coach, Graham Henry, with the perfect midfield combination of strength and flair.

Henderson's teammates weren't so appreciative of his off-the-field activities though. Rooming with Henderson was the ultimate nightmare, according to Austin Healey, because he smokes like a chimney and snores liked a blocked-up chimney, and because sarcastic is his middle name and he could turn any sentence into a jail term.

Henderson has enjoyed the company of many characters through rugby:

'You could pick any one of the Irish team I played on. Malcolm O'Kelly is a great character. If he was any more laid-back, his head would be touching the ground.'

62

THE TRYING GAME

Ireland v Australia, 1991

From an Irish point of view, the tournament was a story of what might have been. The 1991 World Cup quarter-finals approached and the rugby world, despite the underdog success of Western Samoa earlier in the tournament, expected it was part of the natural order that the Wallabies would cruise comfortably into the last four. Ireland had often proved a handful at home, but few genuinely believed they would push Australia for the full eighty minutes.

Historically, Lansdowne Road never was a natural home for rugby logic. A full-blooded brawl among the forwards set the tone for a match in which the Aussies, despite two scores from David Campese, the undisputed player of the tournament, never managed to finish off the fighting Irish. Twelve points from the boot of Ralph Keyes kept Ireland within striking distance but never in front – until a moment never to be forgotten.

With Ireland behind 15–12, full-back Jim Staples hoofed up field in the dying moments and winger Jack Clarke set off in pursuit, then fed the charging Gordon Hamilton. The flanker stormed past Campese, leaving him leaden-footed as he sprinted forty yards to score in the corner. Hamilton was mobbed by his teammates and a swarm of fans in some of the most jubilant scenes Irish rugby had ever seen. Then Keyes, who had kept Ireland in the match with yet another fine kicking display, slotted the conversion between the posts from the far left to give Ireland a three-point lead.

Before the crowd could catch their breath, the game turned decisively once more. Ireland conceded a penalty and Michael Lynagh seemed set to take the penalty to level the scores. Fortune favours the brave and instead, the Wallaby great opted to take a quick-tap penalty. The stunned Irish defence rushed to cover but in the process gave too much space for Tim Horan and Jason Little, who each gained invaluable ground. Then Little whipped the ball out to Campese and Campo surged for the line, only to be stopped just short. He had just enough time to loft the ball to Lynagh, who crashed over for a try and a heartbreaking loss for Ireland, as Ralph Keys explained to me.

'The Australian match was the greatest disappointment of my career. We had the match won, but we lost it. I remember our bus got stuck in a traffic jam on the way to the match, which meant that we literally ran in off the bus, got togged out and ran on to the pitch. It was a tremendous performance.

'I genuinely believe we had a chance of beating New Zealand in the semi-final in front of our home fans. Our form had been poor up to that match and nobody expected us to do well. Had we won that game, I think it would have generated a whole new level of interest in rugby throughout the country. It could have been like the mass hysteria which the Irish soccer team generated during the World Cup in Italia '90.

'It's funny the things that go through players' minds during a big game. During the 1991 World Cup quarter-final, Australia's great centre Tim Horan was in a panic. After Gordon's try, Tim thought it was all over for them and they would be on the plane home the following morning. He had put a lot of his clothes in the laundry that morning and his big fear was that the clothes wouldn't be ready for the following day! Then Michael Lynagh intervened and took them out of jail with his try.'

In the World Cup final itself that year, Horan had an even more pressing distraction. In the build-up to the final, the Australian team had an amazing amount of support from well-wishers, not just the fans who cheered them on their way but many who sent messages to the team hotel. In the lead-up to the final, the players went into the team room in the hotel to read the messages from time to time. The messages were incredible: some offered free accommodation at five-star hotels, free evenings at massage parlours, free beach holidays, but then came the classic. A woman from Adelaide had faxed in: 'To whoever scores the first try in the final, I will offer you fantastic free sex.' Then she added her phone number.

Once the game started, the first break in the match happened to come from Horan. He was racing down the right-hand side with only Will Carling between himself and the try line, also at stake this incredible offer. Was he about to get lucky twice in the one moment? He decided to chip through, but the ball went into touch. From the ensuing line-out, the Australians managed to pilfer possession, and the forwards drove over the line. The prop, Tony Daly, crashed over the line to score this crucial try, and became an unexpected hero, scoring the only try of the match. Tony was a wonderful old-fashioned prop, who won forty-one caps for Australia, but had no future as a male model and was no George Clooney.

As the whole of Australia watched the game on television, the nation's telephone company had its quietest two hours ever.

They only took a single call. A lady from Adelaide had rung in to say that she wanted her number changed immediately!

Another amusing postscript to the match came over twenty years later when Ollie Campbell collected Michael Lynagh at the airport when he was visiting Dublin to attend a dinner. The legendary Australian out-half had his young son with him. When they drove past the new Aviva stadium, Ollie told the boy, 'Your dad scored a famous try in the old stadium here in the last minute of the 1991 World Cup quarter-final and the Irish people were so disappointed they knocked down the stadium.'

The young boy blurted out, 'Dad, how could you do that to the Irish people?'

63

MEETING MANDELA

A Rugby Friendship

Few people get the chance to meet a global hero. Tony Ward was one of the lucky few to do so.

'Because of my decision to boycott Ireland's tour of South Africa in 1981, in 1990 I was invited with fellow former international Donal Spring to a special meeting with Nelson Mandela during his visit to receive the freedom of the city of Dublin. We had all heard about this man who has been locked away for twenty-six years, and then suddenly he appears. I met him and his then wife, Winnie, with Donal Spring and the Dunnes Stores' workers when he received the freedom of Dublin in 1990. He just shook hands and thanked us. It's a memory I will always treasure.'

The power of this encounter is trumped by another one for Ward.

'When I look back at that experience in 1980, one of my fondest memories of the tour was of a friendship I formed with one of the most exciting talents in South Africa, Errol Tobias. I suppose because we were both out-halves we developed a special bond.

He told me that he owed everything he had to rugby. He could become the first black player to play for the Springboks. But he had his feelings too, and when we were talking together, he was always very careful in case anybody was listening. I knew he wanted to speak his mind but could not. He had to move from Cape Town to Johannesburg to get the chance to play rugby in a "non-racial" team.

'Years before Chester Williams, Errol Tobias earned his place in rugby history by becoming the first black player to start a Test match for the Springboks, when he lined out against Ireland on 30 May 1981. He was thirty-one at that juncture and his selection came not at out-half but in the centre, following an injury to Willie du Plessis.'

Tobias was born in Caledon, a township in the Cape Province sixty miles east of Cape Town. He began playing rugby as a seven-year-old at the township's Holy Trinity School. The pitch was merely a stretch of weeds and gravel. At first, he lined out at full-back, and, after leaving school, he worked his way up from the thirds of a club called Progress to the first team. The change to stand-off was an experiment that worked brilliantly.

'Errol's elevation to the Test side provoked hostility on two fronts. Many within his own community felt he shouldn't play because it would be an act of collusion with the system of apartheid. Meanwhile, many whites who were committed to apartheid did not want to see him on the team. This was an era when white and black players used different pitches, pavements and shops, so his selection by national coach Nellie Schmidt was, in the real sense of the term, revolutionary.

'Ten years previously, Tobias had tasted international rugby in the UK with the Proteas, a team affiliated to the South African Rugby Football Federation. In 1979, he again made a huge impact when he starred in the South African Barbarians team.

In 1981, he played a key part in both Tests against Ireland, with South Africa winning 23–15 at Newlands and 12–10 in Durban.

'Later that year, he also took part in the Springbok tour to New Zealand, but for reasons best known to the selectors, he didn't make the Test side and was limited to playing for the midweek team. Many saw him as a "token Springbok", whose function was to show to the world that South African rugby was not run along racial lines. Without the presence of a black player, it was believed that the tour would not go ahead.

'His next two caps came in 1984 when his skills as an out-half were at last shown to the rugby world on the international stage, when he starred in the two victories over a touring England side. With Tobias calling the shots, South Africa recorded two big wins, 33–15 in Port Elizabeth and 35–9 in Johannesburg. Later that year, Tobias starred in his two final Tests for South Africa. The Springboks beat a touring South American side, 22–13 in Cape Town and 32–15 in Pretoria. This meant that Tobias has the nice distinction of never having played on a losing Test side. An interesting footnote to that South American series was that Avril Williams, the Western Province centre, became the second black player to line-out for South Africa. This points to the historical importance of Tobias. He broke the mould and opened the door for rugby integration in South Africa. He opened the eyes of the South African public to what talent they were denying themselves by allowing the system of apartheid to influence their rugby selection policy.

'However, it's not just because of his skin colour that Tobias is best remembered but because of his genius on the pitch. To colour-blind rugby fans he was a running out-half, with great physical presence and a keen eye for a gap, where his devastating breaks past one opponent after another would often send buzzes of excitement through the crowds. Above all, he had the skills to release the players around him with his electric pace and quick hands, not unlike Paul Dean. There are lies, damn lies, and statistics, but the records speak for themselves.'

Errol told Ward of his mission in life: 'Needless to say there were people who were saying that a black man shouldn't be playing for the Springboks. I knew that there were people who were thinking that, but I decided I was going to show South African people that all men are born equal. I wanted to show them that colour doesn't matter – if you have the skills, then you should play for your country.'

He was not fazed by those in his own township, where, because of his silken skills, he was referred to as the 'hero among heroes', who felt he shouldn't turn out for a sport so associated with the apartheid regime.

'Some people reacted furiously to my selection. They felt that the apartheid laws should be removed before I played for South Africa, but from a sports point of view, I was no politician. We had no say in politics. We didn't even have a vote, so all I knew at this stage was to play rugby. My goal was to show the country and the rest of the world that we had black players who were as good as, if not better than, the whites, and that if you were good enough, you should play.'

Initially there was scepticism from his teammates on the Springboks.

'I have to admit that at the beginning of the tour to New Zealand in 1981, the atmosphere was very tense. But as the tour progressed, we started to talk to one another. Whether you are black or white, you have to prove yourself to your teammates and gain their respect. I remember one of the white players said to me: "Errol, the strangest thing is happening here – you don't even look as black as you did when you started in this group."

They saw the rugby I played was of a high quality and they respected me for that.'

Tony Ward situates him in his historical context.

'His importance was also in blazing a trail for others like Chester Williams and Breyton Paulse to follow. I suppose the best way of summarising Errol's career was to say that he was a man whose real struggle was more off the pitch than on it.'

64

A DROPPING AND PROMOTION

The Jim and Tony Show

A different type of rugby friendship was that between Irish rugby legends Jim McCarthy and Tony O'Reilly. Cork born wing-forward Jim McCarthy was a product of CBC Cork. He won a Munster Senior Schools Cup medal with the school in 1943. With his club Dolphin, he won Munster Cup medals in 1944, '45 and '48. He was capped twenty-eight times for Ireland between 1948 and 1955, captaining the side four times in 1954 and 1955, and scoring eight international tries. He was also omnipresent in the Irish team which won the international championship in 1951, and toured Argentina and Chile in 1952 with Ireland.

He is best remembered as a breakaway forward of the highest quality, playing in all four matches in the 1948 Grand Slam year, and for the entire season of 1949. He brought a new dimension to wing-forward play, particularly in relation to helping the out-half breach the opposing half. A flying redhead, he was an invaluable ally to Jack Kyle, combining with him to devastating effect.

McCarthy explained his unusual friendship with O'Reilly to me.

'Tony came down to take up his first job in Cork and joined us for afternoon tea, which led him to stay a few days, which became two years, and in the process, he became one of the family. When he first came, he would say "your house, Jim, and your children and your wife", but he quickly changed the "yours" to "ours". I had no problem with "our kids" and "our dog," but when he started saying "our" wife, I showed him the door!

'I knew the first time I saw him that he would be a success in anything he turned his hand to. He had it all and more. Having said that, I don't envy him.

'I believe he was never fully exploited on the Irish team. I think he should have been selected at full-back to get the best out of his attacking abilities. There are two sayings which I think apply to Tony: "The bigger the reputation, the smaller the gap," and "To be good, you've got to be twice as good." Everybody wants to cut the guy with the big reputation down to size.

'I was best man at both his weddings! I only played one season with Tony at international level though. When he arrived on the scene, he was the darling of the media and could do no wrong. After his first match against France, the *Irish Independent* said that I had played poorly and had not protected Tony well enough, even though I wasn't playing in the centre! I was dropped for the next match after that report and never played another international. Twenty-five years later Tony put me on the board of the *Irish Independent* just to make up for their injustice to me all those years ago!'

PART VI
Controversial Moments

Irish rugby has produced a number of pantomime villains down through the years – none more so than Martin Johnson, who infamously snubbed Irish president Mary McAleese on the red carpet in Lansdowne Road in Ireland's 2003 Grand Slam decider against England. It has also generated many controversies, some more sensitive and complex than others. For example, we do not know all the behind-the-scenes machinations about Ireland's failed attempt to host the Rugby World Cup – although that hasn't stopped many people from speculating. However, there are no shortage of other tales which do not require the same caution. Simon Zebo, in exile, in France with Racing 92 revealed in February 2019 that he keeps two phones to ensure that if he ever gets the phone call to return to the Irish squad, he will be ready to answer it. There has been a controversy about Joe Schmidt's policy of not selecting Irish players, who, like Zebo, play abroad.

We don't believe in conspiracy theories but ...

Before Ireland played Scotland in the 2019 Six Nations, Joe Schmidt resurrected the 'Busgate' controversy when the Ireland bus arrived late for the Scotland match in 2017, which may have contributed to Ireland's surprise defeat on the day.

This section explores some of these controversies.

65

THE SCUMMY IRISH

Eddie Is Not Steady

Days before the 2018 Grand Slam decider, a major controversy erupted. English coach Eddie Jones and the Rugby Football Union both issued apologies after video footage emerged of the England head coach referring to 'the scummy Irish' and Wales as a 'little sh*t place' during a speech the previous year. Jones said he was 'very sorry' for remarks he conceded were inexcusable.

Jones had made the comments during a talk on leadership for the truck-manufacturing company Fuso, the Japanese sister company of the England team sponsor Mitsubishi, the previous July, but they only came to light that week. Jones had said, 'We've played twenty-three Tests and we've only lost one Test to the scummy Irish. I'm still dirty about that game, but we'll get that back, don't worry. We've got them next year at home so don't worry, we'll get that back.'

Joe Schmidt, though, was unfazed by the noise.

'I wasn't going to get distracted by anything Eddie said. I know Eddie of old and the idea of him saying controversial things is nothing new at this stage. I am very thankful to Eddie though. Eddie had tried to play it clever and had extended the dead-ball line by two metres behind the goalposts, thinking it would suit England. That's where the luck came in because without those extra two metres, Jacob Stockdale would not have scored his try. It was a delicious irony which I loved – but Eddie not so much.

'There was another irony. Because they changed the lines – they had to change the colour of those lines – but the referee was colour-blind! You couldn't make it up!'

66

A CLEAN SLATE?

Gerbrandt Grobler Signs for Munster

Gerbrandt Grobler's controversial stint with Munster is likely to be the last time an overseas player who has served a ban for performance-enhancing drugs will come to play in Ireland.

The South African lock's signing in July 2017 sparked huge debate, given that Grobler served a two-year doping ban between 2014 and 2016. The arrival of Tadhg Beirne from Scarlets always made it likely that he would move on after a year. However, there was concern that his presence would damage the Munster brand and could have a detrimental impact on their capacity to attract new sponsors or to retain the existing ones.

For Tony Ward, ethical considerations were a priority. 'I was of the opinion that he shouldn't have been signed on day one. I recognise that he's a good player. He's a big, athletic man. I stand by my belief, though, that bringing the former Racing 92 man in was a bad call. It just sends out the wrong message about what we think about drugs in sport.

'In fairness, because of his performances, he had his defenders in Munster, but as a former player with the province myself,

I was happy when it was announced that he was going to Gloucester. I genuinely think it closes a chapter on what had been a poor decision from Munster and the IRFU to start with.

'The key point though is its long-term significance. I will be shocked from a policy point of view if we see another player signed up from overseas who has served a ban for performance-enhancing drugs play for one of our provinces ever again. If one good thing has come out of the Grobler controversy, it's that.'

67

THE PRINCES OF WALES

Warren Gatland Drops Brian O'Driscoll

Such was the Welsh dominance of the Lions third Test team in 2013, that Johnny Sexton joked that it was a matter of enormous pride to him to have finally made his Welsh international debut.

Warren Gatland's sensational decision to drop Brian O'Driscoll for that game was the main talking point. To add insult to injury, O'Driscoll wasn't even selected for a place on the bench. Despite the controversy of being dropped for the final Test, Drico had some sweet moments after the game. He was able to bring his baby daughter Sadie on to the pitch. Then he met James Bond himself when Daniel Craig went into the Lions changing room. The bad-pun police were called when someone suggested he was in 'Double-O-Heaven'.

Weeks after the tour, O'Driscoll told Shane Horgan in a TV interview that Warren Gatland wouldn't be on his Christmas card list after he dropped him. O'Driscoll's comments got huge media attention, and shortly afterwards he realised that he was going to meet Gatland at a function. Not wishing the 'feud' to develop further, O'Driscoll took the wind out his coach's sails by presenting him with a Christmas card, even though it was only September.

After the Lions tour, Drico went into a hi-tech electrical store to buy a car radio and the salesman said, 'This is the very latest model. It's voice-activated. You just tell it what you want to listen to and the station changes automatically. There's no need to take your hands off the wheel.'

On the way home, O'Driscoll decided to test it. He said, 'Classical,' and the sound of the BBC orchestra filled the car. He said, 'Country,' and instantly he was listening to Dolly Parton. Then suddenly a pedestrian stepped off the pavement in front of him, causing him to swerve violently and shout at him, 'F**king idiot.' Then the radio changed to a documentary on Warren Gatland.

Gatland's decision to drop Drico immediately put the focus on Ireland's next game against Wales. Ireland's call was answered resoundingly with a 26–3 win. The *Sunday Independent* had the best take on it with their headline: 'Wales left to sink up Schmidt creek'.

68

THE DEMON DRINK

Rugby Sponsorship Controversy

Ireland arrived at the 2007 Rugby World Cup with great expectations. Like the 1999 tournament, though, their campaign imploded in ignominious failure. It would mark the beginning of the end for Eddie O'Sullivan's reign as Irish coach. One of the many disappointed Irish fans was Suzanne Costello.

Suzanne has a unique place in Irish sporting history: she is one half of the first brother and sister duo to represent Ireland at senior athletics. Her brother Victor competed for Ireland in the shot-put at the Barcelona Olympics in 1992. He then turned his attention to rugby and won thirty-nine caps for Ireland. On the way, he earned the nickname 'Pizza Robber' – for having the temerity to steal Neil Francis's pizza when they were sharing a room on an Irish tour. Through Victor, Suzanne became friendly with other Irish players like Denis Hickie.

Suzanne was responsible for the only funny moment of the 2007 World Cup from an Irish perspective. After another Irish capitulation, she sent Hickie a message with words of consolation. At the time, she was executive director of Samaritans

Ireland. Denis said: 'You know things are bad when you have to ring the Samaritans, but you know things must be unbelievably bad when the Samaritans are ringing you!'

Subsequently Suzanne went on to become a major critic of one aspect of the IRFU's activities. In her former role as Alcohol Action Ireland chief executive, she was scathing of what she considers the 'ongoing failure to introduce effective regulations and legislation' which has meant the alcohol industry has 'become Irish children and young people's primary educator on alcohol'. Moreover, she contends that an opportunity to make a major difference to the health of future generations will be spurned by failure to tackle alcohol marketing.

She also claims that existing voluntary codes governing alcohol advertising and alcohol sponsorship of sport on a statutory footing are 'deeply concerning', arguing that children were 'continuously exposed to positive, risk-free images of alcohol and its use' and that sponsorship of sporting events by alcohol brands is 'a particularly potent form of sales promotion'.

She insists 'comprehensive evidence' had shown children are not only exposed to a lot of alcohol promotion through sports sponsorship, 'but that their beliefs and behaviour in relation to alcohol are influenced by the alignment of alcohol brands with their sporting heroes and everything they represent'.

She believes that the alcohol industry 'writes the rules it sees fit to adhere to and decides whether they are being obeyed or not. Like most systems of self-regulation in Ireland, the alcohol industry's codes have proven to be wholly ineffective and have done nothing to protect the young and vulnerable members of our society from alcohol harm.'

She continues: 'I am a huge rugby fan. I am very proud that both my brother and father played rugby for Ireland. Yet I equally believe that sporting bodies like the IRFU have a duty of care, particularly to the young people of Ireland. Through sponsorships like the Heineken Cup, for many people there is a clear association between rugby and alcohol companies in Ireland and abroad. Is that the message we want to give our young people?'

69

THE WEST WAS NOT ASLEEP

The IRFU Seek to Disband Connacht

In 2003, Tony Ward created a media storm.

'There are times when I have been the architect of my own destruction. I still cringe at one memory. The first time Ireland played Italy in the Six Nations, I rang Ken Ging, the former Leinster manager, and asked him about getting tickets for the game in Rome. He immediately told me that the match had been refixed for the Colosseum because it had been revamped and was now the best rugby stadium in Italy. I was very surprised and replied: "I never knew. It will be very hard to win there. It's been very difficult for visiting teams to win there."

'Ken interjected: 'The Lions have a great record there."

'I replied with shock in my voice: "I never knew the Lions played there." At that moment, I realised Ken had been winding me up and that I had made a total fool of myself. I made him solemnly swear that he would never repeat the story to a single soul. He promised me faithfully. Ken is the doyen of the after-dinner circuit and of course he has told that story to large gatherings over 150 times since!

'Long after my playing days were over, I never expected that a routine visit to Tesco in Dún Laoghaire would land me in the middle of controversy – but it did. I met Eddie Wigglesworth, IRFU director of rugby there. We were in school together in St Mary's, though he was a few years ahead of me, and he informed me that he had something to tell me and asked me to come and see him. I duly did, and he told me that the cold financial facts of modern-day professional rugby dictated an end to the traditional nurturing of the four-province system. The IRFU's plan to cope with the financial drain of contracting 120 professional players was to disband Team Connacht.

'After I broke the story in my column in the *Irish Independent*, there was a massive outcry and it became a major news story. It was covered on the *News at One* that day and snowballed from there on. The IRFU had not expected a reaction of that magnitude. Of course, the public became hugely engaged with the plight of Connacht, and there was a massive march on the streets of Dublin, which people like Jim Glennon were involved in. With the tide of public opinion so heavily against them, the IRFU had no option but to back down.'

The reaction to Ward in Connacht was not all positive.

'The IRFU were understandably unhappy with the leaking of the story to me. It wasn't as if I was sniffing round for a story, though. According to those guiding the Union through the early days of professionalism, four professional entities into an optimum three just wouldn't go.

'The Saturday after I broke the story, I went with Ned Van Esbeck to Ericsson Park in Athlone, where Connacht were in European action against Pontypridd. I remember meeting a few Connacht fans who had a shoot-the-messenger philosophy and they laid into me with some very unparliamentary language for daring to show my face at the game.

'I spoke with Eric Elwood, who was coaching Connacht at the time, and he was unhappy with me breaking the story the week of such an important match because it broke the players' focus. The two of us were coming at things from different perspectives. He was only interested in winning the match, and rightly so. As a journalist, my concern was to bring an important story into the public domain and to look at the bigger picture.'

Ward was defending what he believes is an important principle.

'I feel very strongly that you need a shop-window team in every province because it provides an incentive for young players. If they don't have a top team to play on, what is there for young players to aspire to? When my daughter Nikki was a teenager, she and her friends regularly went to see Leinster play, and after the games they could go and get autographs from Brian O'Driscoll or Gordon D'Arcy or Denis Hickie.

'There is such great talent in the West at the moment, and I have no doubt that this assembly line has been fuelled in part by young, talented players seeing their provincial side in the flesh. Forget the history or tradition argument – to have that window of opportunity for young players to aspire to is vital if we are to continue to have the game humming in the province as never before.'

70

BACKHANDER

Leicester v Munster, 2002

Munster's Heineken Cup defeat to Leicester is shrouded in controversy.

La mano de Dios, 'the hand of God', is one of the most famous incidents of ethical dimensions in world sport. This was the explanation given by Diego Maradona of Argentina after he deflected the ball with his hand over the advancing England goalkeeper Peter Shilton in the 1986 World Cup. His goal helped Argentina to victory and they went on to take the World Cup.

Perhaps the most talked about ethical incident in rugby occurred in the final moments of the Heineken Cup final in 2002. Munster were trailing Leicester and were driving hard for their opponents' line when they were awarded a set scrum, some five metres out from goal. It was crucial to win this ball and set up a final drive for possible victory. As the Munster scrum-half was about to put the ball into the scrum, Neil Back's infamous 'hand-of-God' backhander knocked the ball from Peter Stringer's grasp into the Leicester scrum and the ball was lost to Leicester. The referee had taken up a position opposite the incoming ball and did not see the incident.

The controversy spawned a new joke:

Q: What's the difference between Tim Henman and Neil Back?

A: Neil Back is much better with his backhand.

One Munster fan's reaction was to say: 'The Leicester Tigers should be renamed the Leicester Cheetahs.'

71

DUNCAN DISORDERLY

Ronan O'Gara Is Assaulted

One of the defining sporting images of 2001 was the sight of blood streaming from Ronan O'Gara's eye. During the Lions tour to Australia in 2001 Duncan McRae had repeatedly beaten him in the left eye during the match against the New South Wales Waratahs with an eleven-punch attack. O'Gara's popularity with the squad after the McRae episode was indicated when everyone wanted to go and sort out 'Duncan Disorderly'.

Two and a half years later, McRae publicly pronounced his contrition for his actions and his intention to apologise to O'Gara the next time they met. By an amazing coincidence, that admission came two weeks before McRae, as the new Gloucester out-half, was due to play against Munster in Thomond Park. The previous year, the Zurich Premiership leaders Gloucester had lost 33–6 in Thomond Park in the never-to-be-forgotten 'Miracle Match'.

How does O'Gara feel about McCrae now?

'I don't have any feelings about him to be honest. There were all kinds of rumours about what freaked him out. It's not for me to comment. What was great, though, was the support I got afterwards, both from within the squad and from back home, and to know that people were thinking of me and wanting things to work out well for me.'

O'Gara had been chosen for the tour ahead of Scotland's Gregor Townsend. While the focus of the media attention on O'Gara's Lions tour was on the McRae incident, Ronan himself has very different memories from the tour.

'Other people seemed to be more affected by the sight of my blood than I was. I look back on that tour with good memories, and I found it to be an enriching experience. I learned a lot from that tour and have taken a number of things from that trip and incorporated them into my game. It was great to see at first hand the way players like Jonny Wilkinson train. He was so professional and went about his game with such dedication and attention to detail. Another person I really admired was Rob Howley. He was a great player, and Brian O'Driscoll had such a wonderful tournament – that famous try in the first Test will never be forgotten. I get on very well with Brian personally. As the out-half, it's important that you get on well with all the backs and forwards because you are the link between them.'

Austin Healey or, as the Aussie press branded him, 'Lippy the Lion' claims that Rog was considered the funniest man on the tour because his sayings became squad sayings. He answered questions like how was he feeling with replies like: 'Oh, I'm unnaturally good today.'

72

SIMON'S SUSPENSION

Simon Geoghegan's Suspension from the Irish Team

The ultimate test of a player in any sport is whether they have the power to make the pulse skip a beat when they're in full flight. Once they get the ball, a buzz of expectancy goes around the ground. Before Brian O'Driscoll came on the scene, the one player who constantly had this effect was Simon Geoghegan. Unlike O'Driscoll, Geoghegan didn't have the good fortune to play with a strong Irish team. Indeed, sadly he seemed to spend much of his international career waiting for a pass. It's surprising that he never got the nickname Cinderella because it often seemed nobody wanted to take him to the ball. However, in full flight he lit up the stage like a flash of forked lightning, blazing brilliantly, thrillingly and, from the opposition's point of view, frighteningly. He scored eleven tries in his thirty-seven caps for Ireland.

Geoghegan was born and bred in England so why did he play rugby for Ireland?

'My father is from Killimor, County Galway, a great hurling area, and growing up, I spent most of my summer holidays there, so I got a great love for places like Ballinasloe and all the Galway area. Because of that, I always had a sense of being Irish.'

Great tries in 1991 against Wales and England established the then Baker Street resident as the rising star of Irish rugby. However, the following season, as Ireland lost every game, he got no chance to impress. Things went from bad to worse the following season – when he hoped to make the Lions tour to New Zealand. His ability as a defender wasn't just questioned, it was derided – particularly after the way Derek Stark scored a try 'on him' in Murrayfield.

'Yes, 1993 was a bad season for me. My club form was poor and that probably affected my confidence when playing for Ireland.'

His problems at the time weren't just on the field. He was temporarily suspended from the Irish squad. What prompted this exclusion?

'I'm not the most diplomatic person in the world. When I give my opinion, I tend not to mince my words. I was unhappy with the way the team was playing and the fact that I was getting so few opportunities, and I made my views known in a public way – but that's all water under the bridge now.'

A prominent rugby journalist openly questioned his commitment to the Irish team because of an incident in which he threw his Irish jersey on the ground. Did this type of criticism hurt him?

'Not in the least. Anybody who knew me knew of my commitment to Ireland and judged me by what I did when I was wearing my green jersey on the pitch, not by what I did with it in the dressing room.'

73

MONEY, MONEY, MONEY

Ireland Prepare for the 1991 World Cup

Ireland's build-up to the 1991 World Cup tournament wasn't ideal on a number of levels, as Ralph Keyes has recalled to me:

'The second World Cup didn't seem to be real because we were based in Ireland. Our preparations were dreadful, especially when we lost warm-up matches to club sides, which really saps away confidence and morale. We played poorly in the tournament but came right in the quarter-final against Australia.'

Not for the first time, money raised its ugly head. In the build-up to the World Cup in 1991, Philip Matthews, Des Fitzgerald and Brendan Mullin formed the players' chosen triumvirate which negotiated with the IRFU over the way players were to be remunerated for their efforts.

'The IRFU wanted us to sign a participation agreement, where we would sign over all rights about the use of our photographs, etc. to them. In effect, we were being asked to give them a blank cheque. They wanted to squeeze everything out of our commercial appeal but give us nothing in return. It was a bitter pill for them to swallow but we said no. We heard that at one stage in South Africa, Naas Botha had led his teammates in a mini-revolt against his club officials. A short while before they were due to go out on the pitch for a crucial match, they said they wouldn't play until they got a better deal. The authorities gave in to their demands.

'In 1991, it went down to the wire as to whether the Irish players took part in the World Cup or not. A deal was only worked out at the eleventh hour after some frenetic contacts with Ronnie Dawson. In fact, at the time of the inaugural dinner for the tournament, we were still meeting Ken Reid to negotiate an agreement. It was probably the first evidence of player power in Irish rugby because we got a deal that was to our satisfaction. We put ourselves under pressure in a way, but that made us more determined. In the end, I think we could and should have done even better.'

74

THE BLOW-IN

The Brian Smith Affair

Tony Ward was very exercised by an Irish rugby import.

'When I started back in the late 1980s as a regular columnist with the *Evening Herald*, I pulled no punches when it came to dealing with the issues of the day. One of the areas where I nailed my colours to the mast most visibly was with Brian Smith's brief "flirtation" with the Irish rugby team.

'I deny that I went over the top about Smith, who of course succeeded Conor O'Shea as director of rugby in London Irish in more recent times. I must emphasise I was not begrudging in the least. It's just a point I feel very strongly about. Indeed, whatever faults may lie with soccer's rules in relation to qualification to play for one country or another, the situation relating to Brian Smith on the Irish rugby team was indefensible. If a player has declared and played for his native place of birth, unless there are extraordinary circumstances, then that should be his lot. To think that Smith, having played for Australia against Ireland in the '87 World Cup, could have ended up playing for Ireland against Australia in the World Cup in 1991 if he'd hung around a bit longer doesn't bear thinking about. The entire principle was wrong. It must be said that the fact that Smith didn't exactly set the world of Irish rugby alight had nothing to do with my feelings. Whether it was Brian Smith or Dan Carter, the principle – I emphasise again – was wrong. At least in those years "Seán" Aldridge, "Antóin" Cascarino and "Micheál" McCarthy declared their hand and opted for the Irish soccer team not having represented their countries of birth.

'When news broke of his defection to rugby league in March 1991, Smith lashed out at both Mick Doyle and me: "Ward and Doyle didn't want me in the first place. Their attack has been a personalised one."'

Ward reacts angrily to the suggestion that his criticism of Smith was personalised.

'Why would it be? I didn't even know the chap. It was the principle of his selection I objected to. It was a mistake by the IRFU. The whole idea of playing for your country is a matter of national pride. Brian Smith was opportunistic. He was just passing through. But I would like to stress that I criticised other players too. I was always careful to analyse him as a player. I had no axe to grind. That system of players "defecting" to other countries still goes on in the professional era and it continues to annoy me.

'Samuel Beckett said: "There are only two kinds of Irish joke – ones that were once funny and those that were never funny." I still feel the situation held us up to ridicule, and I recall the London Irish RFC programme note in 1993 explaining the Irish links of Hika Reid, former London Irish coach: "His grandfather once went out with a Polish girl whose uncle once saw Ollie Campbell play."

'Having said that, I was delighted when Ralph Keyes took Smith's place on the Irish team and made such an impression on the 1991 World Cup, when he was at last recognised as the class player he assuredly was, when he became the top scorer in the competition, coming out ahead of such luminaries as Grant Fox, Gavin Hastings and Michael Lynagh with sixty-eight points.

'I found it extraordinary that the selectors continued to choose Brian Smith ahead of Keyes for the Irish team when Paul Dean retired, as Keyes was such a great all-round player. After Smith switched to rugby league, the door opened for Ralph in the 1991 World Cup to show his talents to the rugby world. I was genuinely thrilled for him that, at last, he had the proper stage to showcase his talents. He grabbed the opportunity literally with both feet. I would go so far as to say that he was the best two-footed player we have ever had, certainly in my lifetime.'

75

IT WAS NOT LOVELY AND FAIR

'The Rose of Tralee' Is Played as the Irish Anthem

As coach Mick Doyle conceded subsequently, Ireland made a major blunder in the build-up to the inaugural World Cup in 1987 by trying to wrap their players in cotton wool and not allowing them to play any club matches after March, whereas the Welsh players were involved in club rugby right up to the first half of May. Ireland looked very rusty in that opening match in Wellington, while Wales were sharp and incisive and ran out comfortable winners 13–6.

The match is as much remembered for an incident before the game as for the action on the field. Tony Ward watched the events unfold before his eyes with a mixture of incredulity and horror.

'I will never forget the version of 'The Rose of Tralee' which the band played before the game instead of the Irish National Anthem. It was horrendous. I love James Last's version of that song, but this was excruciatingly painful and embarrassing to us all.'

After the defeat to Wales, changes were inevitable for the

second game – a 46–19 victory over Canada. Tony Ward was recalled at out-half in place of Paul Dean – who came in for a lot of criticism for not using the strong wind in Wellington against the Welsh.

In the press conference to announce the team, Mick Doyle was asked why he hadn't picked Ward for the first game. Doyle replied, 'Well it's very simple. We couldn't be sure if he knew the words of "The Rose of Tralee".'

76

DON'T CRY FOR ME ARGENTINA

Willie Anderson Is Arrested

In sporting terms, he is one of a kind. He is famous in the rugby world for playing the bagpipes. Whatever that indefinable quality called charisma is, this guy has it in buckets. He has a keen appreciation of the black humour of life, an easily discernible kindness and sensitivity, particularly for those down on their luck, and his smile signals a warm affection for friend and stranger alike. He lacks one thing – a capacity to dissemble. Despite his twenty-seven caps for Ireland, his then record of seventy-eight caps for Ulster, his achievements as coach and his status as assistant coach to Scotland, Willie Anderson will probably always be remembered as the player who precipitated an international diplomatic incident. He was on a tour of Argentina with the Penguins in 1980 and took a shine to the Argentinian flag and decided to claim it as his own.

'Myself and another player were walking home to the hotel around midnight. I liked the look of the flag and its colours. Shortly after that, six guys came through the door with machine guns. They said: "Someone in here has an Argentinian flag." I

288

immediately handed it back and said I was sorry. I was quickly told saying sorry wasn't good enough in this situation. As I was brought down to the jail, two Irish internationals, Dave Irwin and Frank Wilson, volunteered to come with me for moral support. For their consideration, they were both thrown in jail with me for three weeks!

'I was strip-searched and had thirty sets of fingerprints taken. I was literally in the interrogation chair for a day. Anyone who has seen the film *Midnight Express* will have an idea of the naked terror you can experience when you're in prison and there's a gun to your head. Things got worse before they got better. I was put into this box, which is the most frightening place in the world, before being taken to my cell. The cell was six foot by four and had nothing but a cement bed in the centre. The people who'd been there before me had left their excrement behind. It was pretty revolting. The only blessing was that I wasn't put in the "open" cell with a crowd of prisoners because I would never have survived.'

Then things got even worse.

'The next day I was taken out in handcuffs, which is the ultimate in degradation. I was taken up the stairs and was stunned to discover that there were about sixty or seventy reporters and journalists waiting for me. For three or four days, I wasn't just front-page news in Argentina – I was the first three pages. To me, the press weren't much better than terrorists. As I had a British passport, they tried to whip up a nationalistic frenzy and portray me as an imperialist. They didn't print the truth. Some said I had urinated on the flag. Others said I had burned it. Yet more said I had done both. My lawyer got death threats.'

Irish rugby fans had no sense of what was really happening at the time.

'It was much more serious than anybody realised here. I know for a fact that two or three army generals wanted to have me executed. Others wanted to make sure that I served at least ten years' hard labour. The whole episode cost my parents £10,000 in legal fees and so on, but you can't put a price on the mental anguish that they had to endure. I remember one letter I sent them home that I would hate to have to read again because I had struck rock bottom.

'The two lads and I were taken back to a cell where we came into contact with two South Koreans. They had tried to smuggle some Walkmans into the country. David Irwin taught me how to play chess and we had the World Chess Championships: South Korea v Northern Ireland.

'One of the guards looked like a ringer for Sergeant Bilko. At one stage, he was marching us in the yard and Frank roared out: "Bilko." I said: "For Christ's sake, Frank, just keep your mouth shut." Thankfully the guard didn't know who Bilko was. I think things could have been much worse had not the warden wanted to learn English. His colleagues would have been happy to throw away the keys to our cell. In that country, we were guilty until proved innocent.'

Anderson's life was shaped in many ways by the experience.

'After three weeks, Frank and David were sent home. It was the loneliest day of my life. I had to wait for a further two months before my trial and release. Someone arranged a hotel room for me. I wouldn't wish what happened to me on my worst enemy. All rugby players contributed via the clubs to a fund to pay for the legal expenses. The people of Dungannon rallied around and raised a lot of money also. I owe them a lot. I wrote to my then girlfriend, now wife, Heather every day. The following year we got married. I think the Argentinian experience consolidated our relationship. I also learned a lot about myself. In the beginning of that experience, I prayed intensely, but I gradually realised that I couldn't leave things to God. I had to take control of things myself. I ran every day and made a great effort to learn something about the culture and the political system. Bad and all as things were for me, it was a real culture shock to visit the town square and see all the women who were frantically looking for their sons. It was part of the way of life there that people disappeared and were lost forever. If you were seen as any kind of threat to the state you were eliminated.

'In rugby terms, I was to pay a heavy price for my indiscretion. I was perceived as a rebel and was quietly told later, by a prominent personality in Irish rugby, that my first cap was delayed because of the incident. In fact, I was twenty-nine when I first played for Ireland. I met Denis Thatcher some years later and told him that I could have told his wife the Argentinians were scrapping for a war.'

77

DON'T PICK WARDY

Tony Ward Is Dropped in 1979

Throughout his career, Tony Ward would build two reputations, one for his skill on the field and the other for the controversies which restricted his appearances in the green jersey. In fact, it's somewhat surprising that he never got the nickname 'The Judge' because he spent so much time sitting on the bench.

Ward took the international world by storm, and in both 1978 and 1979 he was voted European Player of the Year. Just as Ward's career was at its height, his world came apart on Ireland's tour to Australia in 1979.

'My scoring achievements made headlines in the Australian papers. I found myself being sought out for interviews; rugby writers seemed to follow my every step. It was never my way to reject media representatives in such circumstances, as I feel they have a job to do, and it's only right that one should cooperate with them. To simply run away or meet their queries with a bland, tight-lipped "no comment" was never my way. I hadn't thought that publicity about me in Europe – winning the European Player of the Year Award and so on – would have been so well known down under. I was rather naive in that. But they knew everything about me.

'In retrospect, I now realise – older and wiser – that if I wanted to make sure of my place on the Irish team for the first Test, I might have acted more correctly if I had gone to ground at that point and ignored the media. It would have spared me a moment that left an indelible imprint on my mind. I have pondered it again and again when reflecting on what developed into a most traumatic experience that shattered my confidence for almost two years.

'We were in the dressing room, preparing to go out for a training session for the match against New South Wales, when Jack Coffey, the team manager, came over to me and said: "This is absolutely ridiculous. It's crazy what's going on – all this media stuff. I suggest that you stay away from these fellows altogether." I looked at him aghast. I didn't know what he was driving at. It was only at the end of the tour that the true relevance of his remarks that day became clear.

'I knew before I left Ireland that I was under pressure and consequently made certain that I played well in the preliminary games on that tour. I suspected certain devious undertones. I knew Noel "Noisy" Murphy was no fan of mine; when he was the Munster coach he used to call me "the soccer player" from the sideline.

'I still feel that it was totally unjustified. Being dropped hit me like a thunderbolt – no warning, no explanation, and nobody wanted to help me. It was extremely traumatic. The immature side of me wanted to come home immediately.

'I reacted like a spoilt brat. I wanted to get on a plane and get out of there. How dare anyone drop me! In the end, I didn't, and I would like to think I learned a lot from the experience. That's what life is about – learning from experience, because if we could all live with the benefit of hindsight that would be great. They picked Ollie (Campbell) and he delivered in spades and Ireland won, so the selectors could argue they were proved right, but I still feel it was unjust to have dropped me at that stage.'

News that he had been dropped sent shock waves through Irish rugby fans. It was like using the Shroud of Turin to clean somebody's porridge dish – a sacrilege. It had a profound effect on Ward's life as a whole. Up to '79 he had led a sheltered life, wallowing in the delight of a successful career which had brought all his childhood fantasies to reality. The greatest tragedy was that he lost his inherent faith in his own ability.

78

THE FOURTH ESTATE

Irish Rugby and the Media

There have been many fraught moments between the Irish rugby fraternity and the media down the years. Who will ever forget the sheer awkwardness of Reggie Corrigan's post-match interview with Peter O'Mahony?

Ireland's 2018 Grand Slam win was bookended with two such controversies. At the outset, there was a spat between Joe Schmidt and the media when he restricted some of his availability for interviews after international games. After the Grand Slam was secured, it emerged that news journalists had been banned from Ulster rugby press conferences because so much time was being spent on non-rugby issues in the wake of the trial involving Paddy Jackson.

Colin Patterson ('Patty') is a gifted storyteller, talking in a way that is delightfully descriptive and wickedly insightful of human foibles. An accomplished mimic, his impression of Noel Murphy is devastating. While studying law at Bristol, he played for English and British Universities. With his fast fingers and his ability to switch the options, he won eleven caps for Ireland between 1980, scoring five international tries.

Patterson immediately struck up an instant rapport with his half-back partner, Tony Ward, on and off the field. It was said that they went together like ham and eggs, and that Patterson could find Ward in a darkened room. The scrum-half was heard to proclaim that Ward was not the first person he would want to meet in those circumstances!

'I later went on *The Late Late Show* with Tony when he was the golden boy of Irish rugby and landed him in big trouble. Wardy was involved in a serious relationship at the time and Gay Byrne asked him if he had a girlfriend. I quipped immediately: "One in every town." Tony had a lot of explaining to do to his young lady after that! He was also asked if he had thought about defecting to rugby league. When Tony rejected the idea out of hand, Gay turned to me and said: "Tony's looking down on rugby league, Colin – how about you?"

'"When you're only five-foot-five you can't afford to look down on anything," I replied.

'The personality difference between Tony and I was also evident on that visit. We were both asked what we would like to drink. I said two Irish coffees please, which wasn't what they normally provided and would take a bit of trouble on their part. Immediately Tony intervened and said: "Oh no. Don't go to any trouble for us."

'"Okay, Tony, I'll drink yours as well," I answered and we both got our Irish coffees.

'I loved winding Tony up. Of course, he gave me the ideal opportunity after the publication of his page-three-style pose in his swimming trunks before the Scottish game in 1979. I pinned the photo up on the wall and kept gushing to him about his fantastic bum and how no woman could possibly resist him.

'People kept asking me why he was dropped. There was all kinds of speculation, including the ridiculous notion that Wardy was caught in bed with one of the selectors' wives, but Tony isn't like that.'

Patterson was a rugby ecumenist singing the national anthem with gusto before matches, even though he wasn't from nationalist stock.

'Wardy taught me the first six or seven lines of the anthem and then I discovered that I could sing it to the tune of "The Sash". I sang the first half of "The Soldier's Song" and the second half of "The Sash" just to give it a political balance!'

When asked about the relationship between players and the media, he uses his own experience as a case study. Patterson made his international debut against the All Blacks in 1978.

'I heard about it a week before the match. I was so nervous I must have thought about ringing up ten times and telling them that I was unable to play. Once we got on the team bus, with the Garda escort, I started to relax and really enjoyed the occasion.

'One of my clearest memories of winning my first cap is of a piece written about me in a local newspaper. The journalist in question had rung my mother a few times but had been unable to contact me. Yet when I opened the paper, I saw a big piece full of quotes from me. I tackled the journalist about this afterwards. He said: "It's the sort of thing you would have said!"

'Throughout my career, the number of quotes attributed to me written by journalists who I had never even met defies belief. I didn't have that problem with *The Irish Times*. In their case, the difficulty was that I never should have been picked for Ireland in the first place. I was described as Ireland's sixth choice.'

79

GET YOUR RETALIATION IN FIRST

Willie John McBride's 99 Call

The Lions won all eighteen of their provincial games and three of the four Tests in 1974, with the other drawn only because the referee disallowed Fergus Slattery's match-winning try. They scored a record 729 points. McBride's philosophy was that the Lions would 'take no prisoners' and 'get our retaliation in first', as he recalled for me.

'South African rugby was always physical, and we had always been dominated, played second fiddle, in years gone by, and they just couldn't believe that we could stand up to this. Of course, we were physical, but we were definitely not dirty. In fact, we went out of our way not to be dirty because we knew we were the better players and the better team when we played rugby football. You can't be a good team and a dirty team at the same time.'

McBride was responsible for a tactic that has now become part of rugby folklore: the infamous '99' call used by the captain as an emergency measure when things looked like getting out of hand. On his signal, all fifteen Lions would 'take on' their nearest opponent, not only to show the South Africans that they weren't going to back down but also to reduce the risks of a sending off, as the referee was highly unlikely to dismiss an entire team. The call was used twice in the bruising third Test but only as a last resort. Willie John explained the background to me:

'The whole thing about the 99 call has been overplayed. I would say there were possibly four incidents in all the games and that was about it. It was a good thing because it showed South Africa that the Lions at last were going to stand up and weren't going to take any nonsense. On previous tours, there's no doubt about it, they were bullied, and there was no way we were going to accept it in 1974.

'My experience on previous Lions tours had taught me that in provincial games you tend to have a bit of thuggery to soften up the tourists. Before the match against Eastern Province, I told the side that I was expecting trouble. I said to them, "Tomorrow, if anything happens, we're all in it together – and I mean all. You hit the guy that's nearest to you as hard as you can, whether he's done anything wrong or not. If that doesn't stop it, you haven't hit him hard enough. My attitude was, hurt one of us and you hurt us all, so we'll stop it there and then. Initially the signal I came up was "999", the traditional alert for all emergency services, but the feeling among us was that 999 was too long, so we cut it down to 99.

'There's no question that Gareth Edwards was one of the best players in the world at the time. So if there was any thuggery, he was always likely to be targeted. At one stage during the game, he got a thump on the back of his head after he'd passed the ball. Within seconds, about half the Eastern Province team were sprawling on the ground. They literally didn't know what hit them. An important marker had been put down for the rest of the tour.

'The 1974 tour was like all my Christmases at once. Winning became a habit, and we liked it. I suppose the sad thing was that there was such controversy about the drawn game, which was the final match. None of us could understand why Fergus Slattery's try was disallowed. The main thing was that we didn't lose the game because of it. If we had, it would have taken some of the gloss off the tour. To beat them on their turf was incredible.'

The tour itself was shrouded in controversy.

'You might say we were under house arrest even before we left home. We came under tremendous pressure, spending three days in London, where the anti-apartheid movement asked us to pull out of the tour. I met the players and told them. "If you don't want to come, please leave now." There wasn't a sound. It seemed like forever but after a couple of moments I could wait no longer and said. "Okay then, we're all in this together."

'Once in South Africa, we discovered that the British government, who were against the tour, had instructed the embassy to boycott us. The opposition helped weld us together, to mould us into one big family.'

80

THE NO-SHOWS

Scotland and Wales Refuse to Play Ireland

In 1972, Tom Grace won the first of his twenty-five caps in the high-pressure zone at Stade Colombes in Paris. To soothe his frayed nerves, he sought consolation from an old hand.

'Team captain Tom Kiernan traditionally spoke at the team talk with each player individually. I recall that he spent a lot of time talking with the wingers. The froth was coming out of his mouth, he was so fired up. He warned us about the way the French would bombard us with high balls. The consoling thing, though, was that he assured us he would be there beside us to take the pressure off us. The match was barely on when the French out-half kicked this almighty ball up in the air between Kiernan and myself. To my horror, I heard Kiernan shouting: "Your ball". So much for all that brothers-in-arms talk, but that's the captain's prerogative! I caught the ball and nearly got killed!

'After the match, I didn't realise how significant our victory was. I could see that players who, to me, were heroes, like Willie John and Tom Kiernan, were very emotional about the whole thing. Now I understand why.

'My second match was at Twickenham. I remember seeing the number of big cars going into the ground and the smoked-salmon-and-champagne parties and how that was used to motivate the Irish side. It was also stressed how important it was for the Irish community in England for us to win. If there was any doubt about that, the Irish fans in the crowd's reaction after Kevin Flynn scored that famous try said it all.'

Johnny Moloney was a very single-minded player. In a schoolboy match, he was charging through for a try when a despairing dive by his marker robbed him of his shorts. True to form, he raced through for the try in his underpants before worrying about getting new togs! Moloney was a most under-rated player, even though he won twenty-seven caps for Ireland. He was the ultimate third wing-forward. With his athletic build, his work rate around the field and ability to read the game, his impact was phenomenal. His peers rate him as one of the best all-round tactical scrum-halves they played with.

Moloney won his first cap against France in 1972.

'The joy of being selected for Ireland was heightened for me because my St Mary's clubmate Tom Grace was also picked for the team. Our careers overlapped a lot. Gracer really had a great will to win. I remember in a match for Ireland against England he was up against David Duckham, who came into the match with a great reputation. The first time he got the ball, Gracer ran into him and knocked Duckham clean over. Every time Duckham touched the ball that day, he dropped it. It was one of the best examples of a player psyching out an opponent I have ever seen. Duckham wasn't at the races that day and Gracer came out a clear winner.

'I can't remember much about the build-up to my first cap. I'm naturally a very calm person, but that quality was accentuated that week. I recall that there was a wonderful dinner after the match. The French subs were in great singing voice.

'I was one of five new caps with Tom Grace on the right wing, Wallace McMaster on the left, Con Feighery in the second row and Stewart McKinney at wing-forward. I always think of that side as a team of three fives. The five new caps, five senior stars (Tom Kiernan, Kevin Flynn, Mike Gibson, Willie John McBride, Ray McLoughlin) and five rising stars (Fergus Slattery, Ken Kennedy, Barry McGann and my two clubmates Denis Hickie and Seán Lynch). It was an ideal blend.'

With typical modesty, Moloney makes no mention of the fact that he scored the first of his four international tries on his debut. In the process, he became the first player to score a four-point try for Ireland, helping his country to a 14–9 win at Colombes. Moloney's memories are almost all happy ones:

'The one regret I suppose was that we didn't win a Triple Crown. I think were it not for the Troubles, we would have won it in 1972 when Scotland and Wales refused to travel to play us, because we won both our away matches to France and England and the Welsh were a coming side rather than the dominant force they were later in the decade.

'I will never forget our match against England the next season. The Troubles were at their height, and it was a brave gesture on the part of the English team to travel to Dublin. The reception they got when they went out on to the pitch was amazing, with a standing ovation. The emotion ran through to the whole Irish team. To the credit of our coach Ronnie Dawson, he was able to channel that emotion into our performance and we won the match.'

PART VII
Hello Darkness, My Old Friend

Life is a mixture of light and shade. Irish rugby is no different. A collection of pieces like these will, of course, focus on the glory days. However, no collection of great moments would be complete without some reference to the really dark days which left enduring memories for Irish rugby fans. This short section considers four of them.

81

A DAY IN SEPTEMBER

The Nevin Spence Tragedy

He was all that we want our sporting heroes to be. Nevin Spence was a talented centre with the Ulster rugby team. At just twenty-two years of age he was on the cusp of making the Irish team. The rugby world was his oyster. But on 15 September 2012 tragedy struck and he lost his life.

In the worst farming accident in over twenty years in Ulster, Nevin was taken from the family he adored in an attempt to rescue a beloved dog after it had fallen into a slurry tank on the family farm in Hillsborough, County Down. His father Noel (aged fifty-eight) and his brother Graham (thirty) also died while trying to rescue each other from the slurry tank. Such were the bonds of family love that Nevin's sister Emma also courageously put her life on the line in an effort to rescue her father and brothers before being overcome by the poisonous fumes and waking up in the recovery position.

Members of the Ulster Rugby team carried Nevin's coffin into and out of the church. The then Irish rugby coach Declan Kidney and Tyrone Gaelic football manager Mickey Harte were among other well-known sporting faces amid more than 2,000 people who attended their funerals.

Emma pays an emotional tribute to the three men: 'Dad was the one you probably saw taking up half the Drumlough Road with the tractor. He is the one that greeted you with a thump on the arm. He is the one who christened you with a new nickname no matter who you were. To me he was the one sitting at the kitchen table with his coffee made in only Mum's best china cup, listening to my every worry and telling me the truth – whether I wanted to hear it or not,' she remembers with a tremor in her voice.

Graham was 'driven by the thought of improving farming' and was 'unashamedly Nevin's biggest fan.

'He was a gentle giant who doted on his two children. He is the one who came alive when he talked about farming. To me, he is the one who protected me as I grew up. To me, he is looking at me when I look at Nathan and I look at Georgia.'

She sums all three up: 'They were hard-working men. They weren't perfect but they were genuine. They were best friends. They were godly men – they didn't talk about God, they just did God. They were just ordinary – but God made them extraordinary.'

Many tributes were paid to Nevin after he died. The Ulster physio remarked, 'I have no son, but if I did, I would want them to be like Nevin and have his values.'

The impression of meeting Emma and her sister Laura is of a shaft of light illuminating the darkness of a family tragedy – two noble natures standing up for people they serve and love. Preserving that cherished image remains important for those who see it at first hand. Their testimonies of faith strike not so much a note of hope as a symphony.

The memory of magical childhood moments with her father

and brothers linger for life in Emma's mind and in the minds of those who grew up with her, leaving a warm afterglow to light up numerous conversations years later. She remains fiercely proud of her brother's achievements on and off the rugby field:

'He was humble. Often, I was congratulated on Nevin's achievements and to hide my confusion, I accepted the praise for him, then headed home to ask at the dinner table, "So, Nev, I didn't get the paper today – what have you done?" The answer would be "Nothing, I don't know" only to find he had been selected to train in the Ireland camp, or won Young Player of the Year! Nevin didn't see these things as important; instead he reflected what Mother Teresa said: "Be faithful in small things because it is in them your strength lies."'

Nevin will always live on in Emma's heart. 'As my mum put it when he was alive and has repeated even more in the past six years, "Nevin was special." Maybe what was even more special was if you had the chance to encounter him in your life.'

Whoever said time heals all wounds has not met the Spence family. 'My dad and Graham worked the farm and were passionate about it, and while Nevin may have been a full-time rugby player, he loved the farming just as much,' she says. 'At night-time here he milked the cows, and the joke was that his best workouts would be standing out in the yard.'

Emma started to see the farm anew, looking at it from the point of view of her dad and brothers. An artist by profession, Emma has literally drawn on her family's farm for inspiration for her paintings. 'To most people, looking at something like hedges, they would see only weeds, but I was stopping to look at them and recognising the beauty in them, which is why I wanted to paint them,' she says with a laugh.

But there were, and still are, plenty of down times as well. 'I remember the first spring after the accident,' Emma recalls. 'It had always been a happy time, seeing the cows going out into the fields after the winter. But that first spring tore me apart because Dad, Graham and Nevin weren't there.

'Now, with the passage of time, I think of the joy that the boys got from something like that. It still hurts, but I'm trying to accept that this is life. I'm not saying I have it all sorted out now, because I think we are all still in the grieving process with the enormity of all that's happened. But I suppose we have no other choice but to try and cope with it and live with it.'

Years on, Emma's sadness at what she has lost is balanced to some extent by her gratitude for what she had: 'Nevin's masseur used a verse from the bible to sum him up. Colossians 3:23 says, "Whatever you do, work at it with all your heart, as working for the Lord not for human masters." Nevin's commitment to his faith was reflected in his life. This was the core of Nevin's life, which mirrored the person he was. He has left a lasting impression on those who knew him. I have heard it said Nevin, along with his brother and father, have spoken more in death than in life.'

82

TROUBLED TIMES

Nigel Carr's Career Ended in Bomb Blast

It was Irish rugby's darkest day.

In 1987, one of Northern Ireland's most senior judges, Lord Gibson (seventy-three) and his wife Lady Cecily Gibson (sixty-seven) were killed by a 500lb IRA landmine at Killeen, close to the border as they drove home to Drumbo, County Down, from holiday. Three prominent Irish rugby internationals, Nigel Carr, Philip 'Chipper' Rainey and David Irwin were in a car travelling in the opposite direction at the time, to attend an Irish rugby squad training session, and were caught in the blast. Nigel Carr was one of the stars of Ireland's Triple Crown triumph in 1985. He would never play rugby seriously again.

I invited the three players to recreate their journey that day with me to help them tell their story fully. David Irwin explained, 'It's the first time we've sat down as friends to talk about it and I'm very aware that the two other guys don't remember it clearly.'

Philip Rainey gave the location: 'To set the scene, we're back in Killeen, a small place between Newry and Dundalk.'

Nigel Carr set the context: 'I was travelling with two of my great friends from university, Davy Irwin and Philip Rainey. We were going on a journey that I had taken many times – but this one changed the course of my life in many respects. It had been a mixed season, better than the year before but not as good as the one before that. That year – 1987 – was a unique one from a rugby perspective with the inaugural World Cup, and we were all terribly excited about it. So, as we drove south for a training session, there was lots of chat, banter and rugby talk. Then everything came to an abrupt end.'

David Irwin took up the story: 'The day began early because we were driving south for a session at 10.30 a.m. I remember I was driving along, chatting to the two guys, when suddenly there was a massive thud and also a giant explosion of light. The only way I could describe it was like facing a hundred flashbulbs going off at once. I was aware enough to think that a bomb had actually gone off underneath our car. My first thought was that the IRA were trying to kill somebody else and they'd made a mistake and we'd got mixed up in it. That sense lasted several seconds, but certainly there was a huge noise and a massive flash of flight.'

Nigel was taken by the description. 'That's the first time I have heard that description in that sort of detail. I don't remember anything. I half imagine I do remember something sometimes, but then I realise I don't. My first memory is heading back to the hospital.'

Philip noted, 'My memories are very short. I remember driving behind David and him saying at one stage: "There's a fire", and that's it.'

David explained how events unfolded: 'Having experienced what I thought was a bomb in my own car, I then realised that I was literally stopped in the same lane and still pointing the same way. I recall that my first thought was to feel my own body, just to check that everything was still there, and when I established that was, in fact, the case, I remember looking to my right and noting that there was a massive crater in the Belfast side of the road. At the same time, I turned around to the left and realised that Nigel had been bleeding quite badly, and that the blood was coming out profusely from a neck wound. He seemed to be semi-conscious. The whole front of the car had been pushed in but particularly over on Nigel's side, and I said to him (though he probably doesn't remember it): "We've been in a bomb. You're okay, you're bleeding from your head but you're fine."

'While I was saying this to Nigel, as I looked past him through the passenger window, I could see another car, parallel to our own, pointing to Dublin, and there was a huge inferno of flames in that car, with two vague shadows of people and fire in the front seat. I assumed that it was possibly an RUC car, and then as I panned around I saw Philip lying sort of across the back seat – motionless. Initially I thought he might be dead, but I wasn't sure. I felt I had to get out of the car and get the guys out in case the petrol tank exploded. I wasn't totally aware of what was going on around me.

'As I managed to get out of the driver's door, one of the things that struck me was that two or three of the cars that had been behind us driving south actually drove around my car and passed us and drove down the road a bit and I remember thinking at the time: how could people drive past this? But in retrospect they were that bit outside the incident and were probably in shock themselves and the natural thing was to drive around it and get to safety.

'As I walked around the front of my car, I was aware of two or three females running up and down the road, screaming hysterically. I found out afterwards that they were part of a group of nurses that were driving north and they were actually behind Judge Gibson's car and that car had gone into the ditch. They were distraught. Again, this all happened within several seconds. A large juggernaut or lorry was driving up the road and I stopped it and told the driver to go up to the garage and ring the police and for an ambulance.'

It was a time when David's medical expertise proved invaluable. 'Having done that, I went around to Nigel and tried to get the passenger door open, which was a wee bit difficult because it had buckled with the impact. Once I sort of got the door open again, Nigel was coming around a bit but was still very groggy. I told him I had to get him out of the car because there was a danger of a further explosion. I asked him if he was in pain. He told me he was very uncomfortable in one of his thighs. I suppose being a doctor I would have been aware that a common road-accident type of injury is where the dashboard is pushed in under the passenger's knees, and that can cause you to fracture your femur. My initial thought was: *Oh my goodness, Nigel has to miss the World Cup 'cos he's fractured his femur.*

'As I tried to get him out on the passenger's side, I realised his ankles and feet were caught underneath the dashboard, and I think between me pulling and Nigel giving some assistance, I managed to drag him out. I think one of his trainers was left stuck in the car. I half-carried him and he half-walked up the road, and then I set him down on the grass verge. I took my belt off and tied his knees together again, assuming he had a leg fracture.

'I went back and spoke to Philip. He had started to come around, though he was still groggy, and I told him the car might explode and we needed to get out of there. He was able to get out by himself with just a little bit of assistance from me. I took him up and sat him beside Nigel.

'At that point, the traffic had stopped about fifty yards either side and people were getting out of their cars and looking around. It seemed fairly clear to me by then what had happened, but I wasn't sure why it had happened. A plain-clothes detective came along, and I asked if it had been a police car that had been blown up. He told me that it was a high court judge and his wife. It became clear that the police had been waiting to escort him the rest of the journey and the Gardaí had escorted him up to the south side of the border, but the car was in no man's land when the bomb had gone off. Then I saw that Philip had got up and was walking around obviously concussed and not sure what was going on.'

David handed over the care to others at that point.

'Shortly after that, the ambulance had arrived to take Philip and Nigel away. The other thing I noticed then was that one of our rugby bags was about forty yards up the road from the impact of the explosion from the car. I couldn't work out how this had happened. The explanation was that the bag flew out with the force of the explosion and then the boot had closed again.

'At that stage, the objective was to get the two guys to Daisy Hill Hospital, and I recall feeling so disappointed that Nigel was going to miss the World Cup. I gathered our valuables and bits and pieces from the car. I was told that I was going to be escorted back to Newry police station in a police car. I remember thinking: *Jeepers, we've all come through that and I'm alive, but now I have to get into a police car.* I knew from living in the north that sometimes when bombs were set off and the police came on the scene, a second bomb was sometimes set off. I was thinking, *I hope this doesn't happen to me on the way back.*'

315

Nigel was taken by the account. 'We've talked before about the day, but I've never heard so much detail about it before. David was saying about my thigh injury. I don't know how he got me out because I was a lot sorer after that! I don't recall any of it. My first memory was of heading in the ambulance and hearing the medical staff whispering. I was conscious of the fact that it was only me and one other patient. I didn't know if it was either Chipper or Davy. I heard the staff talking about people being killed. My first thought was that three of us were driving in the car but there was only two of us in the ambulance. I assumed that one of my friends had been killed. Maybe I went unconscious because my next memory is of being in the hospital.'

Philip recalled, 'That's the second time I've heard the story from David. It still amazes me, and Nigel and I were so lucky we had such a great guy with us. I was in his hands and the next thing I remember was being in a theatre in hospital, getting pieces of glass picked out of me.'

David kept up his duty of care even after the ambulance had arrived. 'Once I got to Newry police station, my first job was to ring our families. Then the police car brought me to the hospital. I met the doctor in the corridor and my first question was about Nigel's leg. I was so relieved and thought, *Great, he'll be okay for the World Cup*, but it turned out later that he had a fracture in his ankle and had what is known as "a rigid abdomen", which meant internal injuries. I then found out that although Philip had taken a bad blow to the head and was unconscious, he was basically okay.'

Nigel continued, 'I think I must have been given some sort of painkilling injection when I was en route. I don't recall feeling that sore. I didn't think things were that bad. I knew I had cuts and bruises, but I also had twisted joints, chipped bones, five broken ribs and internal bleeding. For the next few days I was in acute pain. I would hold on for as long as I could and then get an injection into my backside to give me relief.'

David began to piece the chain of events together. 'That morning, I became more aware of what had happened. Lord Gibson had gone to the same school as me, and over the following days I learned that he and his wife were a very nice couple.'

After their 'success' with the Gibson murders, the IRA sought to repeat their coup the following year. For that reason, I brought the three players to meet the Reverend John Dinnen, the rector in Hillsborough in County Down. Three members of his congregation, the Hanna family from Hillsborough (Robert aged forty-five, his wife Maureen and their six-year-old son James), were killed by a bomb in Killeen, when the IRA mistook their jeep for one owned by another senior member of the judiciary, high court judge Eoin Higgins. The deaths of the Hanna family had a profound effect on John Dinnen.

'I remember hearing the news as if it was yesterday. The first thing I had to do was to comfort the family. Although the father and mother and youngest child were killed, there were two young teenage children in the Hanna family who weren't in the car that day and they needed to be consoled. I can't describe the pain and sorrow that was in their family home when I visited. They were almost numb with grief.

'There was incredible media interest in the story, which surprised me because I would have thought that there were so many tragedies before then in the north that people would no longer see this as an enormous national and international story. Maybe it was because there were two young children left behind that it touched such a chord, but I was under siege with people trying to look for a comment from me. My focus, though, was to prepare for the funeral.

'The church was packed, and there was a massive crowd outside who couldn't get in. It was very hard to say anything that would bring comfort in the face of such a horrific event. I will never forget walking out of the church to the graveyard in front of those three coffins. There were flashlights going off constantly from the press photographers, and there seemed to be cameras everywhere. All I could hear was the click-click of shutters. To this day, every time I preside at a funeral, the memory of that funeral comes back to me. It was just heart-breaking. Heartbreaking.'

The players then gave their reaction to John. Nigel noted, 'In many respects, the things that happened to us were easier than what happened to other people in the Troubles because they only happened to us. If it happened to our close family members, it would have been much tougher to take. When children are involved, as in the case of the Hanna family, it would have been much harder, especially as we now all have children of our own.'

David's medical background was again evident. 'I think that affects me in my own role as a family doctor. I come across death frequently, but the big difference in the Hanna incident was the loss of a six-year-old child. There's an inevitability when a person gets older that they will die, but when a child of that age dies, it's much harder to comprehend. Those who are left behind are left uncertain, worrying if they suffered, and after I heard the news, I felt an urge to write to the remaining members of the Hanna family and try to put into words what we had been through. I think the main thing I was trying to get across to them was that their family wouldn't have suffered because things happen so fast in a car bomb. It happened to the Hannas in nearly exactly the same spot – literally fifty or a hundred yards from the location of our accident. It gave me a closer empathy with what happened.'

In light of their experiences, I wondered what the three former internationals would say if they were to come face to face with the IRA man who had planted 'their' bomb.

David was emphatic: 'I certainly wouldn't be shaking his hand. The intelligence was that the man responsible for planting the bomb was killed somewhere else a few years later. You don't know what you would do 'til you're in that situation.'

Nigel didn't want to go there. 'To be frank, I don't care to think about it. I don't know what my reaction would be.'

Philip was more circumspect. 'I'm ambivalent. If I met the guy, I would probably ask him why he did it and if he felt good about it. We've moved on. We're different people, better people. We're perhaps stronger people.'

83

ER

Two Careers Ended on 1980 Lions Tour

With Rodney O'Donnell, Colin Patterson, Ollie Campbell and Shannon's Colm Tucker, Dr John O'Driscoll was chosen on the Lions tour to South Africa in 1980. Tucker was an interesting selection because he was unable to command a regular place on the Irish team. Tony Ward, Phil Orr and John Robbie subsequently joined the squad as replacements.

The tour ended in failure for the Lions. Colin Patterson contends it should not have.

'I believe we would have won the Test series had Fergus Slattery been chosen as captain. When I came on to the Irish scene, I watched in awe as he did what he did. I would have run through a brick wall if he asked me because I know he would have done the same for the team. I think we would have been better off with an Irish captain rather than an Irish coach because Noel Murphy (one of his instructions to the squad during a training session was: "Spread out in a bunch") was brilliant at motivating the Irish lads but not so good with the Welsh, who require a different type of motivation. We had very light backs on the tour and needed quick ball. When I said this to the forwards, Jeff Squire told me: "You'll get the ball when we've finished with it." We should have been playing a rucking game, but instead our forwards favoured mauling. In the Test matches, we also had two blind-side forwards in the back row which didn't give us the balance we needed.'

Patterson has both happy and sad memories from his trip.

'It was a real education touring with the Welsh. That was the era when you paid for your own telephone calls home. They had three great tricks devised never to pay for a telephone. Plan A was to charm the hotel receptionist into giving them the secret code they could use to make calls without being charged. Plan B was to distract the receptionist and for one of them to sneak in behind the desk and steal all their telephone bills. Plan C was when a journalist asked for an interview, they traded it for a phone call.

'Best of all, though, was when we went into the Adidas factory. We were allowed to pick a bag of our choice and stuff it with gear. Most of us selected the most stylish bags and filled them with gear. All the Welsh guys, without exception, took the biggest bags in the shop and walked out with half of the gear in the factory!

'One night they did a classic wind-up on the English player Mike Slemen, who was the leading try scorer on the tour. All of them gathered in the one room and rang him up, pretending to be from the BBC World Service, with a suitably posh accent. They fed him a lot of compliments, and he started blowing his own trumpet and claimed that he was probably one of the best players on the tour. Eventually the Welsh lads could take no more and shouted: "Slemen, you're a useless bastard." The English man was mortified that he had been caught out so badly.'

John O'Driscoll played in all four Tests. It was an horrific tour, though, for two of O'Driscoll's Irish colleagues. Without O'Driscoll's presence, however, it would have been even worse. Tragedy struck against the Junior Springboks in the penultimate game of the tour when the Lions won 23–19 and Rodney O'Donnell sustained a serious injury tackling the massive Danie Gerber. Although he walked off the field, when he was examined in hospital, it was discovered that he had dislocated his neck between the sixth and seventh vertebrae and that he had come within a fraction of an inch of being paralysed for life. Prompt intervention by O'Driscoll on the pitch prevented more severe repercussions. To compound the problem, when the ambulance finally arrived, the driver got lost on the way back to the hospital, depriving the Irish player of the quickest possible care.

One person literally at the centre of the action that day was the great Welsh centre Ray Gravell.

'It was such a shame that Rodney's career ended so prematurely on that tour. Rodney was actually lucky to still have the use of limbs after breaking his neck. If Dr John O'Driscoll hadn't been playing and shouted to the ambulance men when Rod went down not to move him, then he could have died or been paralysed. Moreover, John was only playing against the Junior Boks that day because Colm Tucker had sprained his ankle.'

With his small stature, scrum-half Colin Patterson was an obvious target for intimidation on the rugby pitch.

'I prided myself on my ability to take punishment. The tougher it got, the better I liked it. Whenever I got crushed by somebody, I got up immediately and said to him, "Good tackle, soldier," which really annoyed them.

'At internationals, there were a number of efforts to verbally intimidate me, but I never let that sort of bullsh*t get to me. The best example of this was when we played Wales in 1980. Where

Stuart Lane wasn't going to stuff the ball up my anatomy, I can't say. I eventually turned around and said to him: "Stuart, you don't mean that." It was my last home game for Ireland so the BBC gave me the video of the match. When I watched it, I saw again Stuart bursting into laughter and saying: "You're a cheeky wee bollocks." The more a player tried to intimidate me, the more I wound him up by waving at him in the line-out and so on. Apart from the fact that it helped me to win the psychological war, it's the only fun us small fellas get!'

In 1980, misfortune swooped like a hawk flying down from the sky, a fearsome beast, ferocious as it ripped and shred and tore, attacking all it saw when Patterson's career was prematurely ended on the Lions tour to South Africa. It was one of those moments, those breaths of time, when sadness and joy share the narrow path of life. Patty was at the height of his powers when all was taken from him in an accidental clash.

'It all began with an innocuous incident. I was screaming in agony, the pain was so intense. My situation wasn't helped by the fact that the referee tried to play amateur doctor with me and started poking around with my leg. I was stretchered off, but they're so fanatical about their rugby out there that two fans rushed on. One took my discarded boot and the other my sock, and he asked me if I would give him my shorts.'

The consequent wrecked medial ligaments from his injury caused Patterson to revise his career plans. Had he not got that injury, he had arranged to go out and play in Australia for a season. In fact, he already had his ticket bought.

84

ALONE IT STANDS

Donal Canniffe's Story

Rugby can be glorious.

Rugby can be tragic.

Sometimes it can even be both on the same day.

Some days, immortality and mortality make unlikely bedfellows

On the most unique day in Irish rugby history, one player had a unique story.

While Moss Keane was lucky enough to win fifty-four caps and be on the Triple Crown-winning side in 1982, and was also on a Lions tour, he once told me a famous Munster victory was the high point of his career.

'It's very hard to separate memories and say one match was more important than another. My first cap was a great feeling; so was my Lions Test appearance. Ginger's try in '82 was memorable, but the highlight was defeating the All Blacks. It was a great, great day, though my clearest memory is the disappointment we all felt when we heard that the father of our scrum-half and captain, Donal Canniffe, died immediately after the match. Donal was a very fine player, and it was a shame that he had such sadness on what should have been the happiest day of his life.'

Dan Canniffe collapsed and died in Cork, listening to the match. At the banquet in honour of the team's victory, a minute's silence was observed, and Pat Whelan, vice-captain, stood in for Donal. The match was one of the biggest highlights of Whelan's career.

'In 1978, Munster rounded off a magnificent season by beating Leinster 12–3 in Lansdowne Road in December to win their first Grand Slam since 1968, their first championship outright since 1973 and to record their first win at Lansdowne Road since 1972. That game was played on a Sunday. The previous day, the All Blacks were playing against the Barbarians, and the Munster team watched the match in the hotel together. The All Blacks only won with a late drop goal, and I still remember the roar that went up when they got that score because it meant that the All Blacks had won seventeen out of eighteen, highlighting the uniqueness of Munster's achievement. It set us up for the performance the next day, without question Munster's finest season. The magnitude of our achievement in defeating the All Blacks only sunk in years afterwards, but the personal tragedy for Donal Canniffe was immediately apparent to us all when we heard the news of his father's passing after the match.'

Donal Canniffe, a former Irish international, had been an inspirational captain to that Munster team. When his team gathered around at half-time leading 9–0, there was an eerie silence because the crowd couldn't cope with a shock of such massive proportions. To keep the team all fired up, Canniffe uttered the words: 'We're forty minutes from immortality . . . believe it.'

PART VIII
Tickle Your Odd-Shaped Balls

If laughter be the food of rugby, play on. On the World Cup and Grand Slam index, Ireland doesn't feature very prominently. Yet no student of the game would disagree that Ireland has given international rugby a disproportionate number of the great characters of the game. In this category are people like Jack Macaulay. He was said to be the first married man to be capped in international rugby in 1887 – according to rugby folk-lore, he got wed just to get leave of absence to play for Ireland! Even club players have entered international rugby's informal hall of fame with their celebrated wit. A case in point is Sam Hutton of Malone, not least because of his famous chat-up line, 'Excuse me, darling, haven't you met me somewhere before?' They may not always have known how to win many titles, but they certainly know how to have a laugh. This section celebrates some of the many funny moments in Irish rugby.

85

MUNSTER BLISS

Andrew Conway's Wonder Try Against Toulon

Paul O'Connell has to get some of the credit for Ireland's Grand Slam win in 2018. Keith Earls was in the form of his life and put his resurgence down to a quiet word from his former Ireland and Munster teammate. Earls observed, 'After speaking to Paulie and having roomed with him for a couple of years, we used to be a bit nervous before games. He said if he had his chance over again, he wouldn't worry as much, and I took something from that.'

In his distinguished career with Munster, O'Connell played in many of Munster's 'miracle matches'. In 2018, he witnessed one in the stands as Munster beat Toulon 20–19 with a stunning Andrew Conway try with four minutes left in a drama-filled European quarter-final. With Munster trailing by six points, hope was starting to fade when François Trinh-Duc kicked to touch from within his own twenty-two. Had the France fly-half made it, that might have been game over, but Conway, on his tiptoes, judged the flight perfectly and grabbed the ball above his head. Wing Josua Tuisova had come up in-field expecting a quick line-out, enabling the Munster winger to set off diagonally. Toulon's kick-chase was ragged and the Irish defender, gathering speed, straightened past Trinh-Duc and Raphaël Lakafia. The Thomond Park roar was deafening as Conway cut against the grain past Malakai Fekitoa's despairing tackle and under the posts. This led to bedlam in the stands. There was only one word to describe it – Munsteresque.

Conway's try has the capacity to become iconic for Munster fans. Footage has since emerged of an almost identical try scored by a fifteen-year-old Conway while playing for Blackrock College against St Michael's College in the 2007 Leinster Schools Junior Cup final.

Immediately after the game, Munster fans started to make their plans for the semi-final in France against Dan Carter and Racing 92. Paul O'Connell was no different.

When he went home that evening, he calmly informed his wife Emily that he would be making the journey. She equally calmly informed him that he couldn't travel because they had to go to a christening that day. Paul shook his head fiercely and less calmly told her that there was no way he was missing a match of that importance for 'just' a christening.

A pregnant pause ensued.

Then Emily gave him the type of withering look that only a wife can give her husband after he has committed a terrible crime in her eyes.

She replied in a calm voice – but with a conviction that was not open to challenge – 'You do realise that it's our child that is getting christened?'

86

SNAKES ALIVE

A Man Apart

Rob Henderson has his fair share of rugby stories, but his favourites deal with the exploits of one former Irish international.

'My favourite character is Ken O'Connell, the former Irish international. His nickname is "The Legend" but you would have to know him to understand why. He gained his legendary status in a different way to Brian O'Driscoll! He went off to India or Thailand to find himself.

'We played together with London Irish. At one stage, we were playing in the European Conference. We were all there getting ready to travel to Bordeaux. We were getting kitted out and were all there with our kit bags as if we were heading to Monaco. We looked a million dollars. Just as we were ready to leave, someone shouted: "Where's Ken?" Half an hour later he shows up with Malcolm O'Kelly. For once, miraculously, Mal had all his gear and luggage. Somebody must have dressed him! Ken turned up wearing a T-shirt and shorts. His T-shirt had a picture of a fella wearing shorts and a T-shirt but with his manhood sticking out. His only luggage was a kit bag which was the size of a big ice-cream tub. I said: "Ken, what are you carrying, mate?"

He replied: "I've got all I need. I've got my boots, my gumshield and my heart." With that, he was off to get the plane. That's Ken boy. That's why he's a legend.

'I will never forget my first introduction to Ken. Before he played his first game for London Irish, he wandered into the changing room with his togs around his ankles. He looked down at his private parts and said to me: "I bet you thought St Patrick chased all the snakes out of Ireland."'

87

THE CLOWN PRINCE

Donncha O'Callaghan Meets Hollywood Royalty

When Donncha O'Callaghan finally retired from rugby in 2018, he did so with a treasure trove of goodwill from his former colleagues. Geordan Murphy is happy to give plaudits to O'Callaghan.

'Of course, there were so many great forwards in the Irish team when I played for Ireland who did such great work and gave us such a supply of good ball. There were some great characters on the team, none more so than Donncha O'Callaghan. He's very funny and is always game for a laugh, and above all he can laugh at himself.'

Gordon D'Arcy rejoiced in the camaraderie in the Irish squad. 'Donncha O'Callaghan is a comedian. He drags fun out of everybody. He was the judge essentially, and if somebody was acting the maggot or arrived in with a new, flash car or had a new girlfriend, he would give them a hard time.'

The most nuanced assessment of O'Callaghan comes from Paul O'Connell: 'Donncha is a great character but was also a fabulous player and really aggressive on the pitch. He has a reputation as a messer, and to be fair he deserves it! Off the pitch and away from the training ground, there was no bigger messer, and when he was around, you knew there was a prank on its way, but when it came to playing, training, diet or getting the proper rest, there was nobody more dedicated. He was a contradiction in some ways, but if you asked anyone within the squad, they would tell you that he was the most focused and dedicated of us all.'

Eric Miller witnessed some strange sights with the Irish team.

'As the tour of South Africa in 2004 was coming to an end. We organised John Hayes's stag party. We dressed John up in a gymslip. The sight of a twenty-stone man in a gymslip is one that I never want to see again! Someone arranged for two strippers to come along, but they weren't the stars of the show because Colin Farrell was filming there at the time and he came to join us for the party. He was a very sound guy and certainly knew how to have a good time! We gathered round in a circle with John in the middle and everyone got to ask Colin a question. Everything was going to plan until Donncha O'Callaghan, as only Donncha can, asked, "What was it like to be the star of *Titanic*?" The whole place cracked up and we nearly fell off our seats laughing.'

88

THE BYRNEING ISSUE

Shane Byrne Wins His 100th Leinster Cap

Many Irish players have given great service to their province over many years. Shane Byrne was one such example.

The former Leinster manager Ken Ging gave a speech at the testimonial dinner to mark Byrne's 100th Leinster Cap. He told the story of two elderly Americans who were finally discovered and, against all odds, found to be alive in a disused Japanese POW camp, having been captured during World War Two. They first asked, 'How is President Roosevelt?'

'Oh, he died a long time ago.'

'And how is Stalin?'

'Oh, he died a long time ago.'

'Please tell us that Winston Churchill is still alive and well.'

'Alas, I'm afraid he died as well.'

'Tell us, is Shane Byrne still playing for Leinster?'

89

THE ITALIAN JOB

Trevor Brennan Saves the Day

Trevor Brennan is one of the great rugby characters. He is larger than life and made a massive impact when he moved to play rugby in France.

Girvan Dempsey recalls one moment when Brennan shocked his Leinster teammates.

'Trevor was responsible for my funniest moment in rugby. It was one of my first starts for Leinster and we were playing Treviso on a pre-season tour in Italy. After we flew into the airport and collected our bags, our manager at the time, Jim Glennon, came in to tell us there would be a delay because there was a difficulty with Dean Oswald's passport and that the problem was compounded by the fact that there was a language problem. Trevor immediately piped up: "I'll sort it out for you. I know the lingo."

We were all stunned because Trevor was not known for his linguistic skills. When we turned to him and asked him when he learned to speak Italian, he coolly replied: "I worked in Luigi's chip shop one summer"!'

90

GUESS WHO'S COMING TO DINNER?

The Irish Team Are Hospitable to Will Carling

Paul Dean very reluctantly denies that he christened Michael Kiernan 'Pepper' because he always got up your nose. Not surprisingly, Kiernan features in Deano's personal favourite rugby story.

'Michael Kiernan was always a terribly bad influence on me! After we lost badly at home to England one year, we went to the post-match dinner in the Shelbourne. Will Carling was the young and up-and-coming captain of England. It was one of his first games as captain. There were 300 people there, all men. It was black tie only and a bit stuffy.

'We were looking forward to having a few beers after the game. At the Shelbourne, there were waiters going around with double gin and tonics on silver trays at the reception before the dinner. Will Carling arrived in a white dinner jacket with his hair gelled back. Everybody else was wearing a black suit. Michael and I steered Will into a corner and grabbed a silver tray full of G&Ts and toasted Will, many times, on England's success. We had been drinking before the reception and were getting pretty sloshed.

'Will's mistake was to think that because we were senior players, he was safe with us. The English manager was Roger Uttley and he had been looking for Will and grabbed him and took him away, after he said forcefully to him: "You're captain of England. You have to be careful. You have responsibilities. You have to give a speech."

'The dinner was structured with English and Irish players around circular tables. I was completely dwarfed sitting between Paul Ackford and Wade Dooley. It's a very stuffy environment and so before the dinner we entertained ourselves with drinking games. The problem was that we were terrible drinkers.

'Roger Uttley was minding Carling for the meal, but during the dinner Will slipped away from him and he came down to us, from the top table, and sat between Paul Ackford and myself. The English players weren't too happy with Will wearing a white dinner jacket as well, being very prim and proper. We pushed him under the table and closed in our seats. It was a big table and Will was under the middle of it shouting: "Lads, let me out." His voice, though, couldn't be heard in the noisy room.

'Roger Uttley was looking for him frantically because it was coming close to the speeches. Will started kicking us to get out. We couldn't see him so we started kicking him back. The next drink was a glass of red wine, so in uniformity, one after the other, we threw it under the table on top of his white dinner jacket and gelled hair.

'Will started screaming, "Lads, let me out or I'll turn over the table."

'We all put our elbows on the table. We were laughing away and eventually Roger Uttley saw what was going on and dragged Will out from under the table. There were big red-wine stains dripping off his lovely white jacket.

'A few minutes later Will gave his speech. Carling subsequently went on to make a fortune going round companies giving inspirational speeches, but let's just say his address that night wasn't his finest moment!'

91

MURPHY'S LAW

Johnny Murphy Captains Leinster

Former Irish full-back Johnny Murphy was a great captain of Leinster. He had a bus and hearse business and turned up for training one night in his hearse with a coffin inside. Some of the Leinster players found it disconcerting to be doing their press-ups beside a coffin and grumbled to Johnny. He just said, 'She's not going anywhere and doesn't mind waiting.'

Johnny's speeches were memorable, not least because he was great at taking off posh accents. His opening sentence after a Connacht match was, 'Mr President of Leinster, Mr President of Connacht, players and the rest of you hangers-on.' He made more politically incorrect remarks and was told by the 'blazers' to tone down his speeches.

The next week, Leinster played Llanelli and beat the pants off them. Everyone was dying to know what Johnny would say. He began, 'Well, lads, I've got to be very careful what I say this week. It was a great honour for us to have the privilege of playing against such a famous side. My only regret is that BBC's *Rugby Special* wasn't here to see us beating the sh*te out of ye.

'I know people will say ye were missing some of yer star players but don't forget we were missing one of our greatest stars – Hugo MacNeill. He couldn't get his f**king place – I have it.'

The whole place was in stitches and Ray Gravell in particular had to be picked off the floor, he was laughing so hard.

92

CAMPBELL'S KINGDOM

Campbell v Ward

It was Irish sport's first civil war.

It took place twenty years before Keane v McCarthy in Saipan.

The Irish sporting nation was split right down the middle.

After he was sensationally dropped by the Irish rugby selectors on the tour to Australia in 1979, Tony Ward became embroiled in one of the most keenly argued controversies in the history of Irish sport. For three years, a fierce debate raged: who should wear Ireland's number ten jersey – Ward or Ollie Campbell?

Ollie Campbell thought he had finally resolved the Tony Ward issue with a series of stunning performances that ensured Ireland broke a thirty-three-year famine and won the Triple Crown in 1982. A few weeks later, Ollie was leaving Westport one morning when he picked up a lady of mature years who was visiting a friend in Castlebar Hospital. After an initial flurry of small talk, the conversation unfolded as follows:

Her: 'And what sports do you play? Do you play Gaelic?'

Ollie (as modestly as possible): 'No, I play rugby.'

Long silence.

Her: 'Do you know there's one thing I'll never understand about rugby?'

Ollie (with all due modesty): 'What? I might be able to help.'

Short silence.

Her: 'The only thing I don't understand about rugby is why Tony Ward is not on the Irish team!'

Even after his retirement from rugby, Campbell still found his name linked with Tony Ward's. He was invited on Mike Murphy's radio show at one stage. Before the broadcast, he was asked if there were any subjects he didn't wish to discuss. He said: 'Tony Ward and South Africa' because he thought they had been flogged to death. The first question Mike asked him was: 'I see here, Ollie, that the two areas you've said you don't want to be questioned about are South Africa and Tony Ward. Why is that?'

93

HOLD ON TIGHT

John O'Desperate

Rugby is the only game where a man sticks his head up another man's bum and the referee allows it. Yet Irish rugby players have often had more specialist knowledge of human anatomy.

Dr John 'O'Desperate' O'Driscoll is the consummate gentleman and a top dermatologist, but he liked to enjoy himself on tour. He was a very committed, driven player but a real Jekyll and Hyde character. His party piece was to hang out of windows late at night. During Ireland's tour of South Africa in 1981, this got a bit boring after a number of weeks. For the sake of variety, he decided he would hang someone else out of the window, so one night he dangled Terry Kennedy by the legs outside the hotel window – seventeen storeys up. It's the only time his teammates had ever seen Terry quiet.

Then Willie Duggan came into the room, puffing his cigarette, with a bottle of beer in his hand and with his matted hair that hadn't being combed since the tour started. As Willie was such a senior player and a close friend of John's, people assumed he would talk some sense to him. All he said to John before turning and walking out was, 'O'Driscoll, you don't have the guts to let him go.'

He was right too!

94

BELLY UP

Barry McGann Lends His Weight

Barry McGann always had a bit of a problem with the battle of
the bulge. Ray Gravell recalled his experiences of Barry for me:
'With Ollie Campbell, another superb kicking out-half I came
across for Ireland was Barry McGann. Barry was the fastest out-
half I've ever seen over five yards. The problem is that he was
completely f**ked after five yards!'

The nice thing about McGann is that he can talk about being
'calorifically challenged' with a smile on his face.

'The rugby scene was very different in my time. I missed
out on the beauty contest! I do recall, though, that at one stage
the ladies column in the *Evening Press* referred to me as "our
chubby hero". My own mother was delighted with the final line
in the feature: "Every mother should have one." Now because
of Sky Sport and so on, rugby stars are treated almost the same
way as Kylie Minogue or Kim Kardashian!

'What I most remember is the slagging I used to get whenever
I went back to play in Cork. One time we were playing Cork

Celtic. As I ran on to the pitch, I heard a voice saying on the terraces: "Who's that fella?"

"That's McGann the rugby player."

"Oh, you wouldn't know it by his stomach!"'

95

OUT OF SOUTH AFRICA

Freddie McLennan's Wind-Up

A depleted Irish side toured South Africa in 1981. The tour saw one of the great wind-ups of Irish rugby. Freddie McLennan was 'duty boy' (the player in charge of informing players about travel arrangements, etc. for a particular day during a tour abroad – each player takes it in turn) one Saturday. The squad had been given the day off and had to decide how to spend it. Freddie, himself a keen golfer, offered two choices. They could either go for a game of golf or take a trip around Johannesburg harbour. Eighteen players favoured the harbour trip on the basis that they could play golf any time but wouldn't always get the chance to do some sightseeing in Johannesburg. The next morning the players were ready at 8 a.m. for their trip around the harbour, only to be told that since the city was 5,000 feet above sea level, it didn't have a harbour and that the nearest seaside was a massive bus trip away.

Johnny Moloney, though, once saw the tables turned on McLennan: 'Mick Quinn would sometimes involve me as his partner in crime. He had this trick he played on every player gaining his first cap. A lot of players before their debut start to feel that they are a bit sluggish and not at their best. Quinny would pretend to be very sympathetic and tell them he had the solution. He would inform them in the strictest confidence that the top players always took a freezing cold bath to give them an edge in a big match. The only reason why this wasn't generally known was that it was a trade secret.

'The biggest casualty in all of this was Freddie McLennan. We put him in a cold bath and added buckets of ice. We told him he had to wait in there for twenty minutes otherwise it was no good. He was squealing like a pig. When his time was up, he couldn't move and had ice on his legs.'

Colin Patterson was a big fan of McLennan.

'Freddie is a great personality. Once when we played England, Freddie and John Carleton were having a real jousting match. At one stage, John sent Freddie crashing to the ground in a tackle. As he was going back to his position, Freddie shouted at him, "John, John. Is my hair all right?" If you watch the video of the game, you'll see John cracking up with laughter and Freddie straightening his hair.'

96

SNORING BEAUTY

Willie Duggan Takes a Nap

Ireland's tour to Australia in 1979 provided perhaps the funniest moment in Ollie Campbell's rugby career.

'The night before the first Test we had a team meeting. Our coach, Noel "Noisy" Murphy, always got very worked up when he spoke at these meetings. The problem was that he generally said the same thing each time. He always started with: "This is the most important match you will ever play for Ireland."

'The night before the first Test, sure enough Murphy's first words were: "This is the most important match you will ever play." We were just after eating dinner and the room was very warm because there were twenty-five of us. Murphy was talking away for about five minutes and just as he said, "Jesus Christ, ye're wearing the Irish jersey and do you realise this is the most important f**king game you will ever play?", there was a massive snore. It was, of course, Willie Duggan. Murphy said, "F**k it. I'm not doing this." Then he stormed out.

Willie's Lions captain Phil Bennett loved Duggan's willing-ness to take on physical confrontation in the most intimating of environments. Hence his joking description of Willie as 'a fuse deliberately seeking a match'.

Scottish referees, like their goalkeepers, sometimes get a bad press. A Scottish referee, who will remain nameless, was making his international debut at Twickenham in an England–Ireland Five Nations fixture in the 1970s. Willie Duggan was having a fag in the Irish dressing room. The time had come to run on the pitch, but Duggan had nowhere to put out his cigarette. He knew that if he ran out in the tunnel with the fag in his mouth, the cameras would zoom in on him straight away.

When the referee came in to tell the teams it was time to leave, the Irish number eight went over to him and said, 'Would you hold that for a second please?'

The obliging referee said yes but Duggan promptly ran out on the pitch – leaving the ref with no option but to put out the fag. He went out to face the glare of the cameras, and the first sight the television audience had of him was holding a cigarette! Asked about the incident afterwards, the referee said, 'I've had a wonderful day – but this wasn't it!'

The referee did have the last word, though, at the post-match dinner when Duggan asked him if he minded his smoking. He said, 'I don't mind your smoking, if you don't mind my being sick all over you.'

Duggan sometimes got into trouble with referees. He was always phlegmatic about it: 'I don't consider I was sent off. The referee invited me to leave the pitch and I accepted the invitation.'

97

ON AIR FORCE ONE

When Ollie Campbell Met Bill Clinton

There is a strong perfectionist streak in Ollie Campbell as he admits.

'Rugby, not academic matters, was my focus in school. This was probably best reflected in my oral Irish Leaving Cert exam. "*Suigh síos*," said the examiner. "*Gracias*," I replied.'

In 1984, Ollie found himself the main topic of conversation among the chattering classes. When he pulled out of the England game in 1984, it was suggested by some that he was giving up rugby and joining the priesthood! He has absolutely no idea where this particular rumour emanated from. To this day, though, former Irish scrum-half John Robbie still calls him 'Father Campbell'!

To highlight just how absurd that fabricated story was, two weeks later, after Ireland played Scotland, Ollie turned up dressed as a priest at the post-match dinner! Not only that, he persuaded a female friend of his to accompany him dressed up as a nun! He went around all night with a fag in one hand (and he has never smoked) and a pint in the other (and at the time he didn't drink) and danced away with this 'nun', although he's never been much of a dancer. All of this was so out of character for him that he assumed that people would immediately see that the priesthood story was entire nonsense. What staggered him was the amount of people who came to him and, apologising to 'Sister' for interrupting, sincerely congratulated him on his big decision! Instead of putting this little fire out, all he succeeded in doing was to pour fuel on it!

Some sports personalities are renowned for their immodesty. Ron Atkinson famously said, 'I met Mick Jagger when I was playing for Oxford United and the Rolling Stones played a concert there. Little did I know that one day he'd be almost as famous as me.'

Ollie, though, is known for his modesty. He's rugby's nice guy and is renowned for his good manners and clean living almost as much as his achievements in the game. The story goes that such is his legendary status within rugby that when Bill Clinton was president of America and wanted to promote the game in the States, his first choice to spearhead the campaign was Ollie. Clinton flew over to Ireland and brought him back on Air Force One. It was shortly after the Monica Lewinsky scandal broke. After they took off from Dublin, an air hostess came over to Ollie and Bill and asked them if they would like a drink. Bill replied, 'I'll have a scotch on the rocks.'

She immediately got him his drink. Then she turned to Ollie and asked him if he would like a drink. Ollie replied, 'I'd sooner be ravaged by a loose woman than have a drink pass my lips.'

Straight away, Bill handed back his drink and said, 'I didn't know there was a choice.'

98

THE FRENCH CONNECTION

Moss Keane's Irish Debut

On Moss's first cap in Paris, Willie John McBride, sensing that his huge frame needed extra nourishment, took him out for a bag of chips the night before the game. They were coming back to the team hotel via a rough area and one of the locals decided to do the unthinkable and steal the chips from Moss. The Keane edge surfaced immediately and Moss floored him with a right hook. His friends, though, all ganged up on the two Irish players and a brawl broke out. Before long, there was a trail of bodies on the ground – all of them French. Within minutes four gendarmes arrived. Moss explained the situation: 'They started it. They stole my chips.' One of the officers responded, 'Messieurs, we didn't come to arrest you. We came to save the mob.'

Moss made his debut in the Irish scrum in the cauldron of Parc des Princes in 1974. He was stamped on and was feeling very miserable. Consolation came in the form of his colleague Stewart McKinney: 'Cheer up, Moss – it could have been a lot worse. You would have suffered brain damage if you'd been kicked in the arse.'

99

DOCTOR'S ORDERS

Phil O'Callaghan Gets Injured

Long after his retirement as a player, Karl Mullen was involved in one of the most famous incidents in Irish rugby. During a match he was attending, one of the great folk heroes of Irish rugby Phil O'Callaghan was in the thick of the action.

Philo is famed in story for his experiences playing for Dolphin. One goes back to a match played on a bitterly cold November day. He was lifting one of his forwards Eoghan Moriarty in the line-out. The big man shouted down at him: 'Philo, let me down. My hands are frozen.'

After Philo put out his shoulder, Karl Mullen was to experience his tongue at first hand when he ran on the pitch to give him medical care. Dr Mullen said: 'I'll put it back, but I warn you it will be painful.'

He did and it was. According to the story, Philo was screaming his head off with the pain. The doctor turned to him and said: 'You should be ashamed of yourself. I was with a sixteen-year-old girl this morning in the Rotunda as she gave birth and there wasn't even a word of complaint from her.'

Philo replied: 'I wonder what she bloody well would have said if you tried putting the f**king thing back in.'

PART IX
True Grit

This section is a celebration of a special game in Irish rugby history which showcased all that is marvellous, magnificent and magical about one of Ireland's favourite sports. An epic tale of guts and grace; skill and style; character and courage.

100

NO ORDINARY JOE

Ireland Beat the All Blacks in Ireland

Joe Schmidt has a weakness. In fact, he has two, as he revealed to me, 'I have a terrible diet.'

When I expressed extreme scepticism about this fact to him based on his waistline, I asked for evidence. He answered in a guilty voice, 'I ate some chocolate biscuits this afternoon.'

His more recurring weakness is that he's a bad sleeper.

'It doesn't bother me. If I'm awake at 4 a.m., I'll just get up and do something. We had Rog (Ronan O'Gara) with us for a week on our summer tour a few years ago and he told me that I had a lot of energy. I do. I'm like a battery that's on full power, but I know the day will eventually come when the power goes down. Until that day comes, though, I'm going to continue flat out!'

This energy means that he had the intellectual resolve to plan Ireland's first ever win over the All Blacks on home soil on 17 November 2018. Ireland's 16–9 victory was another triumph for Schmidt. He had never experienced such a frenzied build-up to a big match.

'I had a fair bit of contact with Martin O'Neill when he was

Irish manager. When Ireland played Wales in October 2018, even though they gave away a lot of free tickets, they still couldn't fill the ground. The soccer fraternity were very disappointed with that.

'For us, though, our win in Chicago really heightened the demand for tickets when we played the All Blacks in 2018. I have never seen anything like it. I played against Smiley (Kevin) Barrett whose three sons play for the All Blacks, and he's a lovely guy. A few weeks before the match, he rang me and asked me if I could get him eight extra tickets because the family have such strong Irish roots. The ones I had been allocated I had already given away so I couldn't help him, but it really brought home to me how crazy the demand for tickets was.'

The hype was well merited with a pulsating contest. Even before the game started, Ireland signalled their intent by taking a step forward during the haka.

On the day Ireland's passion and will to win, accuracy and aggression was encapsulated by Peter O'Mahony: bruised and battered but not broken – barely walking because of injury, he forced himself through the pain barrier, like the greatest warrior on the battlefield, to make a crucial try-saving interception.

Jacob Stockdale's stock rose even higher with a chip-and-chase try that proved the difference between the sides. It was a day when all around the field, heroes abounded. Devin Toner ruled the roost in the line-out, Cian Healy tore into the opposition like a man possessed and everyone in the green jersey appeared to play the game of their lives. Like a good wine, Rob Kearney gets better with age and was imperious in defence while 22-year-old James Ryan, with no less than seventeen carries and twenty tackles, played like a seasoned veteran. The fact that it was the first time since 1995 that the All Blacks had failed to score a try against a Northern Hemisphere side was a massive affirmation of the Irish defence. The only mystery that remained unresolved at the end of the game was: how was it possible, given his consistent brilliance, that Tadhg Furlong had not been nominated for World Player of the Year?

Tony Ward was very taken by one aspect of the end of the match. 'The last man off the pitch was the All Blacks' captain Kieran Read, and he was clapping everybody. People talk about the arrogance of the All Blacks, but he showed such humility and sportsmanship. When we beat the All Blacks in 1978, their players came into the function afterwards singing: "Hi ho. Hi ho. It's off to work we go." They were so gracious in defeat, and it was lovely to see Read continuing that sporting tradition.'

Gregor Paul's verdict in *The New Zealand Herald* was: 'Ireland can now claim to be the best team in the world after producing a stunning performance that was brave, creative and relentless. They deserved the win and, with it, they deserve to be seen as world rugby's best team, even if the rankings don't agree.'

The game had been billed as a showdown between Johnny Sexton and Beauden Barrett for World Player of the Year. It would be the Irish man who would win the game of thrones on the day and then go on to win World Player of the Year, with Ireland winning team of the year and Joe Schmidt winning coach of the year.

The All Blacks victory was a big milestone in the trajectory of Schmidt's career.

'There are a lot of things we can't control. Injuries are an obvious example. You don't choose to go and play some of the best teams in the world with some of your world-class players watching in the stands. All we can do is prepare well and work hard to give the best performance we possibly can.

'For some games, there is a big burden of expectation. People forget that the week before we won the Grand Slam in 2018, we had won the Six Nations. The fact that we won the tournament for the third time in five years should have been a big deal, but nobody cared. The week before the England game, the only thing people were saying was: will ye win the Grand Slam? So, although it was minus five degrees, it was a red-hot atmosphere at Twickenham because if we lost, winning the Six Nations would have been a total anti-climax.

'I think 2018 was an important year for the team because it showed that the higher the stakes, the better we performed – which wasn't always the case with Irish teams in the past.

'We were obviously delighted to finish the year with the Autumn Series as all forty-one players in the squad got match time and acquitted themselves well. Plus, getting our first home-soil win over the All Blacks was special, especially with the raucous and supportive crowd, which created an incredible atmosphere.'

THE LAST WORD

Beating the All Blacks on home soil was one of the climactic moments in Irish rugby's story of great moments.

For many Irish people, rugby has been the one fixed point in a fast-changing age. Those years have not been without their troubles, but even when the storm clouds gathered, Irish rugby has not withered before their blast and a greener, better, stronger movement lay in the sunshine when the tempest was past.

Our economic system values measurable outcomes, but what is deepest about us transcends what can be said and outstrips what can be analysed. There are moments when we know that there is more to life – and to us – than the grim and grasping existence of seeking and striving and succeeding. There are moments of wonder, hope and grace that give us hints of ecstasy and lift us out of ourselves. They are, in Yeats's phrase, the soul's 'monuments of its own magnificence'. These moments take us to the heart of the deep mystery of being a person, the subterranean stirrings of the spirit, the rapid rhythms of the human heart. They have to do with remembering who we are, enlarging our perspective, seeing ourselves whole.

These 100 moments capture a flavour of that larger story of Irish rugby.

ACKNOWLEDGEMENTS

My special thanks to the great Jack McGrath for writing the foreword.

I also wish to express my gratitude to Ollie Campbell, Tony Ward, Keith Wood, Paul O'Connell, Tadhg Furlong, Jacob and Janine Stockdale, Philip McKinley and Emma Spence for their assistance.

My profound thanks to the many players, past and present, who generously shared their stories and thoughts with me and who made this book possible.

A very particular thanks for many kindnesses to Joe Schmidt.

As this book was being written, we lost the much-loved June Ward. She will be greatly missed by her devoted family. Sadly she missed out on the wedding of her adored granddaughter Nikki to Robbie Doyle. May they both discover that love is all around.

Likewise, Old Belvedere lost one of its greatest ever stalwarts Paul Reddy. The Irish rugby family will be much poorer without him.

Irish rugby gained a new fan this year with the birth of

Tamara McKinley. May her days as an Irish rugby supporter be merry and bright.

Thanks to Simon Hess, Campbell Brown and all at Black & White for their help.

Thanks to Ali, Emily and Robbie Henshaw for their assistance and congratulations to them on their outstanding achievement with their wonderful fundraising CD with the iconic Sharon Shannon for the South Westmeath Hospice, 'The Secret Sessions'.

Our family cat is called Jack as an homage to Roscommon rugby's greatest son, the Connacht out-half Jack Carty. Thanks to Jack for ensuring that in rugby terms the West's Awake. One of the few highlights from the 2019 Six Nations was watching Jack win his first three caps for Ireland. It coincided with another important milestone for the county when Roscommon CBS qualified for the Connacht Schools Cup Final for the first time. Then Jack Carty became the highest points scorer in the history of Connacht rugby with a try against Benetton Treviso.

One of Ireland's national treasures Tom Dunne missed the 2018 victory over the All Blacks. In fairness, he had a decent excuse. He was undergoing life-saving heart surgery at the time. Much of this book was written burning the midnight oil with Tom's wonderful programme on Newstalk for company. After a short hiatus for recovery, Tom was happily back to light up the airwaves. May he continue to reign supreme for many, many years to come. Thank you for the music.